From Margie and me
to our grandchildren
Andrew, Eric, Matthew, Will,
Owen, Lauren, Melody Faith…
in full confidence that their futures
and those of their fellow Canadians
will be human capital futures.

INSTITUTE FOR RESEARCH ON PUBLIC POLICY

INSTITUT DE RECHERCHE EN POLITIQUES PUBLIQUES

IRPP

F OUNDED IN 1972, THE INSTITUTE FOR RESEARCH ON Public Policy is an independent, national, nonprofit organization.

IRPP seeks to improve public policy in Canada by generating research, providing insight and sparking debate that will contribute to the public policy decision-making process and strengthen the quality of the public policy decisions made by Canadian governments, citizens, institutions and organizations.

IRPP's independence is assured by an endowment fund, to which federal and provincial governments and the private sector have contributed.

F ONDÉ EN 1972, L'INSTITUT DE RECHERCHE EN politiques publiques (IRPP) est un organisme canadien, indépendant et sans but lucratif.

L'IRPP cherche à améliorer les politiques publiques canadiennes en encourageant la recherche, en mettant de l'avant de nouvelles perspectives et en suscitant des débats qui contribueront au processus décisionnel en matière de politiques publiques et qui rehausseront la qualité des décisions que prennent les gouvernements, les citoyens, les institutions et les organismes canadiens.

L'indépendance de l'IRPP est assurée par un fonds de dotation, auquel ont souscrit le gouvernement fédéral, les gouvernements provinciaux et le secteur privé.

iRPP

INSTITUTE FOR RESEARCH ON PUBLIC POLICY

INSTITUT DE RECHERCHE EN POLITIQUES PUBLIQUES

A State of Minds

Toward a Human
Capital Future for
Canadians

by

Thomas J. Courchene

Copyright ©
The Institute for Research on Public Policy (IRPP) 2001
All rights reserved

Printed in Canada
Dépôt légal 2001

National Library of Canada
Bibliothèque nationale du Québec

CANADIAN CATALOGUING IN PUBLICATION DATA

Courchene, Thomas J., 1940-
A state of minds: toward a human capital future
for Canadians
Includes bibliographical references.
ISBN 0-88645-188-4

1. Human capital—Canada. 2. Manpower policy—
Canada. 3. Globalization. 4. Information society—
Canada. 5. Information technology—Social aspects—
Canada.
I. Institute for Research on Public Policy.
II. Title
HD4904.7.C68 2000   331.11'0971   C00-901568-X

Suzanne Ostiguy McIntyre
VICE PRESIDENT, OPERATIONS

COPY EDITOR
Brian McIntyre

DESIGN AND PRODUCTION
Schumacher Design

COVER PHOTO
Mitch Hrdlicka

PUBLISHED BY
The Institute for Research on Public Policy (IRPP)
l'Institut de recherche en politiques publiques
1470 Peel Street, Suite 200
Montreal, Quebec H3A 1T1

T HIS BOOK BEGAN AS *CANADA IN THE NEW GLOBAL ORDER*, THE TITLE OF MY 1999 Mabel Timlin Lecture at the University of Saskatchewan. While substantially reworked over the interim, chapters 2 through 8 retain their original Timlin flavour. However, I found myself unwilling to produce a text of the Timlin Lecture. The problem was that while I had addressed the challenges emanating from globalization and the knowledge/information revolution, I had little in the way of a creative response to the challenges.

About that time, I had the good fortune of having Hugh Segal invite me to be become IRPP's Senior Scholar. Not only did I readily accept, but it was not long before we agreed that the Timlin Lecture should be converted into a more comprehensive monograph that would be published by IRPP. Thankfully, Duff Spafford, who had orchestrated the Timlin Lecture, graciously agreed to this arrangement and, in the process, the Timlin Trust became associated with this publication.

Over the fifteen months since that turning point, the current manuscript began to take shape. One of the major catalysts in this process was the Public Executives Program of Queen's School of Business, where successive presentations of the material served to advance my thinking and writing. I also benefited from comments generated by numerous presentations of the lecture in Canada, the USA, Mexico and Germany. A summary of the analysis constituted my keynote address to the May 2000 IRPP Conference *Creating Canada's Advantage in an Information Age* and appeared in the July-August edition of *Policy Options*. Somewhere along the way, it became obvious that the "solution" to the globalization challenge was a human capital society and, appropriately perhaps, while en route to an IRPP conference in Saskatchewan, I stumbled on the title *A State Of Minds*.

It is a pleasure to acknowledge those who played important roles in the development of this book.

Hugh Segal's contributions have been as important as they are appreciated. He commented on all the drafts, listened to at least half a dozen presentations, provided encouragement at all stages and generally has been this book's, and my, biggest booster. Many thanks, Hugh.

In terms of the book's University of Saskatchewan origins, I appreciate the support and comments of Duff and Shirley Spafford, David Smith, John Courtney and Cris de Clercy. I also owe a debt of thanks to Dan MacNamara of Queen's Public Executive's Program for inviting me to present successive versions of the manuscript as well as for his comments.

France St-Hilaire, Daniel Schwanen, Donald Savoie, Marcel Côté and David Zussman provided copious and valuable comments and recommendations on the first draft. And France and Daniel did the same for the second draft. The final product is much better because of their comments and concerns.

At the Queen's end, Sharon Alton managed the manuscript through its several drafts and coordinated the many associated presentations en route, and always with her cheerful efficiency.

IRPP's Suzanne Ostiguy McIntyre orchestrated and oversaw the entire production of the book from cover design to table and chart production, editing etc, through to the printing and distribution process. It is a pleasure to see a professional at work. I would also like to acknowledge the staff at IRRP who helped in the production of this book — Chantal Létourneau, Stéphane Baillie, and Nikolas Bjerre.

I want to single out my copy editor, Brian McIntyre, for special recognition and gratitude. Authors need confidence that editors have not only the requisite skills but also the ability to adopt an overarching perspective of the work. Brian excels in both and in the process managed to make the author-editor relationship most comfortable and rewarding.

Margie Courchene's role in the book has been most significant. Apart from her unreserved support and encouragement during what effectively turned out to be a year-long "dash" to the finish line, Margie read the various drafts and provided important insights and needed breakthroughs. By way of example, her earlier research on the theories of Maria Montessori and early childhood development pointed me in the direction of a human capital bill of rights for children. In turn, this led me to the mission statement as well as to the "state of minds" title. And it was she who suggested the way to finish the book was to update the Laurier quotation to apply to "Canadians." Our collaboration extends to the book's dedication.

Given the highly subjective nature of much of the analysis, responsibility for what follows rests entirely with me.

I RPP's mission is to contribute to Canadian public policy by generating timely research, providing analytical and practical insight, and by fostering open discussion and debate. The goal is to inform the decision-making process and, ultimately, enhance the quality of policy outcomes.

It would be hard to imagine a research monograph that better resonates with this mission than *A State of Minds: Toward a Human Capital Future for Canadians*. Nor could the motivating thrust of Tom Courchene's work be timelier: What are the implications of the emerging information era for Canadian policy and governance in the 21st century? This question triggers a comprehensive, far-reaching analysis, one focused on the interaction between the principal societal agents of citizens, markets and governments, and their effect on critical policy issues, including social cohesion, international competitiveness, income polarization, North American integration and digital divides, among others. Moreover, in assessing the implications of globalization and the knowledge/information revolution, Courchene draws on the perspectives of many disciplines — economics, law, politics, sociology, business and public administration.

But Courchene does not stop here. In the full spirit of IRPP's mission, he distills these implications and uses their essence to weave a policy and governance tapestry designed to ensure Canada's socio-economic distinctiveness (and success) in the upper half of North America. And what is the essence of the analysis? The 21st century will inherently be about people — human capital and knowledge — and that the democratization of access to skills and human capital formation is of utmost importance to both social cohesiveness and economic competitiveness. Or, as Courchene puts it, our policy priorities must change from boards and mortar to mortarboards. The remainder of his analysis addresses the critical policies, instruments and governing institutions consistent with Canada becoming a "state of minds."

I want to take this occasion to express the Institute's gratitude to the University of Saskatchewan Timlin Trust for cooperating in the publication of *A State of Minds*. As Tom Courchene notes in his acknowledgments, this book began as the 1999 Mabel Timlin Lecture at the University of Saskatchewan.

And it is a pleasure to recognize and thank the entire IRPP staff for their various roles in contributing to the design, production and distribution of *A State of Minds*.

I now have the privilege of introducing you to an engagingly creative and thought-provoking analysis of the challenges and options facing Canadians as we embrace the information era in the upper half of North America. That this advances IRPP's research agenda superbly is obvious. But what is truly intriguing, and most important, is that Tom Courchene is inviting us all to join him on an intellectual journey intended to advance our national agenda and define what being a Canadian ought to mean in the 21st century.

Hugh Segal
President, IRPP

part I

Introduction and Overview

Introduction

G LOBALIZATION AND THE KNOWLEDGE/INFORMATION REVOLUTION ARE SIGNALLING THE
advent of a new socio-economic order with profound and pervasive implications for citizens, governments, markets and, therefore, public policy. At the core of
this new paradigm is a truly exciting development: the emergence of information-
and knowledge-empowered citizens as the lead actors and agents of future societal
progress on both the economic and social fronts. Indeed, Globalization and the
knowledge/Information Revolution — GIR — will privilege human capital in the
same manner the industrial revolution privileged physical capital. Thus, to succeed
in this new global order, Canada and Canadians must make the transition from a
resource- and physical-capital-based economy and society to a human-capital-
based economy and society. Nothing short of privileging the human capital of
Canadians with pride of place on the public policy agenda will ensure the success
of this transition. In short, Canada must become a state of minds so that, updating
Laurier, the twenty-first century will belong not just to Canada but to *Canadians*.
Documenting why Canada must change and what this change implies for Canadian
public policy is the *raison d'être* for *A State of Minds*.

Accordingly, the ensuing analysis begins (chapters 2 through 8) by detailing and assessing the many features and implications of GIR as they affect and in
many cases transform Canadian society. With this as backdrop, the remainder of
the analysis focuses on the range of instruments, governance structures and policies we can deploy to ensure the emerging global order confers maximum benefits on Canada and Canadians. As already noted, the analytical and policy key to
unlocking the benefits of GIR is to ensure all Canadians have equality of opportunity in terms of developing and enhancing their human capital. With a human

capital framework as a beacon, Canada will be able to ensure that the forces of GIR can be harnessed in ways that will promote both economic competitiveness and societal cohesion. To anticipate another key conclusion of the ensuing analysis, we will retain considerable room to manoeuvre in terms of framing our societal goals, but we certainly must rethink our choice of policy instruments.

In order to come to grips with the pervasive influence of GIR, both in its own right and in terms of informing the resulting policy choices, it is necessary to embed the analysis in an appropriate framework. In my earlier research (e.g., 1995), the approach I adopted was to draw out the implications arising from the many possible definitions of GIR. For example, what implications follow from defining GIR variously as 1) the internationalization of production, 2) the shift from multinational enterprises to transnational enterprises, 3) the internationalization of cities, 4) the knowledge/information revolution, 5) consumer sovereignty and/or 6) ultra mobility? A tabular summary of the implications that derive from this framework appears as Appendix B to this monograph.

Encompassing as this approach might appear to be, it is at the same time too narrow in its seeming sweep and too disconnected in terms of its interrelationships to address the issue at hand: the manner in which GIR is influencing and transforming the building blocks of society (citizens, governments and markets) and, in turn, influencing and transforming the manner in which 21st-century Canadians will live and work and play in the upper half of North America. Accordingly, Figure 1 outlines a conceptual framework more attuned to assessing the paradigm-shift implications of GIR. It also provides a convenient outline for the ensuing analysis. Thus, the first order of business is to focus on the implications of GIR for governments, citizens and markets (the rectangular boxes in Figure 1). However, since it is also in the interaction among these three societal building blocks that the full ramifications of GIR become apparent, I shall then focus on the three "interfaces": the citizen-market, the citizen-government and the government-market interface (the three circles in Figure 1). All this prefaces the central challenge posed by the complex and interactive implications of GIR, namely deriving insight in terms of what this means for the design of governance structures, institutions and policy for 21st-century Canada.

A final introductory comment is in order. In many areas the implications arising from GIR are, to say the least, rather disquieting — the erosion of the traditional middle class, the polarization of market incomes and the consequent

GIR and the Policy Challenge

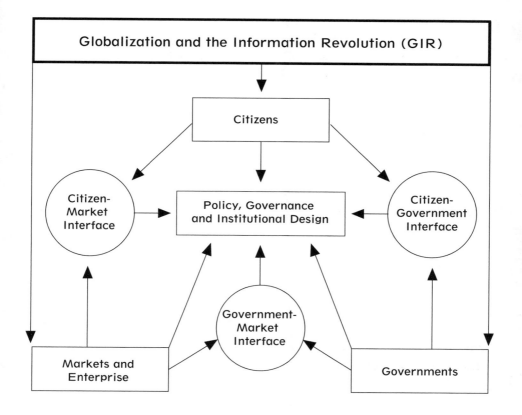

severing of the traditional citizen-market nexus, for example. Several scholars paint an even more troubled picture of the forces at play. Castells (1998: 355) notes that in this new order "nation-states will survive, but not so their sovereignty." Tourraine (1996) goes further: there is an ideology associated with globalization that views it as a "natural force," one that is in the process of reducing societies to economies, economies to markets, and markets to financial flows. If these are the potential downsides of GIR, surely it must be preferable to maintain the good old days and the good old ways. Preferable, perhaps, but largely impossible because the pervasive forces embodied in globalization and the information revolution are to Canada not only exogenous (external) but largely irreversible. Thus, as a small open economy, Canada is effectively a "paradigm taker" in terms of GIR. Phrased differently, *these are the good old days!* There is no status quo to fall back on. But what is possible and what is motivating the analysis is that a comprehensive understanding of the implications of the new global order will allow Canada and Canadians to engage in creative policy and governance so we can ensure these pervasive forces work to our social and economic advantage.

The remainder of this introductory chapter presents a detailed overview of the book. Further backdrop is provided in Appendix A, which elaborates on the definitions and implications of human capital, since it plays such an important role in the ensuing analysis. However, readers may wish to move directly to Chapter 2, *GIR and Governments*.

Outline and Executive Summary

Part II — Globalization and the Knowledge/Information Revolution (GIR): The Anatomy of a Paradigm Shift

CHAPTERS 2 THROUGH 8 FOLLOW THE FIGURE 1 SCHEMA.[1] THE INITIAL EMPHASIS OF the opening substantive chapter (*GIR and Governments*) is on the variety of ways in which GIR is transforming governments: Powers are being transferred upward, downward and outward from central governments of nation-states and, in particular, from central governments of federal states. I shall refer to this as "glocalization." In the popular mind, the domestic implications of these GIR-triggered shifts in powers are frequently viewed as decentralizing. However, reference to the concept of "subsidiarity" reveals that those domestic policy areas that are the most mobile (e.g., capital) are largely being centralized, or passed upward. Thus, while there are important decentralizing aspects to GIR, the larger issue is one of a "reshuffling" of the division of powers within Canada. Chapter 2 concludes with an emphasis on the emerging role of global city-regions as the new dynamic motors of a GIR era. An assessment of how these global city-regions may fit into the Canadian division of powers will be delayed until the penultimate chapter.

Chapter 3 (*GIR and Citizens*) begins with the observation that while GIR is privileging individuals as consumers (one definition of GIR is "consumer sovereignty"), it may be disenfranchising individuals as citizens, although I attempt to make the case that this is only a temporary or transitional phenomenon. Over the longer term, GIR will facilitate global participation and citizenship, with the "Battle in Seattle" as a recent exemplar. But the most disconcerting development for Canadian society is the impact GIR is having on income distribution — not only the polarization of market incomes but also the implications arising from the fact that high-level human capital is progressively more mobile and, therefore, has the ability to "exit." *Inter alia*, this chapter provides one of the key rationales for pursuing a Canadian human capital future, namely Lester Thurow's (1993: 5) penetrating assertion: "If capital is borrowable, raw materials are buyable and technology is copyable, what are you left with if you want to run a high-wage economy? Only skills, there isn't anything else."

Chapter 4 (*GIR and Markets*) focuses initially on the manner in which GIR is simultaneously internationalizing production and dramatically altering the nature of enterprise (e.g., e-business and the ongoing merger mania). While these forces apply to all economies and societies, the remainder of the chapter focuses on a peculiarly Canadian dimension — the dramatic north-south shift in Canadian trade flows. This realignment of Canada's economic geography within the NAFTA environment will feature prominently in the rest of the analysis: for example, how do we Canadians preserve our east-west social union in the face of a progressively north-south trading nexus? The analysis now shifts to embrace the three "interfaces" (the circles in Figure 1). Chapters 5 and 6 address the implications of GIR for the evolution of the market-government relationship.

Chapter 5 (*The Rise of Economic Region-States*) is an extension of the previous chapter's focus on the dramatic rise in north-south trade. Drawing from the

European regional-science literature, and in particular the concept of "untraded interdependencies," the analysis makes the case that Ontario has now donned the mantle of a North American region-state. While this "economic-region-state" status also applies to a greater or lesser extent to other provinces, the analysis delves into a set of selected implications for Canadian federalism arising from the profound shift in Ontario's trade/economic position within North America (e.g., implications for the east-west transfer system, for personal-income-tax evolution and for the future of our east-west economic infrastructure). To broaden the analysis beyond Ontario, the chapter concludes with a "space-of-flows" approach to the new geo-economics of New Brunswick.

Chapter 6 (*Intergovernmental Relations*) initially directs attention to the international dimension of the market-government interface, namely how do we ensure international economic integration does not lead to domestic social disintegration. The focus then shifts to the manner in which this challenge applies domestically. The emphasis here is on recent novel initiatives designed to "manage policy interdependencies" within Canada, namely AIT (the *Agreement on Internal Trade*) and SUFA (the 1999 Social Union Framework Agreement). Also highlighted here is the revitalization of the Annual Premiers' Conference (APC) as a new coordinating and governing instrument to address selected pan-Canadian policy externalities. This leads to a discussion of "corporate governance" and the necessity of ensuring this often-neglected area becomes part and parcel of the manner in which we rethink and rework all aspects of socio-economic policy to maximize the opportunities arising from GIR.

Chapter 7 focuses on the citizen-market interface. The key and disturbing development here is the "simultaneous integration of work and disintegration of workers as a collective." Beyond the obvious erosion of the traditional relationship between citizens and markets, this chapter also directs attention to the tension between the increasingly mobile elites on the one hand and the lower-skilled/immobile segments of the labour force on the other. Since these groups have vastly different preferences for the evolution of Canadian public policy, the eventual challenge will be to forge a societal linkage between these two groups. The analysis concludes with a comparison of how different concepts of capitalism (Anglo-American vs. European) approach the role of training, a key issue in terms of the human capital thrust of the policy section of the study.

The final chapter (8) dealing with the anatomy of the GIR paradigm shift directs attention to the changing citizen-government interface. A major focus of this chapter is the rise of the third, or voluntary, or nonprofit sector as an intermediate organizational form between both citizens and governments, and citizens and markets. This is followed by a discussion of the manner in which e-government is altering the citizen-government relationship. The last section of the chapter addresses the evolving political marketplace: GIR serves to downplay the traditional concept of competitiveness and nation building, namely resource-based economic development, and simultaneously makes "citizen" issues the new political currency. This radically changes federal politics. More to the point, since most of the citizen issues fall under provincial jurisdiction, this sets the stage for a renewed federal-provincial jurisdictional tug of war.

Part III – Bridging Paradigms: From Boards and Mortar To Mortarboards

Part III serves as a transition to the human capital policy focus of the remainder of the analysis: It documents those changes in attitudes and policies that are necessary in our transition from a resource-based (boards-and-mortar) society to a human-capital-based (mortarboards) society. Toward this end, Chapter 9 (*Framing Policy for an Information Era*) begins by enunciating a set of principles requisite for a successful private-sector transition and a corresponding set for public-sector adjustment. The important difference is that while private-sector adjustment will be informed and likely driven by international market forces, no such external influences operate in the public-sector domain. Hence, the key to success in the GIR era will depend on our innate ability to design and implement creative social and socio-economic infrastructure that will resonate well with both our own policy aspirations and the dictates of GIR. The remainder of the chapter elaborates on a variety of further issues relating to public-sector adjustment, including the importance of distinguishing between goals and instruments.

Winds of Change (Chapter 10) addresses two new framework approaches to policy priorities and design in the GIR era: One is from the BCNI; the other is Ontario's economic mission statement. While both frameworks are economics oriented, what is new and significant is the emphasis they place on skills and human capital development as the essential ingredient of the new global order.

The stage is thus set for the principal role of Part III — articulate a socio-economic mission statement for 21st-century Canada. This is Chapter 11, *A Human Capital Mission Statement for Canada*. Since human capital is now key to our competitiveness and since enhancing human capital is also the principal avenue for addressing not only the income-distribution implications of GIR but also the citizenship/democracy potential of Canadians, we have a historically unprecedented window of opportunity to capitalize on the human capital dimension of GIR in terms of advancing *both* economic competitiveness and social cohesion. Accordingly, I offer the following mission statement for 21st-century Canada:

> Design a sustainable, socially inclusive and internationally competitive infrastructure that ensures equal opportunity for all Canadians to develop, to enhance and to employ in Canada their skills and human capital, thereby enabling them to become full citizens in the information-era Canadian and global societies.

The remainder of Chapter 11 elaborates on various aspects of this mission statement.

Part IV — A Human Capital Future for Canadians: Toward Competitiveness and Cohesion

Implementing the mission statement requires nothing short of rethinking and reworking our governance, institutions, policies and priorities in order to ensure that achieving a human capital economy and society becomes Canada's "National Policy" for the 21st century. The obvious corollary is that implementing a human-capital and information-era infrastructure must become the "transcontinental railroad" for this new National Policy. Thus, Chapter 12 (*Building Blocks for a Human Capital Future*) begins with a focus on the characteristics needed to develop new east-west "filaments of fibre" that will provide the same east-west connectedness as did the "ribbons of steel" in John A's National Policy. While this is critical to competitiveness in the new era, it also has a social and cultural dimension, since without an effective information/Internet network presence we will progressively be driven by US standards and regulations and, ultimately, US values.

Devising an information-era social infrastructure appropriate for a human capital future must parallel the information/Internet connectedness. While detailing what this implies for the major components of our existing social network is the subject of Chapter 13, the remainder of Chapter 12 focuses on some fundamental shifts in our societal priorities that must underpin a human-capital-driven social infrastructure. The first of these has to be that of assigning priority to a human capital future. I suggest that the preferred way to accomplish this is to begin with a societal commitment to a "human capital bill of rights" for our children and, then, to follow this up with a recognition that the family is the effective locus for the production of human capital. And at the government level, the bureaucracy should be rethought and restructured via an overarching super-ministry for a human capital future, which would then inform the various policy areas to ensure cohesion and competitiveness.

Chapter 13 (*Human Capital, Societal Cohesion and the Social Envelope*) directs attention to the major social programs: education/training, health, and income distribution. In each of these areas, the thrust of the analysis is to rethink and redirect priorities and programs in ways that contribute to both cohesion and competitiveness. What GIR and the mission statement bring to the analysis is the recognition that, in the information era, these major programs transcend their traditional "social focus" — they are major economic motors and export plat-forms in their own right. If we fail to view them as both social and economic instruments, they will soon fail to deliver state-of-the-art social programs.

Chapter 14 (*Human Capital and Canadian Competitiveness*) then approaches the competitive imperatives of the GIR era. Here the implications are straight-forward economically, although obviously difficult politically: Taxes on mobile fac-tors of production must fall to rates competitive with those of our trading partners, especially the US. In general, this means shifting the tax burden away from income and toward consumption. The first part of the analysis amounts to a case study of federal and provincial budgets in 2000. While Ottawa gets high marks for the social policy dimensions of its 2000 budget (e.g., indexation and lowering the mid-dle-income tax rate), it fairs poorly on the competitive dimension. The result is that it has fallen to selected provinces (in economic region-state fashion) to sharply reduce taxes on mobile factors in order to preserve and advance their economic future in North America and beyond (Ontario, for example, is cutting its corporate tax rates in half). But this is triggering a sea change in both federal-provincial and interprovincial fiscal and economic relations, the implications of which are far from salutary. The underlying problem is that Ottawa has not embraced (or perhaps more appropriately, has not *yet* embraced) the competitive implications of or aris-ing from the knowledge/information era. The remainder of the chapter deals with other macro policy issues and areas (the debt burden, monetary policy and exchange rates) and then directs all-too-brief attention to the rest of the economic policy arsenal (trade, regulation, competition policy). To anticipate aspects of this analysis, the monetary policy and exchange rate sections will broach the issue of greater exchange rate stability and buying more fully into US monetary policy as the appropriate strategy for a human capital era. And in terms of trade and competitiveness the analysis will limit itself to a set of principles that ought to inform policy evolution, e.g., where there are degrees of freedom in policy design and implementation, this freedom should be directed toward ensuring that economic policy becomes more consistent with developing, enhancing and employing-in-Canada the human capital of Canadians. In effect this is the necessary corollary to the earlier approach to our social infrastructure, namely that it become more consistent with the emerging economic opportunities (in the health and post-secondary-education (PSE) areas especially) of the new information order.

There is, however, an underlying message that is never far from the surface in chapters 12 through 14. It runs as follows: Global forces are sufficiently pervasive and powerful to ensure Canada *will* eventually become competitive on the economic front. However, what is far from clear is that we will forge a societal commitment to implement a GIR-consistent social infrastructure. Thus, the fear is that as we fall into line competitively with the Americans, our social policy will drift south as well. In this sense, embracing a human capital approach to our social envelope is by far the most difficult political challenge facing Canadians. Intriguingly, should we succeed in this, there will be important further economic implications from a societal commitment to a human capital future: Apart from the obvious fact that knowledge and human capital are on the cutting edge of competitiveness, a full acceptance of a human capital future will allow Canadian tax rates to move much more quickly to competitive levels, i.e., we will be able to generate an important "first-mover" advantage over the Americans.

The final substantive chapter (*GIR, Canadian Federalism and Human Capital*) focuses on "who should do what" in terms of the federal-provincial implications relating to the implementation of the mission statement. The analysis is informed by two key observations. The first is that federalism is the ideal form of governance in a fast-changing world since it can accommodate the advantages of decentralization and creative adjustment under the umbrella of pan-Canadian principles. The second is that, setting aside the decade or so following the *Constitution Act, 1982*, we Canadians were highly creative in terms of redesigning federalism to accommodate both domestic and international challenges. It is time to fall back on our innate creativity.

In terms of substance, as distinct from the above comments on process, the story thus far is not particularly encouraging on the federal-provincial front. Ottawa (as noted in Chapter 8 above) has recognized that the core of nation building in the 21st century no longer rests with traditional resource-based policies (energy, mining, forestry etc.) but rather with citizen and human-capital-related issues which tend to fall under the constitutional purview of the provinces. Meanwhile, those provinces with fiscal flexibility are being forced to lend policy priority to maintaining and enhancing their economic futures within North America. The result, thus far at least, is more in the nature of a dysfunctional commingling of substance and process, since Ottawa appears to be emphasizing the social side and the provinces the economic side. The underlying problem is our collective failure to recognize the socio-economic essence of the new global order.

However, even were we to embrace the human capital mission statement, the challenges on the federal-provincial front would remain daunting. While the constitutional ball on the social side is currently in the provinces' court, they will have to utilize their Annual Premiers' Conferences to generate pan-Canadian principles and oversight to manage the policy interdependencies arising from the creation of a human-capital-consistent social infrastructure. If they fail in this endeavour, this will amount to an open invitation to Ottawa to provide this pan-Canadian infrastructure. My bottom line here in terms of Canadian federalism is that if there is a "collective will," we Canadians will ensure that there is a "collective way." But the collective will has not yet emerged.

The final substantive section of Chapter 15 (and of the study) refocuses attention on the role of cities in the distribution of powers. The emergence of cities, especially global city-regions, as the dynamic motors of the new economy means their political star is also on the rise. Indeed, the proposal for a Toronto *Charter* is a key catalyst in this direction. The constitutional ball is again in the provinces' court, but in a very different way. Either the provinces will accommodate the rising stars of these cities, or the cities themselves will force a common front to lobby Ottawa to play a more direct role in providing them with GIR-consistent infrastructure, both physical and human.

Going Forward, the final chapter of the study, reiterates a few selected themes of the foregoing analysis.

Before launching into Chapter 2, which addresses the implications of GIR for governments, readers may want to familiarize themselves with the concepts in

Appendix A, *A Primer on Human Capital, Social Capital and Social Cohesion*. Given how much attention in what follows is placed on human capital, the role of this appendix is to elaborate on the full implications that attend my use of the term "human capital." Also included in Appendix A is the relationship between human capital and the more recent emphasis on "social capital" and social cohesion generally.

Globalization and the Knowledge/ Information Revolution: The Anatomy of a Paradigm Shift

GIR and Governments

G LOBALIZATION AND THE KNOWLEDGE/INFORMATION REVOLUTION ARE DRAMATICALLY transforming the traditional nation-state and its governance. Specifically, powers are being transferred upward, downward and outward from central governments of nation-states and, in particular, from central governments in federal nation-states. Paquet (1995) refers to this as the "Gulliver Effect" — nation-states are no longer able to deal effectively with either the dwarfs of Lilliput or the giants of Brobdingnag. This follows the earlier insight of Daniel Bell (1987): Nation-states have become too large to tackle the small things in life and too small to tackle the large things. I have labelled this passing of powers upward and downward from national governments as *glocalization*, the contraction of globalization and localization (Courchene 1995). However labelled, the opening sections of this chapter focus on the erosion of the traditional Westphalian nation-state both from above and from below. In terms of the former, emphasis will be directed first to the emergence of supranational regulation as a national response to the increasing integration of economic space, then to the nature of the underlying process that drives this integrating economic space. In terms of the downward transfer of powers, the analysis focuses on the roles played by markets (e.g., privatization), by subsidiarity (e.g., devolving powers to lower levels of government) and by information-empowered citizens.

This glocalizing impact on nation-state governance leads rather naturally to a brief discussion of the new and altered role of nation-states in the emerging global era. Rounding out the implications of GIR for governments and governance is an initial discussion of the emergence of the role of cities or, more appropriately, of "global city-regions" as the new economic and institutional drivers of the new global order.

Transferring Powers Upward

The Global Regulatory/Countervail Perspective

T HE TRANSFER OF POWERS UPWARD IS STRAIGHTFORWARD: ECONOMIC SPACE IS transcending political space. Perhaps not surprisingly, mobile capital, typically under control of transnational enterprises (TNEs), has been fast off the mark in terms of taking advantage of GIR and has integrated economic space in the process: In countervail fashion, nation-states are transferring selected powers upward to supranational agencies and institutions. While this is not a new phenomenon, the pace of this transformation is clearly accelerating: the Bank for International Settlements' capital-adequacy rules for global banks; the various GATT/WTO rounds which now address services; the EU, the FTA and NAFTA; and, most recently, the advent of the Euro as a pan-European currency under the control of a pan-European central bank.

While these developments obviously represent a transfer of powers (and sovereignty) from the national to the supranational level, individual nation-states do nonetheless have considerable flexibility in terms of both the degree to which these powers are transferred as well as *how* they are transferred. In terms of the latter, for example, the "national treatment" provision in the FTA and NAFTA is far more sovereignty preserving than is the trend toward "home country rule" as the operating principle of the EU. National treatment implies Canada is free to design its own domestic policy, with the important proviso that this will also apply to US and Mexican enterprises operating in Canada. Under national treatment, an American firm can do in Canada exactly what a Canadian firm can do. On the other hand, home country rule (as exemplified by the hundreds of EU "directives") effectively implies, if carried to its limit, that a German firm can do in Holland exactly what it can do in Germany. This is an operating principle that will lead in the direction of regulatory uniformity. To be sure, this EU vs. NAFTA difference reflects the fact that the former has undertones of a political blueprint, whereas NAFTA is largely an economic blueprint. Yet the underlying issue is important for the remainder of the analysis: While many of the pervasive impacts of GIR cannot be avoided, they can be accommodated in quite different ways.

This relates to another recurring theme in the ensuing analysis: what is at issue in a GIR era is not so much the choice of *goals* we set for ourselves as a society, but the choice of *instruments* we deploy to achieve these goals. Consider, for example, the international regulatory system as it applies to trade, competition policy and the like. One approach to reconciling international differences would be to embark on what has been referred to as "deep structural integration," code for ensuring the international regulatory regime extends deep into national regulatory systems, e.g., uniformity of competition policy rules across countries (Ostry 1997). An alternative approach here would be to transfer effective powers to an overarching international organization. To a degree at least, this would characterize the aborted attempt to monitor and regulate key aspects of foreign direct investment under the aegis of the Multilateral Agreement on Investment (MAI). But this degree of uniformity may not coexist well with national autonomy, especially for nation-states like China whose values, culture and institutions go back 2,500 years and which are not likely to have their domestic policy driven by the dictates of supranational capital. Hence, there is a need for new instruments that ply some middle ground between the "shallow integration" of GATT and the WTO on the one hand and the pressures under GIR for "deep structural integration" on the other. In the jargon of regulatory reform, a need exists to move from "negative integration" (e.g., a series of "thou-shalt-nots") toward "positive integration" (e.g., a proactive meshing of national rules and regulations) without simultaneously embracing uniformity. Among the possible intervening instruments are "national treatment" and "mutual recognition" of other countries' standards. For an insightful analysis of this whole area of international "regulatory diplomacy," readers can consult Wolfe (1999).

The "Electronic Herd" Perspective

While governments are everywhere under pressure to acquiesce to the unfettered interplay of markets, the focus on transnational enterprise (TNE) capital as the dominant driving force is far too narrow a concept of the underlying challenge. In his insightful global best seller, *The Lexus and the Olive Tree*, Thomas Friedman views TNEs and their capital as only a part of the larger "democratization of technology, finance and information" that has given rise to what he calls the "Electronic Herd":

> The Electronic Herd is made up of the faceless stock, bond and currency traders sitting behind computer screens all over the globe, moving their money around with the click of a mouse from mutual funds to pension funds to emerging market funds, or trading from their basements on the Internet. And it consists of the big multinational corporations who now spread their factories

around the world, constantly shifting them to the most-efficient, low-cost producers. (Friedman 1999: 90-91)

In terms of the impact of the Electronic Herd, Friedman adds,

> They [the Electronic Herd] blew away all walls. They are what created net-
> works which enable each of us now to reach around the world and become
> super-empowered individuals.... They blew away all ideologies, other than free
> market capitalism. They are what created the incredible new efficiencies that
> every business has to adapt to or die...they are what is forcing people to change
> from thinking locally first and then globally, to thinking globally first and then
> locally. (116-17)
>
> [It is the Electronic Herd that is] tightening and tightening the systems
> around everyone, in ways that will only make the world smaller and smaller
> and faster and faster with each passing day (118).

By way of further elaboration, Friedman asserts that a successful state (or a successful government of a nation-state) will have to implement "operational software" consistent with the dictates of this Electronic Herd:

> Software is a measure of the quality of a country's legal and regulatory systems,
> and the degree to which its officials, bureaucrats and citizens understand its
> laws, embrace them and know how to make them work. Good software
> includes banking laws, commercial laws, bankruptcy rules, contract laws, busi-
> ness codes of conduct, a genuinely independent central bank, property rights
> that encourage risk-taking, processes for judicial review, international account-
> ing standards, commercial courts, regulatory oversight agencies backed up by
> an impartial judiciary, laws against conflicts of interest and insider trading by
> government officials, and officials and citizens ready to implement these rules
> in a reasonably consistent manner. (129)

While most developed nations fare rather well in terms of this operational
software, the implication is that the pervasive Electronic Herd will strive to make
this software more uniform across nations. Indeed, in the wake of the Asian currency crisis, striking the G-20 Committee (with Canada's Paul Martin at the helm)
is explicitly designed to ensure that this vision of accountable and transparent
"software" becomes the norm for all nations.

In any event, there is no denying the impact of the dominant, pervasive
and irreversible forces of global capital on the fortunes of nation-state power and
sovereignty, forces that are likely to intensify as you and I harness the power of
our own PCs and, in effect, become an integral part of this Electronic Herd. But
just as the economic role and power of nation-states is being eroded from above,
as it were, there are correspondingly powerful forces that are undermining
nation-states from below.

Transferring Powers Downward

Markets in Ascendancy

P OWERS ARE ALSO BEING PASSED DOWNWARD FROM CENTRAL GOVERNMENTS OF nation-states, especially from central governments of *federal* nation-states. Partly as a result of technology, fiscal (deficit and debt) considerations, efficiency concerns, and partly as a result of what might be termed the "ideology of globalization," governments everywhere are in the process of privatizing, deregulating, contracting out and downsizing — all of which are serving to constrain the traditional economic and regulatory sweep of national governments. Intriguingly, this downward transfer of powers, like the upward transfer discussed above, is also partly associated with greater reliance on markets, since markets are inherently impersonal and decentralized coordinating mechanisms.

However, there is also a technological aspect to this downward transfer of powers. The information/technological revolution is progressively blurring the lines between the public and private sector, for example. Specifically, the availability of technological "by-pass" means it is no longer possible to cross-subsidize local telephone rates from non-competitive levies on long distance rates. Indeed, we are rapidly approaching the day when there will no longer be specific charges for long-distance calls. Similarly, the Canadian Radio-television and Telecommunications Commission (CRTC) is finding its room to manoeuvre progressively constrained, as evidenced by its recent decision to abandon any attempt to regulate the Internet. This harkens back to the earlier reference to goals and instruments. Canadians may still want to subsidize local telephone service or various cultural activities but, increasingly, this will require creative instrument choice. To an economist, there is some good news here. If Canadian society wishes to intervene on the distribution front (as it certainly does, and indeed should, in many areas) then the appropriate instrument is a *distributional* instrument (e.g., the tax-transfer system) rather than an *allocative* instrument (e.g., cross-subsidization of activities).

This represents an enormous shift in the historical role of governments in Canada. Unlike Americans, we Canadians traditionally held a much more benevolent view of governments and government intervention. At the core of much of our original nation building was a host of Crown Corporations at both levels of government. Hardin (1974) refers to these commercial crowns as the "chosen instrument." However, they are fast disappearing, with Ontario Hydro among the latest to be broken up and subjected to more competition. Again, this is a goals-instrument trade-off. To the extent that the original goals of these commercial crowns remain relevant today, it is increasingly clear that crown corporations are progressively a less effective instrument for pursuing these societal objectives. To return to a recurring theme, we need new instruments to reinvigorate enduring goals.

The Sovereign Individual and the Denationalization of Citizenship

The typical lament for the nation-state, especially the economic nation-state, is linked to capital hegemony, internationally, and to the market pressures for commercializing key aspects of public goods and services delivery, domestically. But there is another fundamental force at play that erodes the nation-state from below: the rise of "the sovereign individual" (Davidson and Rees-Mogg 1997). The reason is straightforward: Information-empowered citizens have broken the nation-states' monopoly on information and, therefore, power. This democratization of information, already referenced in terms of the Electronic Herd, will be developed in more detail in Chapter 3. However, some elaboration is appropriate in the present context.

Under the traditional Westphalian model, states, by virtue of their control over territory, effectively created "nations" or national citizens. With globalization and the information revolution, we are witnessing a shift "away from purely territorial political forms" and toward "a greater role for non-territorial organizations and identities" (Elkins 1995: dust jacket). In other words, nations or citizens will transform the nature of nation-states. Elkins employs a restaurant analogy to press this point: "The unbundled world of the twenty-first century may be more like an *à la carte* menu, even as regards political authorities, than the *table d'hôte* menu of nation-states (237). Thus, instead of accommodating themselves to a powerful state, citizens will begin to reverse this relationship and progressively become valued "customers" of governments. While the Davidson and Rees-Mogg vision of the "denationalization of citizenship" may be taking things too far, it is nonetheless the case that the information-revolution is having a profound and permanent impact on the traditional citizen-state relationship. The June 24, 2000, issue of *The Economist* ("A Survey of Government and the Internet") insightfully refers to one aspect of this emerging relationship as *E The People*, a relationship that has the transmitters (government) attempting to engage the receptors (citizens), who will progressively drive the content of this *E The People* revolution.

Fiscalamity and Decentralization

While this analysis of the downward transfer of powers in nation-states is rather general in that it applies to virtually all OECD countries and not just Canada, we Canadians exacerbated the challenge facing governments in the emerging global era *via a set of policy initiatives that were entirely of our own making.* Foremost among these was a societal decision to saddle future Canadians with an inordinate debt load. One can mount a plausible case that this disregard for the implications of debt and deficits was a reaction to the emerging global order, in that the resulting fiscal excesses represented a futile effort on our part to maintain the last generation's socio-economic paradigm.[2] In any event, the result at the federal level was a mushrooming debt-to-GDP ratio. From a post-war low of less than 20 percent in the early 1970s, the federal debt/GDP ratio exceeded 70 percent in the mid-1990s, before dropping back slightly. If one adds provincial debt into the equation, Canada's aggregate debt/GDP ratio broke through the 100 percent level in the mid-1990s. The immediate problem here was that the deficit was out of control, exceeding $40 billion when Paul Martin assumed the fiscal helm. Recognition that the deficit and debt overhang was unsustainable has dominated federal budgeting since Finance Minister Paul Martin's 1995 budget. As an important aside, one should add that this was not without some help from the Electronic Herd: A few months prior to the path-breaking 1995 federal budget, which put Canada on a course to restore fiscal integrity, Moody's put Canada under a "credit watch."

Among the many results of recent federal budgets were and are the following:

- ◆ The inauguration of the CHST (Canada Health and Social Transfer) as a "super" block fund, integrating the former Established Programs Financing (for health and post-secondary education) and the Canada Assistance Plan (for welfare) replete with a seven-billion dollar decrease in cash transfers to the provinces.
- ◆ A reduction in the role and size of the federal government — a decrease of 45,000 in the federal civil service.

- An intensification of the moves toward contracting out, deregulation, privatization and the like.
- A devolution of power from Ottawa to the provinces: the CHST itself, and the transfer of forestry, mining, tourism and training, among other areas, to the provinces.

The process did not end here. Faced with declining revenues, the provinces also began a roughly similar process of fiscal retrenchment and most of them introduced their own fiscal stringency programs.

In tandem, these and related initiatives represent the most thoroughgoing devolution of government expenditures in the post-war period, and perhaps in our history. As a result, government program spending as a percent of GDP has fallen from 36 percent in 1994 to a forecast 26 percent by the turn of the century, a decrease to 11 percent from 17 percent on Ottawa's part and to 15 percent from 19 percent at the provincial level. This dramatic fall in the ratio of government spending programs to GDP represents a change in the citizen-government relationship that is only now becoming fully recognized by citizens.

One significant implication of this period of fiscal restraint (alongside the ongoing period of sustained economic growth) is that there has been a marked turnaround in the fiscal positions of all governments. At the federal level, the budget has now been in surplus for three successive years, with presumably more to come. These improved fiscal prospects, combined with the growing recognition that the earlier federal expenditure paring was too draconian, have led to some new expenditure infusions, especially in terms of intergovernmental transfers. The 1999 and 2000 federal budgets, along with the September 2000 intergovernmental accord on health care, reversed much of the CHST reduction. Moreover, with further projected surpluses in the offing, future budgets at both levels of government will surely ramp up public spending. But the system is unlikely to return to the 1994 high-water mark in terms of the role of public spending in the economy. Historians will surely mark the last half-dozen years of the twentieth century as every bit as much a watershed in Canada's socio-economic evolution as were the formative Pearson years of the 1960s. And in terms of the operations of the federal systems, this period will also be remembered as one where some key powers were effectively transferred to the provinces. In particular, Chapter 14 will document this process as it relates to the operations of personal and corporate income taxation.

Transferring Powers Outward

IN TERMS OF THE "OUTWARD" OR HORIZONTAL TRANSFER OF POWERS, READERS ARE referred to entry F of Appendix B which focuses on international "regimes," where regimes are defined as formal or informal international institutional devices through which economic and political actors organize and manage their interdependencies. As noted, the activities of regimes run the gamut from setting standards, performing allocative functions, monitoring compliance, reducing conflict and resolving disputes. While regimes have long been with us, the increased interdependency in the GIR era implies they will proliferate, especially in terms of setting industry standards in the high-tech sector. Admittedly, the line between an outward transfer of powers and an upward transfer is blurred: Is the WTO an exercise in sharing sovereignty or does it qualify as an upward transfer of power? For purposes of the ensuing analysis, this distinction is not all that important. What is important is that there are increasing constraints placed on the economic and regulatory scope of governments, some of which arise as the result of international private-sector and public-sector initiatives and arrangements designed to coordinate and monitor activities across national boundaries. Indeed, one may well want to view the recent pan-Canadian initiatives undertaken by the revitalized Annual Premiers' Conference as a domestic version of this horizontal or outward transfer of power, in this case an attempt by provinces to coordinate and internalize the policy interdependencies arising from an enhanced decentralization of powers.

Subsidiarity, GIR and Decentralization

TO THIS POINT IN THE ANALYSIS, THE IMPLICIT IF NOT EXPLICIT ASSUMPTION IS THAT GIR is triggering decentralization within federations, the Canadian federation in particular. On the surface, this accords well with the principle of subsidiarity, which posits that powers and competencies in a federal system should, other things being equal, be assigned to the lowest level of government that can effectively implement these powers. And the information revolution aspect of GIR clearly facilitates this since the falling costs of access to information and to mechanisms for monitoring and control imply that these functions can now be located closer to the people. This is evident in the healthcare area with the proliferation of regional health authorities.

However, there is a flip side to the principle of subsidiarity. In policy areas where externalities and spillovers exist, these policy areas should be transferred upward to that jurisdictional level where these externalities can be internalized. Hence, subsidiarity carries a double thrust: While the information implications of GIR suggest further decentralization, the externality implications of GIR indicate some policy areas should be transferred upward in order to internalize any resulting spillovers.

To convert the principle of subsidiarity into an operational concept, let us associate the likelihood of the presence of externalities with the degree of "mobility" inherent in the specific policy area. With this in mind, consider the three traditional factors of production: land, labour and capital. Land is clearly the least mobile of the three factors of production and, not surprisingly, responsibility for this area is being passed downward, e.g., privatization of various sorts of infrastructure, including the devolution of airports to local authorities. Capital (and finance) is by far the most mobile and, as a result, there are pressures to transfer jurisdiction upward. Indeed, on acquiring power in 1995, the Ontario Conservatives offered to transfer the regulation of the Ontario securities industry to Ottawa, although complications subsequently stalled this transfer. More recently, however, the various provincial stock exchanges have rationalized their operations and, more recently still, they have begun integrating their operations with US stock exchanges (e.g., the Montreal Stock Exchange has linked up with NASDAQ).

The remaining factor, labour, falls in the middle in terms of mobility and, again not surprisingly, responsibility for labour market policy is moving both upward and downward. For example, the training component of labour market policy has been formally devolved to the provinces. However, even though the provinces are generally responsible for occupation accreditation, the concern that citizens be able to ensure portability of their skills accreditation across provinces has led to an upward, or at least an outward, transfer of responsibility (i.e., the mutual recognition provisions of SUFA).

Relatedly, the framework for the new environmental legislation can also be viewed as following the "mobility" dictates of subsidiarity — provincial monitoring of "on the ground" aspects of environmental oversight with pan-Canadian (interprovincial or federal) regulation of those aspects embodying cross-province spillovers. This is subsidiarity in action.

One often hears that subsidiarity points in opposite directions in Canada and in the European Union — toward greater decentralization in Canada and toward greater centralization in the EU. But one must be cautious here, since the Europeans are in the process of creating an integrated market and, to a degree, some common political institutions. Moreover, the "home country rule" in the EU is inherently more centralizing than the "national treatment" provision of the FTA and NAFTA. Thus, one would expect selected powers to be transferred upward in Europe as part of the process to embrace aspects of political integration. Yet, one can make a case that subsidiarity is also alive and well in Europe. For example, in implementing the many EU single-market "directives," the responsibility in Germany frequently falls to the Länder. Indeed, Germany represents an intriguing example of powers being passed upward and downward from central governments of federal nation-states. Specifically, the EU directives are monitored from Brussels, and often implemented by the Länder, and thereby by-pass Berlin. More generally, the Germans have recently amended their Basic Law (Constitution) to the effect that where further EU integration involves the competencies of the Länder, they will take a lead role in the negotiations. Many Canadian provinces would wish to have this degree of commitment to, let alone constitutional recognition of, the principle of subsidiarity.

In summary, the principle of subsidiarity provides an important reminder that even though the recent trends in the Canadian federation have, on balance, been in a decentralist direction, some mobile policy areas are also, and appropriately, being transferred upward in our federation. Beyond this, the subsidiarity principle will play an important role in the design of new governing instruments in the face of GIR: Indeed, it already has in the case of the social union framework (much more on this later).

With powers passing upward and downward from central governments of federal nation-states, what is the role for nation-states in a progressively GIR era? While this is jumping ahead in terms of the flow of the analysis, it seems appropriate to offer some initial reflections.

GIR and the Future of
the Nation-State

DOES GLOCALIZATION SIGNAL THE "DEATH KNELL" FOR THE ECONOMIC NATION-STATE, as Reich (1991) contends? The increasingly porous borders combined with the increasing national intrusiveness of the Electronic Herd on the one hand and the global outreach of national citizens on the other suggest this may well be the case. Nonetheless, the prevailing literature tends to assert that the evolving nation-state need not be less important, but only that its role will be very different. The question is, how different?

The starting point is to recognize that globalization affects nation-states differently. The US appears quite willing to transfer greater powers to markets, but appears quite unwilling to transfer real powers upward to supranational organizations. Smaller and more open nation-states have little option but to do both. But the difference goes beyond this. Louis Pauly (1999) reminds us that international markets may not be as "global" or "cosmopolitan" as one is led to believe. In particular, multinational enterprises (MNEs), especially US MNEs, remain reflections of their deeper national histories, identities and cultures.

> The phenomenon of corporate multinationalization across the leading industrial states essentially remains a process through which still-national corporations, and the innovation and investment systems within which they remain rooted, are inserted into the home markets of their competitors. Those corporations then adapt themselves at the margin, but not at the core. Ultimately, leading multinational corporations (MNCs) continue to reflect that concatenation of variables commonly depicted as their dominant national cultures....Indeed, a commitment to defending distinctive national cultures was hard-wired into many of the world's leading MNCs. (Pauly 1999: 104-06)

This would suggest that what we are witnessing is not globalization, *per se*, but Americanization or Europeanization in the wake of the policies and influences of their home-based multinationals.

Castells (1996: 192) agrees that the concept of transnational corporations as "citizens of the world economy" does not seem to hold quite yet. Nonetheless, he views the networks formed by MNEs as eventually transcending national boundaries, identities and interests. Ultimately, he contends, these MNEs will evolve "from multinational enterprises to international networks." This is in line with his earlier (1989) "networking" concept of the emerging nature of economic geography — from a *space of places* to a *space of flows*. In the interim, Pauly's assessment merits consideration, namely that multinationals of the major nation-states do transfer some of their home culture and values to host countries.

The second and related point is more fundamental, namely this fear that the vision of smaller and more open economies as "paradigm takers" in the GIR era is the effective death-knell for the traditional nation-state, and not only in the economic sphere. In the Canadian context, by far the most comprehensive and passionate lament for the passing of the Westphalian order is York University's Harry Arthurs' *Constitutionalizing Neo-Conservatism and Regional Economic Integration* (1999). Recognizing, implicitly at least, the power and sweep of the Electronic Herd, Arthurs foresees the demise of the activist interventionist state and, as it applies to Canada within NAFTA, concludes that Canada has precious little "room for manoeuvre." Underpinning this conclusion for Canada is a three-pronged series of rationales, two of which fall under the acronym TINA. The first TINA — There Is No Alternative — reflects the pervasiveness of the ongoing philosophy of neo-conservatism. While this TINA is *specific to our time*, as it were, the second TINA — Trapped In North America, or continentalism — is *specific to our place*. These are related in the sense that one reason why There Is No Alternative for Canada is precisely because we are Trapped In North America. Accommodating the challenges of GIR is one thing; doing so with the world's foremost superpower on our doorstep is quite another.

Arthurs' third rationale relates to an additional set of emerging forces — decentralization, juridification and populism — all of which tend to undermine the policy ability of the Canadian federal government: decentralization because the centre becomes less relevant; juridification because Canadians are increasingly turning to the courts as policy arbiters; and populism because, in its current variant (balanced budgets, tax cuts, referenda etc.) it views the state as alien, even hostile. In effect, the totality of these influences is more than the sum of the component parts: Populism speaks to the means while neo-conservatism speaks to the ends, for example.

Arthurs' view is that, together, these forces are influencing our belief systems and constraining our options to such an extent that this belief system is effectively becoming institutionalized and, in a broader sense, *constitutionalized*. In short, there appears in Arthurs' view to be no room to manoeuvre and, unless we counter all of this somehow, the emerging Canadian nation-state will presumably resemble the paradigm-compatible-software vision articulated by Friedman (as quoted earlier).

My view is that both perspectives are correct as far as they go: There is an accommodating imperative and there is less room for manoeuvre. The challenge, which I turn to in Part IV, is how to reap the obvious benefits of GIR while devising strategies, policies and instruments that will allow the Canadian nation-state a meaningful degree of flexibility across a key range of policy fronts — in particular, the pursuit of both economic competitiveness and social cohesion.

This caveat aside, the likely evolution of nation-states has another important dimension, that articulated by Castells. The important insight here is GIR alters the decision locus of each policy area differently. For capital flows, the locus is now international, but this is less so for cultural movements, social infrastructure and the like. Thus, the role of the nation-state in areas where the locus of power has shifted to the supranational level is obviously altered:

> The emerging forms of governance of international markets and other economic processes involve the major national governments but in a new role: states come to function less as "sovereign" entities and more as components of an "international polity." The central functions of the nation-state will become those of providing legitimacy for and ensuring the accountability of supranational and subnational governance mechanisms. (Castells 1997: 304-5)
>
> [Nation-states] will increasingly be nodes of a broader network of power (305).

But even in the face of this internationalization of power and decision-making, nation-states remain relevant:

> National competitiveness is still a function of national policies, and the attractiveness of economies to foreign multinationals is a function of local economic conditions...
>
> National human capital markets are essential for the productivity of economic units located in a national territory. (307)

Thus, nation-states still matter. Software (à la Friedman) is important. Yet there remains some freedom to manoeuvre. Even Friedman, in spite of his above quotation with respect to the Electronic Herd and the software dictates of GIR, recognizes that there is room to manoeuvre. Intriguingly, he does this in the context of the term "glocalization," although his definition differs from my earlier definition:

> I believe the most important filter is the ability to "glocalize." I define healthy glocalization as the ability of a culture, when it encounters other strong cultures, to absorb influences that naturally fit into and can enrich that culture, to resist those things that are truly alien and to compartmentalize those things that, while different, can nevertheless be enjoyed and celebrated as different. The whole purpose of glocalizing is to be able to assimilate aspects of globalization into your country and culture in a way that adds to your growth and diversity, without overwhelming it. (Friedman 1999: 236)

This resonates well with the later themes of this study. Nonetheless, the passionate concerns of Harry Arthurs should not be ignored, especially for those of us who wish to preserve the hard-won socio-economic distinctiveness of the upper half of North America.

Were I writing this only a half-dozen years ago, I would conclude at this point and proceed directly to the following chapter, which addresses the implications of GIR for citizens. However, the sweep of GIR is such that it is forcing a renewed interest and importance on an often neglected component of Canadian government and governance: local/municipal government, in particular on what has come to be referred to as "global city-regions." No less an authority on things global than Kenichi Ohmae (2000) has asserted that urban agglomerations in the range of three to five million people are emerging as the primary engines or motors of the new global economic order. Thus, one of the important sub-themes of this study will be to resurrect the role of cities both in their own right and as an integral component of the structure of governance in the Canadian federation. Accordingly, the next section begins the process of integrating cities, and municipal government generally, more fully and more formally into the analysis of the challenges for government and governance in a GIR era.

Cities and the New Global Order

C ANADIAN CITIES AND MUNICIPALITIES ARE EFFECTIVELY "CONSTITUTIONLESS," OR SO we have been led to believe. Formally, this is not quite correct: Municipalities *are* mentioned in the Constitution. The preamble to Section 92 of the *Constitution Act, 1982*, reads: "In each Province the legislature may exclusively make laws in relation to matters coming within the Classes of Subjects next hereinafter enumerated..." Among the enumerated powers is subsection 92(8): "Municipal Institutions in the Province." What this means is that municipalities and cities are effectively the creatures of their respective provinces. As such, cities have not played a major role in the formal Canadian fiscal federalism literature. To be sure, much has been written about the role and governance of cities and about provincial-municipal relations, but this literature does not link up closely with the division-of-powers literature. Nonetheless, one of the many implications of GIR is that cities large enough to fall under the umbrella of "global city-regions" are emerging as major players on the world economic and political stage. Consequently, Canada's potential global city-regions — Toronto, Montreal, Vancouver, among others — will become increasingly important players on the economic, social and cultural stage; one way or another, they *will* acquire greater power and influence. The purpose of this section is to provide some backdrop relating to the nexus between GIR and these global city-regions. This will prepare the ground for integrating this third tier of government, and global city-regions in particular, into the evolution of governance structures in Chapter 15.

In one sense, it is somewhat surprising that cities and city-regions are gaining in importance. Not too long ago, conventional wisdom suggested that as a result of the information revolution the economies of scope and agglomeration typically associated with cities would become less important. The prevailing view was that of the "electronic cottage" linked interactively with the corporate head office. Thus, you and I could be employed by an enterprise in Toronto or Montreal or Vancouver or Calgary but could work from Renfrew or Rimouski or Rockland or Red Deer. While this vision of the electronic cottage has become a reality in some important areas (e.g., computer programmers in Bangalore, India, writing code for Microsoft, or, within Canada, call centres in Moncton serving the needs of domestic and foreign multinationals), the reality is that GIR has enhanced the role of cities, especially the so-called global city-regions. As Scott, et al. note,

> The propensity for many types of economic activity — manufacturing and service sectors alike — to gather together in dense locational clusters appears to have been intensifying in recent decades. This quest for mutual proximity on the part of all manner of economic agents at the present time can in part be interpreted as a strategic response to intensified economic competition, above all because significant economic productivity and performance advantages can often be obtained by clustering together. Globalization has accentuated the

entire process, and with the extension of markets to wider international spheres, the economies of global city-regions have grown accordingly. Large city-regions are thus coming to function as territorial platforms for contesting global markets. (Scott, et al. 2000)

Thus, GIR is enhancing the position and importance of cities both in their original territorial role and in their newer networking role. In terms of the first of these, more and more firms rely for their success on a variety of externalities — local public goods, access to human capital, access to social overhead capital — provided via the interactions among and between firms on the one hand and the "innovative milieu"[3] of the city on the other. Urban geographers have come to refer to these externalities as "untraded interdependencies" (Storper 1995), whereas economists might refer to them as "locational increasing returns." In any event, "the competitive weapons reside more outside the single firms than inside them, more in the local milieu than in a specific firm located in its geographical space" (Camagni 2000).

The second rationale for the increasing importance of cities in the GIR era relates to their role as *nodes* or *interconnectors* in long-distance networks:

Strong synergetic processes originate...whenever the city acts as a node in multiple planetary networks — transport and communication networks, but also immaterial networks centered around specialized activities, professional relationships, power relationships and headquarters functions. What counts more, multiplier and increasing returns effects stem from the interdependence between the size of the city and its nodal role, due to critical mass effects in the demand for external connectivity and effects on competitiveness of local activities coming from the supply of external connectivity. (Camagni 2000)

Indeed, to the extent that the public sector can be viewed as "globalizing," this is occurring via the spread of these international cities. Toronto increasingly resembles New York and Tokyo rather than Kingston and Sarnia. Moreover, the mayors of these international cities are becoming more important internationally than the premiers or governors of the provinces or states in which they are located. And in the domestic context, cities and local governments generally are the jurisdictional locus where the myriad provincial and federal policies are effectively implemented — policies related to welfare, education, training, health, accommodating immigrants, and on and on. If subsidiarity has any meaning at all, it has to begin to incorporate the importance of cities as the optimal jurisdiction for the implementation of a wide range of policies.

Yet, as noted, Canadian cities currently have little in the way of political, economic or fiscal manoeuvrability. For present purposes, the point to note is that this is progressively offside with the internal dynamics of GIR and, in particular, with the fact that the new global era is privileging global city-regions, let alone offside with the principle of subsidiarity. Rethinking the role of cities in the Canadian governance structure will be rejoined in Chapter 15.

Conclusion

GIR IS TRANSFORMING THE WESTPHALIAN VISION AND VERSION OF THE TRADITIONAL nation-state. Rethinking and repositioning the nation-state in the GIR era will be one of the foremost policy challenges of the millennium. But reconceptualizing the role of government and governance is premature at this point in the analysis; we have just begun the process of detailing the many challenges GIR poses for economies and societies.

What is largely absent from the preceding analysis of the impact of GIR on governments in the new global era is the transfer of powers from all levels of government to citizens. While the rhetoric of GIR tends to focus on its internationalization aspects and the global sweep of the Electronic Herd, the reality is that individuals are now, or soon will be, the principal beneficiaries of the information revolution. You and I have access to incredible information flows that we can transform and transmit in ways that governments of all stripes are powerless to prevent. Arguably, and as noted above, this democratization of information is every bit as significant as internationalization in terms of undermining the traditional concept of the Westphalian nation-state. I now turn in more detail to the impact of GIR on citizens.

GIR and Citizens

T HE IMPACT OF GIR ON GOVERNMENTS AND ON MARKETS, ESPECIALLY THE internationalization of markets, has tended to capture the policy limelight, but one of the enduring themes of this treatise is that citizens are really at the centre of the tumultuous changes ushered in by this new paradigm. Key aspects of this have already been broached: the progressive internationalization of citizens (e.g., the "sovereign individual"), and the presumption that democratization of information implies citizens will emerge as the principal beneficiaries of the informatics revolution. In this chapter, I elaborate on these two pervasive implications and address the more daunting challenges for citizens: those associated with the income-distribution implications arising from GIR.

GIR as Consumer Sovereignty

I NDIVIDUALS ARE EMERGING AS THE PRINCIPAL BENEFICIARIES OF THE INFORMATION revolution. Consistent with this observation, Kenichi Ohmae (*The Borderless World*, 1990) actually defines globalization as "consumer sovereignty," i.e., "performance standards are now set in the global marketplace *by those that buy the products, not those that regulate them*" (dust jacket, emphasis added). Indeed, the democratization of technology foreshadows a much more far-reaching sweep for citizens. Not long ago, those transmitting determined the information flow. Increasingly, "receptors" are calling the shots. Moreover, as former NBC News President Lawrence Grossman noted,

> Printing made us all readers. Xeroxing made us all publishers. Televisions made us all viewers. Digitization makes us all broadcasters. (quoted in Friedman 1999: 45)

And once comfortably, psychologically, and culturally ensconced in the driver's seat, citizens will remain at the wheel as the worldwide networking continues its explosive expansion. This is obviously the case in terms of consumer goods and services where the household PC effectively becomes a global catalogue and, increasingly, a global e-commerce supermarket. But information-empowered citizens will also fundamentally alter the design and delivery of *public* goods and services as *E The People* becomes a reality.

Clearly, GIR has enfranchised individuals as consumers of both public and private goods and services. But GIR may be seen as disenfranchising individuals in some aspects of their roles as political actors and citizens, as we shall see.

GIR and Democracy [4]

THERE IS BURGEONING POLITICAL SCIENCE LITERATURE DEALING WITH THE INTERACTION between GIR and citizens or, more correctly, between GIR and democracy. Since the playing field of political science tends to be nation-state based and since the nation-state is in full evolutionary flight, much of this literature is in the way of a lament for the erosion of citizenship/democracy as more and more of the "stuff" of the nation-state is either transferred upward or privatized. This is true as far as it goes, but it does not go far enough. What is emerging, albeit still in its embryonic stage, is a new, exciting and empowering global citizenship/democracy driven by information-empowered, like-minded individuals from all corners of the globe. It is this movement — let's call it, à la Friedman, the decentralized but internationally networked "Electronic Citizen-Democracy Herd" — that in my view will eventually emerge as an important global countervail to Friedman's "Electronic Herd." This is the emerging framework with which I want to overlay the traditional nation-state-bound democracy literature and its current emphasis on the emergence of "democracy deficits."

First, however, there are areas where citizenship and democracy go hand-in-hand with GIR. Foremost is that the information revolution means citizens are (or can be) much more fully informed (and mobilized) with respect to policy issues than heretofore. Indeed, the era of interactive "direct" democracy is at hand and has already found a place in the design and implementation of government policy, let alone the marketing of new commercial products. At another level, GIR and democracy are also demonstrably compatible: "Globalization has given strength and encouragement to democratizing movements in many parts of the world" (Simeon 1997: 308). Indeed, referencing research by Huntingdon (1991), Simeon (308) notes that between 1974 and 1990, the very period in which globalization was beginning to emerge as the dominant paradigm, at least 30 countries made a transition to democracy. This just about doubled the number of democratic governments in the world and this trend clearly accelerated after the implosion of the USSR and its satellites. In this sense, GIR and democracy are demonstrably compatible.

The more prevalent perspective among political scientists, however, relates to the emergence of so-called "democracy deficits" — the *disenfranchising* of nation-state citizens because an increasing number of policy issues that affect their lives are determined in supranational forums where they have no *direct* representation. Much of the literature on democracy deficits arose in the context of the EU, where the powerful "confederal" Council of Ministers oversaw the articulation of hundreds of directives which were then binding on the individual nation-states and their citizens.[5] For example, the British are now subject to the binding rulings of the European Court of Justice. To be sure, this remains an exercise in *indirect* democracy, since the ministers on the Council are duly elected politicians in their own countries. But it is not an exercise in *popular* democracy, since there is no forum in which French citizens, for example, are directly represented in these decisions. Friedman has aptly cast this issue as follows:

> When all politics is local, your vote matters. But when power shifts to...transnational spheres, there are no elections and there is no one to vote for. (Friedman 1999: 161)

Admittedly, the European Parliament is struggling to enhance its power and scope, but a federal EU is still a long way off. Were it to come to fruition, it would still differ from traditional nation-state democratic participation since there would be no "national vetoes" in the EU parliament. Intriguingly, where unanimity still holds sway with the decision-making of the Council of Ministers, there obviously *are* national vetoes.

What are the likely avenues through which citizen input can be brought to bear on supranational decision-making? The issue can be rephrased as follows: Given that transnational capital was fast off the mark in terms of accommodating itself to the emerging GIR environment, where is the likely source of countervailing power? Governments themselves are constrained to a large degree since it is they who are parties to most of these supranational arrangements, although the decision to be a party is frequently the result of an exercise in popular democracy. This is especially the case in terms of the FTA, given the 1988 free-trade election.

I think that a key component of this countervail will come increasingly from powerful citizens' lobbies organizing themselves at the transnational or global level. Canadians are already well aware of this international citizen power. Brigitte Bardot, and the anti-sealing lobby, is a case in point. Likewise, the good burghers of the US northeast have stalled Hydro Quebec's construction aspirations, and the BC lumbering interests must now answer to citizens' lobbies in Britain and Germany. At a more general and more important level, Canada's Maude Barlow and the associated transnational-citizen-related NGOs can lay claim to being the first successful citizen effort to harness the potential of democratized information in the context of derailing the MAI (Multilateral Agreement on Investment), an agreement that had the support of both national governments and multinational capital.[6] And the Battle in Seattle was a more recent demonstration of the growing power and influence of the Electronic Citizen-Democracy Herd. This clearly speaks to the earlier dictum that digitization will make us all broadcasters.

Along these lines, Stanbury and Vertinsky (1995) survey the impact of the new information technologies on interest group behaviour and policymaking, and emphasize the role of Greenpeace in harnessing the Internet. But the role of Greenpeace itself is becoming "democratized." A few well-targeted e-mail messages related to company X's inappropriate actions in country Y can have wide ramifications for the company's operations everywhere. As detailed later, the corporate response here has, appropriately, been to rethink key aspects of corporate governance and/or corporate responsibility.

Indeed, just as GIR is serving to shift powers upward and downward from national governments, it is also having similar impacts on citizens:

> While globalization can produce an enormous sense of alienation, as power
> keeps moving up to more and more abstract levels that are difficult to touch

and affect or even see, it can also do the opposite. It can push down to the local level and to individuals more power and resources than ever before. (Friedman 1999: 293)

Two caveats are in order here. First, this transfer of "more power and resources" to citizens can be, and increasingly will be, harnessed collectively and/or via NGOs to bring pressure to bear on policies and practices everywhere, one aspect of which will be to play a countervail role on the international scene. Second, GIR implies that citizens will also increasingly direct their traditional political activity in a direction where it has the most impact, namely at the local level. Horsman and Marshall elaborate:

> As the diminution of single-state power becomes evident, and as embryonic supranational political arrangements come only slowly into being, citizens will tend to think more closely...about their own communities (variously defined...), seeking local political reflections of their concerns, even as the economies in which they are consumers move ever closer toward global integration. They will seek political solutions, and democratic accountability, at ever more local levels as the world economy moves toward an ever-greater level of integration. (Horsman and Marshall 1994: xv)

This message serves to breathe life into the principle of subsidiarity, and it has implications for the unbundling of "nation" and "state," which will feature prominently in the chapter on the citizen-government interface.

While it is far too early and perhaps too optimistic to proclaim the implications of GIR for enfranchising individuals as consumers will also be carried fully over to individuals as citizens, it is not premature to suggest that the Westphalian concept of citizenship and democracy needs some rethinking. As Drucker (1993: 10) has appropriately pointed out, by and large, "political theory and constitutional law still know only the sovereign state." We are in need of a new concept of democracy and, indeed, a new approach to sovereignty that recognizes the profound evolution of the nation-state. Kymlicka sheds insight on all of this:

> Decisions about how to relate to other countries are themselves an important exercise of national sovereignty. It is not always true that we are "forced" by globalization into entering into transnational agreements and organizations. In many cases, entry into transnational arrangements is actively desired. This is perhaps clearer in the European context than in North America. It is quite clear, for example, that the desire of Spain or Greece to join the EU was not simply a matter of economic gain. It was also seen as a way of confirming their status as open, modern, democratic and pluralistic states, after many years of being closed and authoritarian societies. Similarly, the decision about whether

to admit new countries from Eastern Europe to the EU will be decided not just on the basis of economic gain, but also on the basis of moral obligations to assist newly democratizing countries, and on the basis of aspirations to create a Europe free of old divisions and hatreds.

In other words, decisions about integrating into transnational institutions are, in part, decisions about what kind of societies people want to live in. Choosing to accept globalization is not necessarily a denial of people's national identity or national autonomy, but may instead be an affirmation of their desired identity, and a deliberate exercise of their national autonomy. Being open to the world is, for many people, an important part of their self-conception as members of modern pluralistic societies, and they autonomously decide to pursue that self-conception through various international agreements and institutions. (Kymlicka 1997: 316)

Aspects of this will resurface in the context of the citizen-government interface in Chapter 8.

GIR and Income Distribution

THE MOST DAUNTING CHALLENGE ARISING FROM GIR AS IT RELATES TO INDIVIDUALS and, indeed, to society as a whole is not the impact on them as consumers or citizens but the implications for individuals as breadwinners — the impact of GIR on income distribution. Starkly put, market incomes are polarizing, with profound implications for societal cohesion and public policy alike. As a general introduction to this distributional issue, Thurow merits highlight:

The returns to capital are up and the returns to labour are down. On a global basis, labour is more abundant relative to capital than it is in the developed world. Therefore the earnings of capitalists grow, and the earnings of labour fall. Similarly the returns to skills are up and the returns to raw unskilled labour are down. On a global basis, the supply of unskilled workers far exceeds that of skilled workers. At the same time, technology is raising the demand for skilled workers and lowering the demand for unskilled workers. Supply and demand matter. (Thurow 1999: 279)

Moreover, this polarization is not only reflected in earnings but also evident in employment data. As Williamson (2000) notes, virtually all employment growth in Canada during the 1990s was for workers with a post-secondary degree, and this holds for all sectors of the economy. Specifically, over the 1990-1999 period, employment for Canadians with at least a post-secondary education rose by 2.26

million. In stark contrast, employment growth for persons with only a high school diploma rose by only 139,000 and it *fell* by 947,000 for Canadians with less than a high school diploma. In tandem, this earnings and employment polarization is one of the key determining factors that informs the underlying thesis of the analysis: A human capital future for Canada and Canadians is the principal way to accommodate and capitalize upon the challenges generated by GIR.

To delve further into the income distribution implications, it is convenient, initially, to focus separately on the globalization aspects and the knowledge/information aspects of GIR. In terms of the former, the internationalization of production implies that the routinized aspects of labour input can be progressively outsourced offshore. This creates both employment and income challenges for the lower end of the skill grid. And often it is not just the lower end of the wage grid that is being affected, since some of the jobs outsourced internationally are erstwhile middle-income positions shielded by the old-paradigm's protectionist environment. Intriguingly, economists' traditional focus on the role of the *minimum* wage is, to a degree at least, giving way to the new concept of a global *maximum* wage: If wage rates for a given routinized activity exceed this notional global maximum, then this activity becomes a candidate for outsourcing internationally.

At the other end of the income-distribution spectrum, the impact of the knowledge/information revolution is such that the returns to human capital are rising. This is complicated further by the fact that human capital is becoming more mobile internationally, so that in addition to garnering higher wages, human capital is now more difficult to subject to taxation. This follows from the general proposition that enhanced mobility (or the availability of "by-pass") means that mobile activities, both footloose industries and factors of production, can simply "migrate" in response to onerous taxation or regulation. What is new here is that not only physical and financial capital can opt out of a high-tax jurisdiction, but also skilled labour (i.e., human capital). Hence, in comparison with the *status quo ante*, market incomes are polarizing, and *after-tax incomes* will tend to exhibit even more polarity. This can be generalized: As Rodrik (1997) reveals, the evidence suggests that it is the immobile factors (land and unskilled labour) that, relatively and even absolutely, are bearing much of the costs of GIR. While these troubling income distribution challenges will be elaborated further in the context of both the citizen-market and citizen-government interfaces, three further observations are now relevant.

First, while market incomes are polarizing in *developed* countries, matters are quite different in *developing* countries:

> Indeed, for all the churning that global capitalism brings to a society, the spread of capitalism has raised living standards higher, faster and for more people than at any time in history. It has also brought more poor people into the middle classes more quickly than at any time in human history. So while the gap between rich and poor is getting wider — as the winners in today's globalization system really take off and separate themselves from everyone else — the floor under the poor has been rising steadily in many parts of the world. In other words, while relative poverty may be growing in many countries, absolute poverty is actually falling in many countries. According to the 1997 United Nations Human Development report, poverty has fallen more in the past 50 years than in the previous five hundred. Developing countries have progressed as fast in the past thirty years as the industrialized world did in the previous century. (Friedman 1999: 287)

For those among us whose frame of reference includes the welfare of peoples everywhere, this is something to cheer about. For others whose perception is national, this may be viewed as a most disconcerting development, one that might suggest a turning inward on globalization. For better but mostly worse, the sheer size of the American market means that the US has some scope to turn inward. Smaller and more open economies do not.

The second observation is related. While skilled labour has indeed become more mobile, so has "work," indeed probably more so in many cases. Thus, thanks to the information revolution, skilled workers in Bangalore, India, do "American" work like writing code for Microsoft, as already noted. In other words, outsourcing, writ large, now extends well into the category of skilled labour, not just routinized or assembly-related tasks. In other words, *"work" is becoming internationalized even if "workers" are not*. This harkens back to the altered nature of economic geography — the geo-economics of the global era is as much a "space of flows" (global networking) as it is a "space of places" (Castells 1989).

The final observation is probably the most relevant in terms of the implications for the evolution of Canadian society. It follows from the earlier assertion that the new global order will privilege human capital in the same way the industrial revolution privileged physical capital. Specifically, with knowledge increasingly at the cutting edge of competitiveness, important aspects of social policy are becoming progressively indistinguishable from "traditional" economic policy in terms of growth and competitiveness. Lester Thurow (1993: 5) effectively focused on the essence of this issue:

> If capital is borrowable, raw materials are buyable and technology is copyable, what are you left with if you want to run a high wage economy? Only skills, there isn't anything else.

Hence, any meaningful mission statement for 21st-century Canada must fully embrace the notion of a human capital society. I shall articulate a mission statement along these lines in Chapter 11. For now, it suffices to note that this will be a tall order for Canada. Among other things, it means that we must make the difficult transition from a resource-based economy and society to a human-capital-based economy and society. We are a long way from this perspective. Incredibly, we still associate terms like investment, investment tax credits, and depreciation only with the physical- and resource-capital domain, reserving for the social sphere such "economically incorrect" terms as subsidies, transfers and welfare. Unless and until we get our rhetoric consistent with the new reality, we will never make this fundamental transformation. While this is arguably the most significant policy challenge facing Canada in the millennium, it is also among the most complex, because effective implementation of a human capital strategy must be embedded within a framework that recognizes the pervasive impact of GIR in all its dimensions and not just on its income distribution or social policy ramifications.

GIR and Markets

I N THE POPULAR MIND, GIR IS TYPICALLY ASSOCIATED WITH THE INTERNATIONALIZATION of production and the advent of integrated global financial markets. This feature of the new economic order has already been highlighted — with economic space transcending political space, we have seen mobile capital and MNEs (i.e., the Electronic Herd) don the mantle of the new hegemonic force spanning the globe. Indeed, these integrated financial capital markets are essentially sophisticated technology-driven information and coordination systems able to bridge both *space* (e.g., currency swaps) and *time* (e.g., financial options and futures markets) on a virtually instantaneous basis. Hence, apart from a brief further focus on the internationalization of production, this section will direct attention first to selected consequences relating to the transformation of enterprise and then to a most profound development for Canada: the integration of the Canada-US or North American economic space.

The Internationalization of Production

I N *THE BORDERLESS WORLD*, KENICHI OHMAE (vii) ASSERTS THAT "NOTHING IS 'overseas' any longer." Alternatively, everything is! Global capital markets and the shift from multinational corporations (MNCs) to transnational enterprises (TNEs)[7] have ushered in an era that decouples enterprise from the factor endowments of any single nation. Hence, locational advantage becomes associated more with national "software" (as defined earlier), including human capital, than with the notion of "endowments" that dominated the earlier paradigm. Among other things, this is serving to wreak havoc with national welfare states everywhere. This is so because the typical welfare state designed its institutions, policies and incentives to mesh well with its national production system. However, with the internationalization of production, these welfare states will have to be rethought: What is the optimal nature of a *national* welfare state in an era of *international* production? Over a decade ago, Peter Drucker reminded us that all economics is now international. Is the same becoming true of all social policy? Since we Canadians do not even address these issues, it is not surprising that we have not made much headway in defining the challenge, let alone in finding a solution.

It is intriguing to focus on the evolution of social policy in light of the progressive integration on the economic and trading fronts. Not all that long ago, social policy was largely a matter of family, church and locality. With a deft selection of incentives (e.g., shared cost programs for hospitals, medical care and welfare) we not only "provincialized" social policy but also created or generated pan-Canadian social policy networks. With the shift toward human capital as the wellspring of economic success and competitiveness, this necessarily implies an enhanced national presence in key aspects of the social policy envelope. However, something new is now afoot — social policy is becoming internationalized! The European literature is replete with references to "social dumping," defined as producing goods and services with a level of wages and fringes *below that level* which would leave the country competitive. On this side of the Atlantic, we have built a "social policy rider" into NAFTA. Moreover, as social policy moves up the jurisdictional ladder, its focus is altering. At the local level, social policy was largely about maintaining body and soul. At the provincial level, the issue became one of rights and equity. At the national level, the focus has shifted toward economics — developing human capital. But in the global arena and in the era of internationalizing production, social policy will progressively come to be viewed as an instrument in competition policy and/or trade policy.

Note that this is part and parcel of the "complexity" I referred to in the earlier context of ensuring human capital issues become the defining feature of 21st-century Canadian social and economic policy. The potential interaction between social policy and commercial or trade policy may well overlay an additional set of constraints on the design of our social infrastructure. Once again, this need not influence our overall goals in this area, but it does call for new and creative instruments. However, it also highlights the unavoidable policy interdependency that promises to be an enduring feature of the new global order. We will no longer have the luxury of relying solely on the social envelope to deliver our social policy goals and aspirations: other policy areas, ranging from regulatory policy to commercial policy, will have to play an integral role in furthering a human capital future for Canadians. If we fail to recognize this emerging policy interdependency, the force of the internationalization of economic activity may well imply that human capital will become one of our principal "exports," with enormous consequences for our economic future, let alone the public purse.

Enterprise and
e-Business

T HE *ECONOMIST* BEGINS ITS SURVEY OF E-BUSINESS WITH THIS QUOTE FROM THE Chairman of Intel: "In five years' time all companies will be Internet companies or they won't be companies at all." Hence, while GIR facilitates the global reach of businesses, it also dramatically alters their operating procedures and strategies. The survey goes on to note three acknowledged facts about e-commerce:

- ◆ First, it shifts power from sellers to buyers by reducing the cost of switching suppliers (the next vendor is only a mouse-click away) and freely distributing a huge amount of price and product information. (Note that this resonates well with the earlier comments that the information revolution is enhancing consumer sovereignty.)
- ◆ The second is that the Internet reduces transactions costs and thus stimulates economic activity. A banking transaction via Internet costs one cent, compared with 27 cents at an ATM or 52 cents over the telephone.
(These two factors lead naturally to an enhanced role for "infomediation.")
- ◆ The third fact is that the speed, range and accessibility of information on the Internet and the low cost of distributing it create new commercial possibilities. Infomediaries, sitting in between buyers and sellers, are uniquely placed to collect information, add value to it, and distribute it to those who will find it most useful. (*The Economist* 1999: 23-24)

In this context, Canada's Internet guru, Donald Tapscott, continually emphasizes the key point that the Internet is not merely an aid or a tool to facilitate existing ways of organizing and producing output. Rather, it is itself a new production and organizational technology, one that may well sweep away existing approaches. Thus, the Internet is not only an integral part of the new techno-economic paradigm, for key areas it is the new techno-economic paradigm.

Indeed, as if in anticipation of these developments, Manuel Castells chose *The Rise of the Network Society* (1996) as the title of the first volume of his already-classic trilogy on the new global order. Networking is emerging as the key organizing principle of the new global order and it applies to governments, citizens and markets (enterprises) alike.

Not surprisingly, this dramatic decrease in transactions and monitoring costs of information is altering the internal structure of firms in myriad ways. Hierarchical structures are giving way to horizontal, flexible structures. The traditional theory of the firm was premised largely on the information and control advantage of "internal" (within-firm) markets over external markets. With the fall in information costs, firms are "unbundling," shedding services like payroll, maintenance, legal services and the like. And with the provision of services becoming much easier to monitor and measure, *The Economist* (1999: 20) speculates that governments may be next in line to restructure themselves along networking lines with myriad networked service providers, not all of which will be in the public sector.

Beyond this, the information revolution is dismantling the traditional boundaries of industry. Digitization means that formerly distinct industries such as cable TV and telephones are now part of the same industry. One problem this generates for public policy is that the resulting industrial restructuring has outstripped our current measurement capacity, based as it is on the old paradigm's industrial classification. Potentially much more problematic is that the consequent productivity increases and competitive pressures arising from GIR are fuelling the ongoing merger wave. As Thurow (1999: 11) notes, "merger activity ($2.4 trillion in 1998) is five times as great as it was in 1990 and 50 percent higher than it was in the previous record-high year (1997)." He goes on to note that nine of the ten largest deals ever made were made in 1998, with the other one in 1997. And the AOL/Time Warner deal in 1999 easily surpassed all of these.

This is and will continue to be a major societal issue for a small open economy like Canada, as the bank merger issue and the foreign takeover of MacMillan

Bloedel clearly indicate. Indeed, the recent Canadian merger and takeover data are highly revealing in their own right. Over the first half of 1999, Canadian companies took over 123 foreign firms worth $7.2 billion, a 25 percent drop from the previous year in the number and an 84 percent fall in the value of foreign acquisitions. During this same six-month period, foreigners took over 89 domestic companies worth $19.9 billion, a 10 percent increase in volume and a 45 percent increase in value (Beauchesne 1999). Elsewhere, I have argued that a large part of this reflects the fact that the sharp fall in the value of the dollar (*vis-à-vis* the US dollar) has served to place our assets at fire-sale prices (Courchene 1999a). Whether "monetary sovereignty" in terms of maintaining a flexible exchange rate is in reality serving to erode our sovereignty elsewhere in the policy sphere (e.g., the control of Canadian business) will be addressed later. For present purposes, the issue is what all this means for the future of Canadian-based multinationals. With, say, nine percent of combined Canadian-US income and assets, will the "steady state" under GIR imply that Canadians will own roughly nine percent of all Canada-US enterprises, but control none? This is another issue that will receive attention in the policy section. To anticipate the thrust of this analysis, Canadian-based head offices are essential if we wish to employ in Canada the human capital of Canadians.

Finally, GIR is changing the very nature of capitalism. Increasingly, the assets essential to a company's success go home every night. Boards and mortar are being replaced by mortarboards. This not only creates a whole new set of challenges for corporate governance but also challenges aspects of the rest of the capitalist framework. Banks have spent decades honing their policies and procedures for lending against hard, in-situ, assets. Now they have to completely reconstitute themselves and their policies for lending to "soft," mobile, human capital assets. This too is an integral part of the transition from a resource-based economy and society to a human-capital-based economy and society.

North American Market/Trade Integration [8]

I NTRIGUING AS THE IMPLICATIONS OF THE ABOVE ANALYSIS MAY BE, THE MOST SIGNIFICANT development for Canada arising from the interaction between GIR and markets is the dramatic shift toward north-south trade. From Table 1, all provinces except PEI and Nova Scotia are now more integrated, trade-wise, internationally than they are domestically.[9] In terms of the all-provinces' data (the last row in Table 1) for every dollar exported to other provinces (ROC, or Rest Of Canada) in 1981, 87 cents was exported to ROW (Rest Of World). By 1996, however, $1.83 was now exported internationally for each dollar of interprovincial exports. While ROW exports in Table 1 relate to exports to all countries, with over 80 percent of Canada's overall exports going to the United States, it is clearly the case that north-south trade dominates east-west trade. More recent data (Grady and Macmillan 1998) suggest that from 1989 to 1997 interprovincial exports slid from 22.7 percent to 19.7 percent of GDP. At the same time, international exports grew from 26.1 percent to 40.2 percent of GDP. In other words, international exports are now more than twice as large as interprovincial exports.

Nowhere is this redirection of trade flows more evident than it is in Ontario. As Figure 2 indicates, both interprovincial and international exports of goods and services from Ontario in 1981 were running at roughly $40 billion. By 1998, however, Ontario's international exports were in the range of $190 billion, nearly three times as large as Ontario's 1998 interprovincial exports, and growing nearly a magnitude faster. Figure 3, which expresses the Figure 2 data as a proportion of Ontario's GDP, indicates that as of 1998 international exports exceeded 50 percent of GDP, up from 30 percent in 1981. In contrast, interprovincial exports, also at 30 percent in 1981, have actually fallen to just under 20 percent of GDP in 1998. Since over 90 percent of Ontario's international exports are destined for the US, north-south exports are now within striking distance of 50 percent of Ontario's GDP.[10] In large measure, it is this dramatic shift in Ontario's trade that led Colin Telmer and I to entitle our recent book on Ontario *From Heartland to North American Region State* (1998).

This shift toward north-south trade is further complicated by the fact that Canada's regional business cycles are not synchronized. This is evident from Figure 4, which focuses on the 1980s and 1990s recessions and their implications for employment recovery. From the upper panel of Figure 4, four years after the onset of the 1980s recession, employment in Ontario was 105 percent of its pre-recession peak, whereas employment in Alberta and especially British Columbia was still well below their respective pre-recession peaks. The 1990s recession was entirely different. British Columbia skated through the recession with nary a

negative impact, and four years after the 1990s recession its employment was
nearly 10 percent above the pre-recession peak (although BC appears to be heading for rougher economic times in the current environment). In sharp contrast,
Ontario's employment was still well below its pre-recession high.

More quantitatively, the highest two-province correlation in terms of changes
in provincial GDPs over the 1961-1995 period is 87 percent, for Ontario and
Quebec (Kneebone and Mackenzie 1998: Table 1). On the other hand, "Alberta
stands out in particular with changes in output negatively correlated with five of the
other provinces, including Ontario and Quebec, and low positive correlations with
the other provinces, except Saskatchewan" [which presumably relates in part to the
fact that fossil energy is also important for Saskatchewan, TJC] (10).

Drawing together the evidence arising from increased north-south integration and east-west cyclical asymmetry leads to some rather controversial implications for Canada. Specifically, one can mount a case that, in terms of trading
opportunities, *Canada is progressively less and less a single national economy and
more and more a series of north-south cross-border economies* (Courchene and Telmer
1998). The implications go further, however. Consistent with the earlier concept
of powers passing downward from central governments of nation-states, the
provinces are beginning to assert themselves in those areas that are key to their
respective long-term economic futures. In turn, this is leading to further decentralization and, indeed, to an increased degree of asymmetry in provincial policies. All of this will be an essential ingredient of the later focus on the
citizen-government and market-government interfaces. For example, how do we
mount an east-west transfer system in the face of a north-south trading system?

Recapitulation

W E HAVE NOW COMPLETED A SELECTIVE SURVEY OF THE PERVASIVE IMPLICATIONS
of GIR on society's three key building blocks: governments, citizens and
markets (the boxes in Figure 1). The emphasis has been on how the new global
order is altering the *structure* and *positioning* of these three societal building
blocks. The remaining chapters of Part II focus on the linkages or interfaces (the
circles in Figure 1) among them. In so doing, the emphasis shifts from a largely
structural focus to one that will embrace policy implications.

Table 1   52

	1981		
	ROC **$**	**ROW** **$**	**ROW/ROC** **(ratio)**
Newfoundland	850	1,980	2.33
P.E.I.	500	190	0.38
Nova Scotia	2,970	1,810	0.61
New Brunswick	2,310	2,470	1.07
Quebec	27,600	21,940	0.79
Ontario	47,040	45,070	0.96
Manitoba	5,110	2,650	0.52
Saskatchewan	3,550	4,210	1.19
Alberta	18,200	9,010	0.5
B.C.	8,210	12,510	1.52
All Provinces	116,340	101,840	0.87

Notes: ROC relates to exports from the given province
to all other provinces, or interprovincial exports.
ROW relates to international exports.
Source: CANSIM Data Base (Matrix 4255).
"The 1981 data is reproduced from Courchene & Telmer
(1998, Table 9,1); 1996 data is reproduced from Courchene
(1999a)."

Domestic and International Exports, 1981 and 1996 Goods and Services ($ million)

	1996		1996 Openness	
ROC $	ROW $	ROW/ROC (ratio)	ROW/GDP %	(ROW+ROC)/GDP %
992	3,026	3.05	30.06	39.91
782	442	0.57	16.69	46.22
4,108	3,650	0.89	19.39	41.21
4,696	5,702	1.21	35.41	64.57
34,500	56,249	1.63	32.07	51.74
64,169	140,658	2.19	43.5	63.41
7,311	7,733	1.06	28.29	55.03
6,272	10,444	1.67	39.50	63.22
23,069	33,500	1.45	37.20	62.82
13,580	30,344	2.23	29.2	42.39
159,479	291,748	1.83	36.57	56.56

Figure 2 54

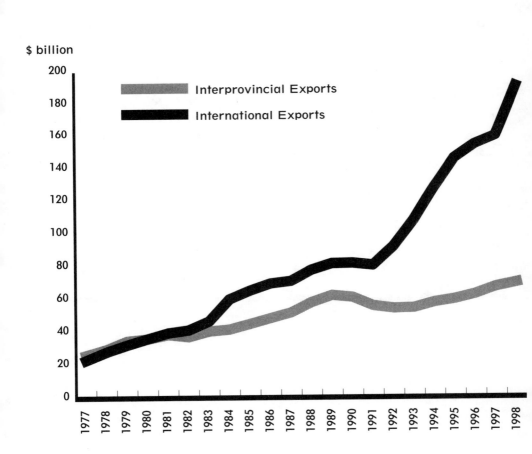

Ontario Trade

1977-1998

$ billion

- Interprovincial Exports
- International Exports

Figure 3

Ontario Trade
as Percent of GDP

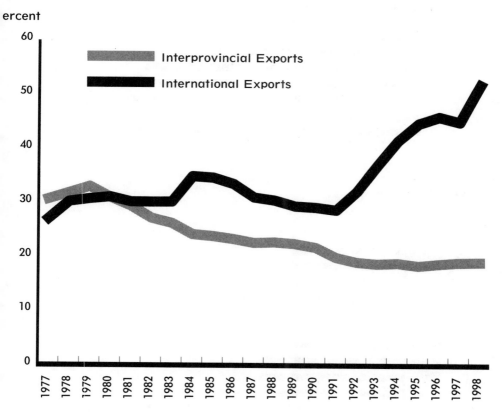

Percent

Interprovincial Exports
International Exports

Source: Ontario Ministry of Finance and
Statistics Canada

Figure 4   56

Employment and Recovery
after Two Recessions

A: 1980s Recession
Employment Recovered Four Years Later?

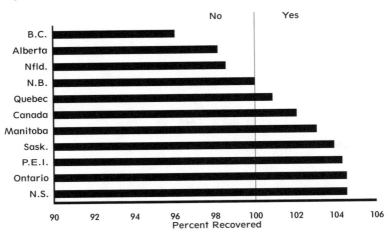

B: 1990s Recession
Employment Recovered Four Years Later?

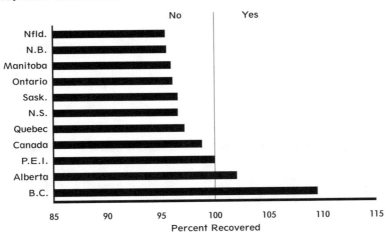

Source: Statistics Canada, TD Bank, Department of
Economic Research. Reproduced from Courchene
and Telmer (1998, Chart 9.2).

To summarize the analysis to this point and to create a bridge to the assessment of the citizen-market, market-government and citizen-government interfaces, I draw upon two capsule summaries of the paradigmatic sweep of GIR. The first, from Lipsey and Bekar, focuses largely on the economic implications arising from GIR. Referring to the new order as the "New Techno-economic Paradigm" (NTP), Lipsey and Bekar reflect as follows:

> A techno-economic paradigm is a systematic relationship among the products that are produced, the methods of producing them, the organization of productive units, and the institutions that support this activity. A typical paradigm is based on: (i) a few *key products* with wide application, (ii) a few *key materials* whose costs are falling over time, (iii) a way of *organizing economic activity*, (iv) a *supporting infrastructure*, (v) a typical pattern of *industrial concentration*, and (vi) a typical *pattern of efficient location*. (Lipsey and Bekar 1995: 58-59, emphasis original)

All of the italicized words or phrases in this quotation are in full paradigmatic evolution, as it were. While some of the basic features of GIR or the NTP have been captured in the above analysis of the direct impacts on governments, citizens and markets, a more comprehensive appreciation of the import and impact of GIR requires the following focus on the interactive linkages between and among governments, citizens and markets (the circles in Figure 1).

The second capsule summary is drawn from the first volume of Manuel Castells' trilogy on the emerging societal order. While it, too, builds on the revolution in the economic sphere, it transcends the merely economic to embrace the larger societal implications of GIR.

> The global economy emerging from information-based production and competition is characterized by its *interdependence*, its *asymmetry*, its *regionalization*, the *increasing diversification within each region*, its *selective inclusiveness*, its *exclusionary segmentation* and, as a result of these features, an extraordinarily *variable geometry* that tends to dissolve historical economic geography (Castells 1996: 106, emphasis original).

With this as both summary and backdrop, I now turn to an analysis of the manner in which GIR is influencing the relationship between governments and markets.

The Market-
Government
Interface I:
The Rise of
Economic
Region-States

A<small>T ONE LEVEL, ADDRESSING THE MARKET-GOVERNMENT INTERFACE APPEARS</small> reasonably straightforward: The focus will be on the interactive links between the evolution of markets and the evolution of governments and governance. What complicates this exercise, however, is "glocalization," the transferring of powers upward, downward and outward from central governments of nation-states. This means that markets now interface with supranational, national and subnational governments. Additionally, it means that intergovernmental relations (national-international, federal-provincial, and provincial-international) as they relate to trade and markets must be addressed. There appears to be no optimal way to order the flow of the analysis.

One approach would have been to create a separate government-government interface to encompass the altered patterns of intergovernmental relations. While this would have had considerable organizational appeal, in this chapter I opt to focus on what I perceive to be the most profound of the developments in the market-government interface, namely the emergence of "regional-international" linkages, i.e., the rise of region-states. Then, in Chapter 6, I focus on a range of other implications arising from the interplay of markets and government-to-government relations in the new economic order. While this division is admittedly arbitrary, it does have the advantage of linking the ensuing analysis with the integration of North American economic space elaborated in the previous chapter.

The Rise of
Region-States

The principal dilemma of contemporary economic geography is the resurgence of regional economies and of territorial specialization in an age of increasing ease of transportation and communication (Storper 1995: 212).

National Boundaries have become increasingly irrelevant in the definition of market and production spaces while regions, rather than countries, are emerging as key policy arenas (United Nations 1990: iii).

On the global economic map, the lines that now matter are those defining what may be called "region-states" (Ohmae 1993).

The European policy literature as it relates to regions is well ahead of its North American counterpart in recognizing the role played by cross-border relationships. In part, this is because all the powerful industrial regions in Europe have economic hinterlands that extend well beyond national boundaries, as reflected in the three quotations above. As a result, there is a growing recognition in policy circles that the traditional "national-national interface" is giving way to a "regional-international interface." Newhouse (1997: 67) notes that two parallel and related processes have emerged: "One is regionalism, the other globalization: instead of working through national capitals, European regions are linking themselves directly to the global economy" and, further, "in this more freewheeling environment, bankers and industrial planners have begun to view Europe at least as much as a group of distinct economic regions as an assortment of nation-states" (69).

A second implication is the recognition that comparative advantage is largely a regional rather than a national phenomenon. The obvious corollary is particularly important: "regionalism is much more than a return to cultural roots or a distancing from national capitals. It has as much to do with wealth creation as anything else" (69).

To the extent that Canadians are familiar with the concept of region-states, it probably stems from the 1988 "Four Motors Association." The four participants were the regions surrounding the international cities of Stuttgart (Baden-Würtemberg), Barcelona (Catalonia), Lyon (Rhône-Alpes), and Milan (Lombardy). As an instructive aside, in 1989 Ontario became an "associate" member of the Four Motors Association, an indication that the concept of cross-border regionalism was wholly familiar to the Peterson Liberals. In terms of selected policy issues relating to industry and trade, these "four motors" may well have more in common with each other than with other regions of their respective countries. Thus the Four

Motors Association serves as a template for coordinating their common industrial and cross-border interests; it also serves to coordinate and enhance their lobbying efforts and influence with Brussels, i.e., within the EU.

These and other efforts in the direction of embracing the concept of a regional-international interface raise a potentially difficult problem for Europe, one with direct carryover to the later analysis of Ontario and Canada. Again, in Newhouse's words,

> If the larger purpose of the Four Motors Association is wealth creation...will the process drive politics in its and other regions to the right, especially as some become richer and others poorer? And who will protect the poor and disadvantaged? Nation-states? The EU? (Newhouse 1997: 72-73)

This brings me to the final reference to the European literature:

> What is clear is that in this age of global trade and capital flows, not to mention information highways and high-speed travel, local entities feel better placed to manage their affairs than distant bureaucracies whether in national capitals or in Brussels. The German state of Baden-Würtemberg, for example, is making its own foreign and trade policies; it has signed several hundred agreements with other regions and entities. (68-69)

As a bridge to the focus on Ontario as a North American region-state and, more generally, on the implications for Canada, it is important to recognize that the North American and European situations differ in several important respects. For example, Baden-Würtemberg (Germany), Alsace (France) and Basel (Switzerland) are now one region for employment purposes. While the FTA and NAFTA provide for freer movement of goods, capital, and to some extent services, labour remains immobile (except for temporary (Trade-NAFTA) visas for the equivalent of knowledge workers or "symbolic analysts"). Moreover, the relationship between Baden-Würtemberg and Berlin is quite different from that between Ontario (or Quebec or Saskatchewan) and Ottawa. One key difference is that the German upper chamber (Bundesrat) comprises delegates from the Länder (provinces, in our terms). Moreover, as noted earlier, negotiations relating to international agreements involving the constitutional competencies of the Länder are handled by the Bundesrat or by representatives of the Länder. This differs radically from the Canadian reality. On the other hand, the Canadian provinces have much more in the way of legislative and policy freedom than does Baden-Würtemberg; i.e., Canada is much more decentralized than is Germany.

With this as backdrop, we now turn to the emergence of North American region-states, with an emphasis on Ontario.

The Essence of Region-States: Creating Untraded Interdependencies

I T IS MUCH MORE DIFFICULT TO SORT OUT THE THEORETICAL UNDERPINNINGS OF REGION-states than it is to document their empirical existence. In general, the relevant literature (again, most of it European) falls into the "evolutionary" economics school rather than the neoclassical school. Specifically, the emphasis is not on equilibria (as it would be if the analysis were neoclassical), but on innovation, agents of change and the role of institutional and structural elements. Indeed, the focus on path-dependency, feedback mechanisms and irreversibilities is central to this literature and predates the appearance of these concepts in mainstream economics as reflected, for example, in the recent literature on endogenous growth.

One important strand of this rich regional literature relates to the role of "local milieux" in generating networking which, in turn, can be characterized by organizational principles and linkages that encourage flexibility, the creation and transmission of knowledge, skill formation, mutual trust among partners, and so on (Lecoq 1991: 239). Thus these *milieux innovateurs* (defined in footnote 3, *infra*) are, at the same time, *organizational* (in the sense that they embody a set of institutions, rules, conventions and practices) and *territorial* (in the sense that they are embedded in the social and economic infrastructure of the region).

Geographer Michael Storper (1995) extends this analysis by postulating that the success of Silicon Valley, Route 128 and other industrial hot spots must reside in what he calls "untraded interdependencies." The "untraded" aspect is critical, since it implies that to access these interdependencies one must be located in the regional economy:

> Thus, regional economies constitute the nexus of untraded interdependencies which emerge and become, themselves, specific but public assets of production communities (assets of coordination, i.e., frameworks of collective action), and which underpin the production and reproduction of other specific assets such as labour and hardware (Storper 1995: 211).

One could, and probably should, expand this definition to explicitly include assets like social capital, although they are implicitly included. Economists may have a difficult time grappling with these concepts because their discipline is inherently market (i.e., tradeables) based. Hence, their focus is typically on "traded interdependencies" which, by definition, are not location specific. Consequently, mainstream economists have not, until recently, played a major role in the development of this literature.

An alternative way to conceive of these untraded interdependencies is to view them as "locational" externalities: One set might relate to the interdependencies at the industry/production level; another could involve the forward and backward linkages among education/training, income support, and labour and product markets; and a third might involve public goods. Focusing, for illustrative purposes, on the last of these, a firm locating anywhere in North America has access to an international public good — NAFTA. If, among Canada, the United States and Mexico, the firm chooses to locate in Canada, it gains access to Canadian public goods (such as medicare for its workers) but foregoes access to the comparable US and Mexican national public goods and/or infrastructures. And if the firm locates in Ontario, it acquires the Ontario set, not the Alberta or Quebec set, of provincial public goods. Because we have focused our example on public goods, it is easy to see they are inherently untradeable — one accesses them by location, not by markets. (In some cases, one could use markets to attempt to replicate another jurisdiction's public goods, e.g., a firm in the US could provide medicare for its workers.) Indeed, one might extend Storper's concept further by viewing the process of competitive federalism as an attempt among subnational units to compete with each other in the provision of these untraded interdependencies or positive locational externalities. The new twist is that this competition is no longer primarily along east-west (interprovincial) lines but rather along cross border (international) lines.

Ontario as a North American Region-State

T HE EARLIER SET OF OBSERVATIONS — THAT THE FEDERATION IS BECOMING MORE decentralized; that the provinces/regions are very different industrially; that they are progressively integrating north-south; and that their business cycles are not synchronous — suggest that Canada is witnessing the emergence of region-states. Quebec probably took the lead here with its mid-1980s "virage vers les marchés" (Courchene 1989). Intriguingly, Quebec's economic star began to shine a lot less brightly when it attempted to move from a "region-state" to a "nation-state," but that is a separate story. Alberta, with its "Alberta Advantage" is leading the way in terms of using fiscal (tax) policy to increase its competitiveness and locational advantage. British Columbia, with its Northwestern US and Pacific Rim orientation, is arguably Canada's most natural region-state but, thus far, BC remains a region-state "in waiting."

However, Ontario is the province that now leads the pack in terms of donning the mantle of a North American region-state. This is especially significant since Ontario has traditionally been viewed as Canada's heartland. Panel A of Table 2 presents my view of the defining features of Heartland Ontario (essentially the Ontario of John Robarts) while Panel B of the table details selected defining features of Region-State Ontario. Beyond these defining characteristics, Ontario's strategic and economic position within North America is very impressive indeed. To be sure, much of the province's economic prowess was built upon the province's dual role as the centre for east-west production and distribution of goods and services and as the principal conduit for north-south trade. In its new role, Ontario is refocusing this economic power north-south. Among its economic advantages now being deployed within the geo-economics of NAFTA are the following:

- Two-thirds of Canada's consumer market and one-half of the US consumer market is within one-day's trucking of southern Ontario.
- A North American consumer market within a 400-mile radius that is as large or larger than that for Detroit, Boston or New York.
- A North American industrial market (within one-day's-trucking) that reaches one-half of US manufacturing firms.
- The third highest concentration of financial services in North America with 47 of Canada's 58 banks, headquarters for nine of ten Canadian investment firms as well as the Toronto Stock Exchange.
- Toronto was (in 1993) headquarters for 91 percent of Canada's foreign banks, 90 percent of top advertising firms, 90 percent of top accounting firms, 80 percent of the top law firms and home to 1,100 multinational firms etc.

Beyond these and other strengths (see Courchene and Telmer 1998: Appendix 9A), including a value of shipments to the US that now equals 45 percent of its GDP and a similarly high proportion of imports, two-way Ontario-US trade is now larger than any other two-way US trade, except for Japan.

By way of a brief detour, while the ensuing analysis is cast in terms of Ontario donning the mantle of a North America region-state, it is clear that much of the ability of Ontario to pursue a north-south economic future is linked to the fact that Toronto and the Greater Toronto Area (GTA, which includes the new megacity of Toronto plus the regions of Durham, York, Peel and Halton) are emerging as a "global city-region." The GTA accounts for roughly half of Ontario's GDP and, therefore, roughly 20 percent of overall Canadian GDP. Thus, aspects of the following discussion probably relate as much to Toronto as a global city-region as to Ontario as a North American region-state.

This caveat aside, a decentralized and north-south-trading Ontario does not, of and by itself, make the province a region-state. For this, Ontario policy must be geared to privileging Ontario and Ontarians in this North American economic space. From my perspective, this is essentially what Harris's *Common Sense Revolution* (CSR) was all about — generating a set of positive locational externalities for Ontario. Among many other features of the CSR, provincial personal income tax rates have fallen from 58 percent of federal tax owing to less than 40 percent, the provincial government's workforce has been reduced by 15 percent, welfare has been reformed, the number of provincial politicians has been reduced from 133 to 103 MLAs, and Ontario Hydro is being broken up an slowly subjected to competition. Following quickly on the CSR was a second revolution: the municipal-institutional revolution with its municipal amalgamations, hospital and school board consolidations and substantial shifts in provincial-municipal functions and financing. In *From Heartland to North American Region State*, Telmer and I suggest that these initiatives constitute an attempt to increase productivity in the public sector, arguably an essential ingredient for Ontario to become an effective North American region-state.

The purpose of all of this is not to sing the praises of Ontario. Rather, it is to focus on the new geo-economics of Ontario as an example of the manner in which GIR is altering the market-government interface. Later, I shall highlight the recent policy thrust of New Brunswick as another way in which GIR is changing the market-government relationship. I now turn to some implications arising from Ontario's new role in the federation.

Table 2   66

Panel A

Heartland Ontario: Selected defining characteristics

- Ontario was so prosperous and so diversified economically — and so powerful politically — that Canadian policy had little choice but to be cast in a pro-Ontario light.
- Relatedly, the management of the big levers of economic power always kept a close eye on Ontario, e.g., if the Minister of Finance was not a Toronto MP then at least Toronto would be well represented in the key economic portfolios.
- Since Ontario could generally count on the federal government to further the province's interests, Heartland Ontario was in favour of a strong central government. For example, Queen's Park did not assume the role of economic policy maker that L'Assemblée nationale did for Quebec. There was no need for this since Rideau Street was essentially an extension of Bay Street, and Ottawa delivered — the auto pact, the NEP, nuclear power for Ontario Hydro.
- Not surprisingly, therefore, Ontarians tended to direct their attention and loyalties to Ottawa, more so than other provincial residents.
- While Ontario obviously desired sufficient influence to defend its own interests, its preference was to block offending legislation of a sister province rather than by acquiring further provincial powers. For example, it did not take up Ottawa's invitation to opt out of federal programs, as did Quebec. Had it done so, other provinces would surely have followed and this would have served to reduce Ottawa's influence.
- With aspects of the National Policy still in play, Ontario's interests were more in the direction of freeing up internal trade than in pursuing freer trade with the US. This was especially true in the high-energy-price era where Ontario wanted full access to the energy-related mega-projects of the energy provinces in tandem with a "buy Canadian" preference.
- Ontario was not a leader in social policy. Some of this related to the economic diversity of the province and some of it to innate conservatism, but there was also an understanding that social policy leadership by Ontario would trigger regional equality concerns from other provinces, with Ontario ultimately playing a large paymaster role.
- In general, Ontario was able to wheel, deal and compromise and to manage its privileged position to ensure that Canada's interests coincided with Ontario's interests.

Source: Courchene (1999c) and Courchene and Telmer (1998, Chapters 2 and 10).

a state of minds

Heartland Ontario vs. Region State Ontario

Panel B
Region-state Ontario: Selected defining characteristics

- Ontario is a North American region-state and the province will advance its interests within this larger, and effectively, global environment. Specifically, Ontario will pursue this new (largely) economic role by actively promoting a regional-international interface and, in particular, by attempting to create a favourable set of untraded interdependencies (positive locational externalities) designed to privilege Ontario and Ontarians within North America.
- Queen's Park is evolving and will continue to evolve in the direction of assuming powers and influence sufficient to deliver on this new role.
- Ontario remains fully committed to the "Canadian dream." But this will not be the former Heartland relationship. For example, Ontario will give high marks to Ottawa policy that maintains fiscal integrity, low inflation and an overall competitive environment.
- Ontario will become much more involved in issues relating to interprovincial redistribution. It will remain a strong supporter of equalization, but will insist on equal treatment for its citizens from other federal redistributive programs ("fair shares" federalism).
- In protecting its own interests, Ontario may still wish to block offending legislation in a sister province (as under Heartland), but it now will have no qualms about acquiring greater powers. This is "provincial rights if necessary but not necessarily provincial rights."
- International free trade is "in." Nonetheless, Ontario will also attempt to preserve and promote east-west markets. Part of this will be via the pursuit of an effective economic union. Indeed, Ontario will likely attempt to link its commitment to the social union to the commitment by other provinces to the economic union.
- As a result of increased decentralization and the likelihood of increased asymmetry as different provinces choose alternative approaches to forge their human capital subsystems, intergovernmentalism or co-determination will emerge as new governance instruments. Ontario will play a leading role here.
- To be a successful region-state, Ontario will have to become a leader in policies related to the creation of human capital. With human capital at the cutting edge of competitiveness and with skills and education the key to a high-wage economy, an integrated approach to this subsystem must become a defining characteristic of Ontario as a region-state. Ontario is not yet on track here.

Implications

B EYOND THOSE IMPLICATIONS OUTLINED IN TABLE 2, IT IS INSTRUCTIVE TO NOW FOCUS on three other generic implications arising from the emerging geo-economics of the upper half of North America: those for intergovernmental transfers, for decentralization and in particular for personal income taxation, and for east-west cross-subsidization. These implications are serving to challenge some long-standing features of our east-west economy and society. The emphasis will again be on Ontario, although the analysis could be extended to incorporate most, if not all, of the provinces.

Intergovernmental Transfers

In terms of intergovernmental transfers, students of Canadian social policy and federalism would no doubt agree that for much of the post-war period Ontario and Ontarians were more supportive of the east-west transfer system than were Albertans or British Columbians (or, at least, than were their respective governments). Public choice analysts would probably not attribute this to any inherent generosity or altruism on the part of Ontarians as compared with residents of British Columbia or Alberta. Rather, their argument would be that the "second-round" spending impacts of these transfers tended to end up somewhere in Ontario, since trade largely flowed east-west and Ontario was the principal north-south conduit. Thus, it was in Ontario's self-interest, to an important degree at least, to support the east-west transfer system.

With generalized north-south trade (as reflected in the data in Table 1) however, these second-round spending impacts may now end up in North Carolina or Minnesota and not in Ontario. This could well serve to alter the distributional priorities of Ontarians *even with unchanged attitudes toward east-west distribution* because the economic costs to Ontarians of these transfers has now increased. Might Ontarians' revealed preferences for east-west redistribution thus tend toward those of British Columbia and Alberta, where there was never much expectation that these two provinces would be the recipients of any significant second-round spending benefits? The answer would presumably be in the affirmative.

A related transfer issue arose in the context of the operations of the Canada Assistance Plan (CAP), Canada's federal-provincial 50 percent cost-sharing program for welfare. In 1990, Ottawa imposed a "cap" on CAP, which limited the transfer growth for the three "have" provinces (Alberta, British Columbia and Ontario) to five percent per year. Initially expected to impose a loss on these three provinces of only $155 million over the initial two years and $365 million in the third year, the loss to Ontario alone in the third year was $1.7 billion (Courchene and Telmer 1998: 166), with cumulative losses to the province eventually exceeding $10 billion. The origins of the cap on CAP presumably related to the enriching of the Ontario welfare system in the late 1980s. The result of this would have saddled Ottawa with 50 percent of any increase in the Ontario welfare bill. The imposition of the cap effectively shielded Ottawa's spending from any such increase in Ontario's welfare benefits. In order to make this politically acceptable, the cap was extended to all three "have" provinces. One might argue, as I have (Courchene 1994: Chapter 4), that this was probably viewed in federal circles as the rich provinces' *quid pro quo* for the earlier imposition of an equalization ceiling on the have-not provinces. In any event, it was the severity of the 1990s recession in Ontario that led to the mushrooming of the costs of the "cap on CAP" to Ontario. This and other transfer programs that discriminated against Ontario (e.g., Ontario receives 38 percent of immigration settlement and training monies even though it is the destination for 55 percent of Canada's immigrants) led Bob Rae's NDP government to launch its "fair shares federalism" campaign. Fair shares federalism also became the rallying cry of the Harris Conservatives. By moving to equal per capita entitlements for the CHST, Ottawa finally removed the cap on CAP from the system (Courchene 1999d).

The message arising from the cap on CAP experience might go as follows: It is wholly appropriate, let alone required by the Constitution, that Ottawa ensure that, via equalization, all provinces have access to a "reasonably comparable level of goods and services at reasonably comparable levels of taxation." What is far less appropriate is that Ottawa extend this preferential treatment to have-not provinces across *other* federal redistributive programs such as EI and the former cap on CAP. Canadians, no matter where they reside, merit equitable treatment from their national government with respect to these other programs. If this is not the case, then popular support for all national redistribution may well begin to erode. As will be broached later in this study, it may be that the forces of GIR will generate increased disparities in terms of the access to revenues across provinces. Should this occur, the appropriate response is to rethink and rework the system of equalization payments, not to embed provincial preferences in other national redistributive programs.

In spite of the above concerns about the altered nature of the cost of equalization to the have provinces (or at least to Ontario), the desire on the part of Canadians to remain a sharing community is, I believe, alive and well. But the instrument for this redistribution across provinces should be the equalization program, not federal programs which are intended to deliver national goods and services to Canadians.

Decentralization and Income Taxation

The advent of region-states implies that provinces will increasingly enact policies that will serve to enhance their ability to compete within the North American economic orbit. This will not only be decentralizing, but also lead to policy and program asymmetries across provinces, since the social and economic infrastructure appropriate for a Pacific Rim province like BC may well differ from that appropriate for a Great Lakes economy like Ontario.

The most recent policy initiative with rather dramatic implications for decentralization or asymmetry is "rate and bracket flexibility" under the provincial personal income tax (PIT) regimes. The catalyst for this was Ontario Finance Minister Ernie Eves' announcement (in his 1997 budget) that Ontario would be considering the option of withdrawing from the tax agreements for the PIT and mounting a separate PIT along Quebec lines (Courchene and Telmer 1998: Chapter 8; Courchene 1999e). This led to the December 1997 federal announcement that, as of calendar year 2001, the provinces would have complete rate and bracket flexibility within the shared PIT, i.e., they would now be able to levy their own rate and bracket structures against taxable income, unlike the present approach where they are required to levy a single tax rate against "federal tax owing." In this terminology of the PIT, this is a shift from "tax on tax" to "tax on base" or "tax on income."

Although Ontario has reduced its personal income tax rates by roughly 40 percent since the advent of the Harris administration, it is Alberta's decision to impose a flat tax, or single-rate tax, of 10.5 percent, thereby generating an "Alberta Advantage," that is sending shock waves through the system. Likewise, Ontario's proposed reduction of its corporate income tax to four percent and eight percent (for small and large corporations, respectively) is a policy initiative designed to privilege Ontario as a corporate location both in Canada as well as in the larger NAFTA context. While virtually all provinces are in a tax-cutting mode, not all have the fiscal ability or political inclination to follow the Ontario and Alberta lead. The result is almost sure to trigger further decentralization and asymmetry across provinces and likely to widen regional disparities in Canada.

For present purposes, the message here is that the enhanced North American trade integration and the rise of economic region-states will significantly complicate the governance of the federation. The more general message, dealt with later, is that these provincial tax initiatives are almost certain to destabilize the economic underpinnings of the federation. Far better for Ottawa to play a more aggressive role to ensure that tax rates on highly mobile factors (capital and "talent") are more in line with those of our neighbour to the south.

East-West Economic Infrastructure

Both the intergovernmental transfer and PIT are part of a larger and much more problematic concern arising from the altered geo-economics of North America: the future of our east-west economic infrastructure. Perhaps the best way to approach this important issue is to remind ourselves that, from the 1879 National Policy onward, we fostered and greatly profited from the creation of an east-west economy and society.[11] But the three building blocks of the National Policy — high tariffs, transportation subsidies, settlement of the West — are no longer in play. Hence (as in the pre-National-Policy era) trade is again following natural north-south geographical dictates. This means that in economic terms much of our east-west economic infrastructure is fast becoming a "stranded asset." Moreover, with the advent of heightened north-south trade, there is diminishing scope within industries or firms for transferring rents from profitable locations to less profitable ones in order to maintain an east-west enterprise. Increased competition, internal and external, will ensure these rents are competed away.

Thus, left to the interplay of markets, private-sector economic agents will begin to aggressively pursue their north-south economic and trading potential, which may mean the abandonment of an east-west perspective and infrastructure. This was highlighted earlier by noting that Canada is less and less an "economic policy railway" and more and more a "social policy railway," and even the "ribbons of steel" are now moving north-south (with CN buying Illinois Central). This represents an enormous policy challenge, one that is sure to impinge on key aspects of our collective identity. How will governments manage this transition? Will they attempt to counter these trends by incentives and/or regulations in an effort to keep our east-west "socio-economic capital" intact? If so, at what long-term cost?

This was precisely the policy issue at the core of the recent federally aborted bank merger proposals. The case for these mergers might be made along the following lines. In the 1970s, many large corporations began to realize that, as capital markets became more developed, they no longer needed their financing through the banks but could go directly to the capital markets. Canadian policy reacted quickly and appropriately to this challenge by striking down the prohibition on banks owning investment dealers. Not surprisingly, the banks gobbled up most of the investment dealers, which allowed the banks to recapture some of the corporate market. But neither time nor markets stand still. In particular, a significant number of corporations are becoming so large they require syndicates of banks to meet their financing needs, and this trend is going to continue.

If Canadian banks do not become larger (in a capitalization sense), they will neither have the capital base to finance many of these corporations nor be sufficiently large to participate in the syndications. A niche strategy might save the individual banks as ongoing companies but, in aggregate, their combined strength and presence will fall short of what Canada needs for future economic development. Increasingly, we will likely have to rely on the US and global financial institutions and financial markets to finance key sectors of our economy, with all this implies for sovereignty and made-in-Canada economic development. One does not have to agree to this assessment of the merger issue to recognize that it has profound implications for Ontario's future as a region-state (and Toronto's future as a global city-region). As noted earlier, Ontario is a major player in the North American financial sector, and with financial power comes a whole range of related services — accounting, legal, advertising etc. Not surprising that Toronto, or at least the Toronto Board of Trade, was a staunch supporter of the mergers.

However, while Ontario may have a north-south view of the evolution of finance and banking, Ottawa had an east-west view. This can be phrased differently: Canada's nationwide banking system is also a key Canadian social or socio-economic institution. In this context, the prospect of the mergers resulting in the closing of branches elsewhere in the country was viewed as unacceptable. To be fair, there is a social or solidarity aspect to our national banks. But what the merger issue highlighted is the deep societal division between the emerging requisites of north-south competitiveness versus the traditional requisites of east-west solidarity. East-west solidarity won this round, but the game is hardly over. On the heels of Finance Minister Paul Martin's rejection of the two bank mergers, CIBC has applied for a US charter. Moreover, the Bank of Montreal has recently announced a quite dramatic cut to its labour force, citing the abortive merger attempt as a catalyst. And several banks have been selling some of their branches to credit unions.

Meanwhile, on the international front, the Americans are now in the process of a wholesale deregulation of their financial sector while the Europeans are bracing for a series of bank mergers where the individual banks involved have assets well in excess of the combined assets of our proposed merged banks. Thus, in a period of a few short years, Canada has moved from a leader to a laggard in terms of competitive financial-sector policy.

To be sure, I may be simplifying the bank merger case. Nonetheless, the underlying point surely rings true: Canadian businesses will begin to pull back on their far-flung east-west enterprises and concentrate their activities north-south, where the market is bigger and closer. This, too, accentuates one of the themes of this paper, namely that pursuing east-west social and socio-economic solidarity in the context of north-south trading arrangements requires new and creative policy approaches. And this challenge will become exacerbated as our diverse regional economies struggle to become competitively viable in the emerging geo-economic reality of North America.

Economic Geography as Networking: New Brunswick

T HE THRUST OF THE FOREGOING ANALYSIS IS THAT GIR IS PERMANENTLY ALTERING THE economic geography of the upper half of North America. However, the emphasis thus far has been on economic geography as a "space of places," albeit regional rather than national. Occurring simultaneously is a "space-of-flows" or networking concept of the new geo-economics. While this is happening everywhere, it has assumed pre-eminence in the policy initiatives of former

Premier Frank McKenna of New Brunswick. Recognizing that federal largesse could not be assumed to continue to flow into the province at existing levels (McKenna and Savoie 1995), New Brunswick decided it had to wean itself from full reliance on federal transfers and strike out on its own in the larger North American context. The industrial sector it chose to spearhead this initiative was telecommunications. Endowed with a bilingual labour force and leveraging off the support of New Brunswick Tel and Northern Telecom among others, New Brunswick's investment in telecommunications infrastructure — digitization and fibre optics — catapulted it into the leading telematics jurisdiction in North America.[12] To be sure, this may be a fleeting advantage since many North American jurisdictions are now following suit. What this means is that New Brunswick is going to have to run to stay ahead, as it were. But as long as New Brunswick's focus is on the North American and not just the Canadian market, it has a fighting chance to succeed. Few Canadians, let alone economists, would have predicted that a so-called transfer-dependent economy like New Brunswick would shift its focus from Ottawa to middle America. This, too, is what the regional/international interface is all about.

A note about the relationship between geography on the one hand and the regional/international interface on the other is in order. Under the old paradigm, New Brunswick was a "powerless place" in the traditional geographical sense. The new telematic infrastructure does not really make New Brunswick a "powerful place." Rather, the province acquires "placeless power" (Graham 1994: 419). One has the image, therefore, of footloose industries being attracted to footloose jurisdictions. Next year, the leadership in terms of placeless telematics power could well shift to Utah, a state that closely rivals New Brunswick in terms of digitization and fibre optics. Thus, geography in this sense is more akin to a "space of flows" rather than a "space of places" (Castells 1989). Indeed, the New Brunswick authorities recognize this:

> The New Brunswick government, NBTel and Northern Telecom recognize that advances in communications technologies have made the physical location of electronic commerce irrelevant. As a result, the marketing campaign has focused on *New Brunswick as a business solution rather than a location.* (Delottinville 1994: 42, emphasis added)

In terms of the earlier analysis, this is New Brunswick's way of generating "untraded interdependencies," i.e., generating the hardware and software environment where an inherently footloose industry can "locate" in a networking space. As an important aside, the New Brunswick experience is significant in another sense. The free trade advocates argued that the resulting FTA benefits were not limited only to those provinces that were ideally positioned initially to take advantage of the opening of markets. New Brunswick is proving them correct.

The general trend toward north-south trade integration in tandem with ongoing decentralization is leading several provinces to aggressively pursue their economic fortunes within the FTA and NAFTA geo-economic reality. While east-west trade remains still vitally important and while our east-west economic space is far more integrated than is the north-south economic space (Helliwell 1998), the reality is that east-west trade is being eclipsed by the sheer volume of north-south trade. The challenge here is to maintain the east-west social and economic union in the face of this growing north-south trading union. Thankfully, we have become appropriately creative in responding to this challenge, as the recent federal-provincial AIT and SUFA bear witness. Now that I have broached the intergovernmental aspects of the market-government interface, I turn to this in more detail.

The Market-Government Interface II: Intergovernmental Relations

T HIS CHAPTER CONTINUES THE FOCUS ON THE IMPLICATIONS OF GIR ON THE MARKET-government interface with attention directed toward within-government and within-corporate relations. Accordingly, the first section deals with government-to-government relations in the international arena, with emphasis on the challenges relating to the erosion of post-war "embedded liberalism." Focus then shifts to the federal-provincial governance challenges, where the analysis highlights two creative initiatives designed to manage socio-economic interdependence: AIT and SUFA. The chapter concludes with a brief discussion of corporate governance in a GIR era.

Nation-States and International Institutions[13]

Post-War "Embedded Liberalism"

T HE GENIUS INHERENT IN THE POST-WAR INTERNATIONAL ECONOMIC ORDER LAY IN what John Ruggie has termed the "compromise of embedded liberalism":[14]

> Societies were asked to embrace the changes and dislocation attending liberalization. In turn, liberalization and its effects were cushioned by the newly acquired economic and social policy roles of governments. (Ruggie 1995: 508)

As a result, the modern welfare state grew apace with increasing international openness because the institutional framework embedded this openness within an activist domestic social democracy and an accommodating international regulatory system. To be sure, this was also the heyday of the Keynesian revolution (with its attendant growth in the size and role of governments everywhere), which served to accommodate domestic priorities and aspirations alongside the increasing internationalism on the trade front. As Rodrik (1997: 65) notes, embedded liberalism served the world economy extremely well: "world trade has expanded phenomenally since the 1950s without causing major social dislocations or generating much opposition in the advanced industrial countries." Indeed, "it is in the most open countries, such as Sweden, Denmark and the Netherlands, that spending on income transfers has expanded the most" (6). All in all, a remarkable achievement!

Under GIR, however, this embedded liberalism appears to be coming unstuck. On the one hand, international markets are becoming dramatically more liberalized, spearheaded by record foreign direct investment and the operations of MNEs and the Electronic Herd. On the other hand, the welfare state appears to be retrenching everywhere, even though the implications of GIR point in the direction of a greater need for social cohesion and for policies to mitigate the resulting costs to immobile factors (i.e., those factors whose options for diversifying against GIR risks are constrained). Thus, while social and labour standards can, admittedly, be maintained if there is a willingness to pay for them, "increased openness to trade and foreign investment does render it more difficult for workers to make other groups in society, and employers in particular, share in the costs" (19).

At one level, the issue can be placed in the context of democracy, accountability and legitimacy. Markets are a social contrivance or institution as well as an economic one so that their continued ability to hold sway is predicated on the perception, and indeed the reality, that their processes and outcomes are legitimate. In the era of embedded liberalism, nation-states were able to provide the accompanying social cohesion and domestic political support that legitimized increasing international trade and openness. Under GIR, it is becoming evident that transactions undertaken in the international marketplace carry the least inherent legitimacy, in large measure because this is the only market that is not regulated by an overarching political authority (71). In terms of the consequences, Rodrik notes,

> Far-sighted companies will tend to their own communities as they globalize. But an employer that has an "exit" option is one that is less likely to exercise the "voice" option. It is so much easier to outsource than to enter a debate

about how to revitalize the local economy. This means that the owners of internationally mobile factors become disengaged from their local communities and
disinterested in their development and prosperity...

What if, by reducing the civic engagement of internationally mobile capital, globalization loosens the civic glue that holds societies together and exac-
erbates social fragmentation? (70)

Thus, the underlying challenge is starkly clear: how do we ensure that "international economic integration" does not lead to "domestic social disintegration?"
(2). If we fail in this challenge, the prospects are for a stalling of selected aspects of
globalization and perhaps even a reversion to some form of old-style protectionism.

But how likely is it that the international order can find a way to put a
human face on the march toward internationalization? Phrased differently, how
likely is it that nations can design and deliver a corresponding "compromise of
embedded GIR?" The European Union is attempting to lead the way here with its
Social Charter and its concern about "social dumping" (alluded to earlier).
Basically, the key concern, as the single European market takes hold, is that this
might trigger a "race to the bottom" in terms of social and labour standards. To
avoid this, the poorer nations are expected to "lever up" their social and labour
policies to the European average, rather than have the social policies in the more
established social democracies "lever down" to the standards in the poorer countries. Rodrik comments on the European initiatives as follows:

> First, it is considerably easier to integrate economically when there are shared
> norms among countries regarding domestic institutions such as labour rela-
> tions or social welfare systems. Second, as integration deepens, it becomes
> more difficult for countries to adopt or maintain social recipes that differ from
> those of their trade partners. Third, even within Europe, where there is sub-
> stantial convergence in income levels and social practices — at least compared
> with the rest of the world — it has proved difficult to strike the right balance
> between expanding economic integration and providing governments with
> room to manoeuvre on the social front. (40-41)

As an important aside, expanding the EU to the east will pose enormous
problems on this front. Wages in Poland are roughly one-sixth of what they are
in Germany, for example.

While recognizing the general thrust of this argument, the fact of the matter is that governments do maintain some room to manoeuvre in terms of social
policy. Keith Banting addresses this issue in a recent paper, "The
Internationalization of the Social Contract". Banting surveys the evolution of

comparative social policy and concludes that while all countries must of necessity adjust their social policies in light of international pressures,

> The global economy does not dictate the ways in which each country responds. Policy is also shaped by domestic politics, and different countries are responding to a changing world according to the rhythms of their domestic politics and culture. (Banting 1997: 264)

As evidence of this room for national flexibility, Banting goes on to observe that the divergent Canadian and US approaches to social policy and redistribution are showing little signs of convergence. Indeed, whereas post-transfer income inequality is rising in the US, in Canada it is not only much lower but also remaining relatively stable. In part, this is because Canada has moved sharply away from universality in terms of income-support benefits and toward greater selectivity (i.e., targeting transfers to those most in need). This is clearly the case for both child benefits and elderly benefits and it is beginning to spread into provincial welfare systems. Perhaps it is more correct to say that existing expenditures for income support now focus more on addressing inequality than was formerly the case. In any event, the message is that, within some obvious limits (and in Canada some of these limits are fiscally induced limits), there still remains national room to manoeuvre.

Among the options proffered by Rodrik (1997: 76-85) for ensuring that the increasing international economic integration does not lead to domestic social disintegration are the following:

- ◆ Introduce a global tax on internationally mobile factors, especially capital.
- ◆ Allow countries to selectively de-link from international obligations when these obligations come into conflict with domestic norms and institutions. [Note that a variant of this would be "mutual recognition" of alternative norms and standards.]
- ◆ Encourage labour to distance itself from protectionist ideas and, instead, advocate a global economy that presents a more humane face — one that recognizes national diversity and leaves room for national differences in institutions.
- ◆ Allow greater access to the WTO's existing "escape clause" for selected restrictions under specified conditions, e.g., tightening the rules on antidumping in conjunction with a reconsideration and reinvigoration of the escape clause mechanisms would make a lot of sense.

Beyond these measures, there may be a case to incorporate social and labour standards/principles more formally into future trade agreements (Scherer 1996). Additionally, the new approaches to corporate governance (elaborated briefly below) are also moving in a "best practices" direction in terms of a range of approaches that relate to social and environmental issues, for example.

Finally, but hardly exhaustively, there is what I earlier referred to as the Electronic Citizen-Democracy Herd, which has significant potential for providing an increasingly effective countervail to any new arrangements which fail to recognize the inherent tension between increased trade/factor liberalization on the one hand and the legitimate concerns with respect to societal cohesion on the other. With the collapse of the first attempt at the MAI, I believe the international economic order (even without a political order) is getting the message that further international liberalization is not an unmitigated "good." If appropriate attention is not directed toward the legitimate issue of preventing further domestic social disintegration in the context of globalization, there may be little in the way of new breakthroughs on the liberalization front.

Enter the WTO, the NGOs and the Battle in Seattle.

Seattle and Globalization

"While it is surely right to say that Seattle was in part the Woodstock of the 1990s" (Wolfe 2000: 9), one needs to step back a bit from the sensationalism and confrontation of Seattle and focus on some of the underlying issues. One major problem here is the absence of a meaningful/relevant international social or socio-economic forum that has the status of the WTO or even the World Bank/IMF combination. Because there is no such international social institution that can mediate the economic implications of enhanced globalization, the Electronic Citizen-Democracy Herd and the myriad NGOs have no alternative but to focus their interests and attention on the operations of the WTO and the Bank/Fund. By default, they become the only game in town.

What the Battle in Seattle demonstrated is that the citizens and NGOs can and did mount an effective "blocking coalition" to the WTO process. While this was an admitted setback for the WTO and a high-profile public relations "win" for the Electronic Citizen-Democracy Herd and the NGOs, it is far from clear that the public relations victory corresponds to a policy victory. This is because the fallback position of a thwarted multilateral WTO process is one where the trading relationships become "bilateralized" and "privatized," i.e., driven by powerful national governments and MNEs, respectively. This cannot be in the interests of the citizen/NGO coalition. One need not go the full way to endorsing Wolfe's view of the WTO — that it is "a leading anti-poverty organization playing a central role in ensuring the full integration of the world's peoples into the global economy on a fair and equitable basis" (2) — to recognize that co-determined multilateralism is much preferable to free wheeling bilateralism and, likely, US standard-setting and dominance.

I remain optimistic that the NGOs will ultimately prove to be a very constructive force in the process of re-embedding liberalism or, more to the point, embedding GIR. Now that they realize they can effectively block new initiatives, they are likely to begin to work more closely with international institutions in ways that bridge competitiveness and cohesion, or openness and community. As Ostry (2001) points out, the Web sites of many of these NGOs offer a range of alternative approaches and ideas that the institutional architects of the new international order would be well advised to give serious consideration to. Moreover, pressures will develop for the NGOs themselves to become more open and accountable, which should enhance their role and status.

Intriguingly, the ball is now in the WTO's court. If it does not become more open, more transparent and more democratic (both in terms of participating countries and the NGOs), the new WTO round is not likely to get off the ground, let alone succeed. For their part, the NGOs need to recognize that the WTO is a creature of the member governments and not an independent, freewheeling, international secretariat with untrammelled policy authority. If both parties recognize each other's roles and responsibilities, then real progress on mutually acceptable multilateral trading arrangements is achievable. While the WTO has dominated the public concern with respect to the manner in which globalization interacts with civil society, there have been other important international institutional developments. The most significant of these from Canada's perspective is the striking of the G-20.

The G-20 and International Stability

In the wake of the contagion or fallout from the recent regional crises, largely currency crises (e.g., the 1994 Mexican peso crisis, the Russian implosion, the 1998 Asian currency crisis, the 1999 Brazilian devaluation), focus has shifted to the "stability" dimension of the international order. Canada, under Finance Minister Paul Martin, provided some early leadership here with the establishment of the

Financial Stability Forum, designed to increase and enforce financial regulatory, monitoring and transparency principles for emerging economies. In September 1999, this initiative was eclipsed when the G7 chose Canada (and Paul Martin in his capacity of Minister of Finance) to head up the new G-20. In addition to the G7, the G-20 will include the European Community (as a single member), the World Bank and the IMF (together as a single member), and eleven other countries: Argentina, Australia, Brazil, China, India, Mexico, Russia, Saudi Arabia, South Africa, South Korea and Turkey. Noticeably absent are nations like Sweden, the Netherlands, Indonesia, Nigeria and Malaysia, among others. This caveat aside, the mandate of the G-20 will be to ensure that industrialized and developing countries alike can better coordinate their economic policies to avoid the kind of global financial panic that rocked financial markets in the late 1990s.

This initiative is occurring alongside a rethinking of the role of international institutions. (Note it is presumably significant in this context that the IMF and the World Bank are part of the new G-20). The July/August 1999 edition of *Policy Options/Options politiques* provides ready access for Canadian readers to some of the latest thinking in this area (James Tobin on financial globalization, former World Bank President Joseph Stiglitz on the financial crisis, Wendy Dobson on the IMF, Barry Eichengreen on capital controls etc). While these initiatives and proposals for institutional redesign are important for Canada, especially since we frequently tend to get sideswiped as a result of currency and economic implosions, they are basically designed to *stabilize* the existing global economic order, i.e., they are geared to managing economic interdependence.

In addition to its focus on international stability, a case can be made that the G-20 should devote at least as much attention to the overarching theme of this section, namely ensuring that global economic integration does not lead to domestic social disintegration. To be sure, the two are related. It is difficult to address the implications for societal or global cohesion when the international system itself is subject to significant and recurring implosions. Hence, the best spin one can put on the ongoing focus of the international community on pursuing "system stability" is that it is the necessary forerunner to a later focus in the direction of imbuing the new global order with a human dimension. Indeed, I may be underestimating the potential of the G-20. The emergence of the issue of Third World debt relief appears to be associated, in terms of timing and perhaps of substance, with the striking of the G-20, so that this new forum may well be the vehicle that begins and/or contributes to the process of embedding GIR.

The good news in all this is that the international order is becoming increasingly aware of the necessity to embed the expanding trading order within a more stable, more social context. This need not take the form of formal social charters as an integral component of future WTO rounds: It could take the form of more flexible arrangements between signatories and the WTO (as elaborated in the second and fourth of the earlier options proffered by Rodrik).

The potential bad news is that the commingling of trade and social issues risks the possibility that the WTO initiative could become deadlocked, leaving the powerful forces of globalization to operate in a non-cooperative international order. This amounts to a call for statecraft and international stewardship to rise to the challenge.

Managing Federal-Provincial Space: Co-Determination

THE MESSAGE FOR CANADIAN GOVERNANCE IN MUCH OF THE PRECEDING ANALYSIS IS that our federation is becoming more decentralized and more asymmetric in the context of GIR, especially because the axes of trade are shifting. These trends have been helped along by the devolution of some of Ottawa's powers to provinces — mining, tourism, training etc. How do we manage this increasing decentralization in the economic and social spheres and, in particular, how do we ensure we will not trigger a "race to the bottom" (on the social policy front) or fragment the economic union across the provinces? While addressing creative approaches to these challenges more appropriately belongs in the later chapters dealing with governance and policy responses to accommodating GIR, the flow of the analysis dictates they be addressed here.

The first step in coming to grips with this GIR/decentralist challenge to the Canadian social and economic union is to devote some attention to what decentralization really means in an increasingly interdependent world. One popular view, developed most fully in Quebec's mid-1950s Tremblay Report (which triggered Quebec's personal income tax system), is that decentralization represents the separation and exclusive assignment of functions between the two levels of government. This has become known as the "watertight compartments" approach to the assignment of powers. Obviously, the more powers assigned to the provinces, the more the system is decentralized. An important corollary is that increased clarity and transparency in the assignment of these powers should lead to the elimination of duplication and overlap. Admittedly, there is much scope for eliminating duplication but, as will be emphasized below, there is precious little room for eliminating overlap and entanglement. Another corollary is that the exercise of an overarching federal spending power is anathema to a watertight compartments view of federalism.

This is not a viable view of what decentralization is all about in modern, integrated and interdependent federal systems. The focus is far too much on structure (i.e., the formal division of powers) and not enough on process. Carl Friedrich's (1968) concept of federalism is more appropriate in the face on interdependencies:

> Federalism should not be seen only as a static pattern or design, characterized by a particular and precisely fixed division of powers between government levels. Federalism is also and perhaps primarily the process...of adopting *joint policies* and making *joint decisions* on *joint problems*. (quoted in Bastien 1981: 48, emphasis added)

Bastien reiterates this view when he suggests that "decentralization does not lead to a separation of powers, as in traditional federalism, but rather to cooperation in decision making"(47). Thus, we have to marry structure and process. With a well-defined structure, one can go a long way, as noted, toward eliminating duplication. But overlap or entanglement is ubiquitous in Canadian-style legislative federations, where both levels of government can legislate freely in areas of their own constitutional competencies.

It is important to note that not all federations fall into the legislative-federalism camp. For example, Germany is an "administrative federalism" (Smiley and Watts 1985) — most laws are legislated federally while their administration or implementation (even those laws relating to federal powers) rests with the Länder. By way of an intriguing example, the nine Canadian provinces that are signatories to the Tax Collection Agreements for personal income taxation are free to legislate their own rate and bracket structures and then have the federal government collect their taxes for them. In contrast, German federal legislation sets uniform rates for all major taxes, but tax collection and administration is left to the individual Länder. Facilitating the operation of administrative federalism in Germany is the powerful upper chamber, the Bundesrat, whose members are direct representatives of the Länder. Thus, much of the challenge of managing intergovernmental interdependencies in the German federal system is mastered by their set of central governing institutions. In stark contrast, Canadian provinces have no direct role in terms of our central governing institutions. In this sense, Canada is by far the most centralized of modern federations (although this is generally overlooked in centralization-decentralization debates in Canada). Consequently, provincial interests tend to be articulated through and by the provinces and their respective premiers. In federalism terminology, Germany is a model of *intrastate* federalism, whereas Canada practices *interstate* federalism. In other words, we need to "negotiate" our way through the inevitable overlap and entanglement (as implied by Richard Simeon's classic book, *Federal-Provincial Diplomacy* (1972)). But negotiation implies, and indeed requires, "process."

Thus, while decentralization in the Canadian context certainly does imply enhanced powers for the provinces, it also requires new governance mechanisms to address or internalize these ubiquitous overlaps and entanglement. Enter "intergovernmentalism" or "co-determination," the apex of which is the First Ministers' Conference (FMC). To be sure, intergovernmentalism, or executive federalism as it is frequently referred to, may not sit well with many Canadians. Gibbons (1997: 43) refers to it as a "retreat from populism" since intergovernmental forums typically "operate beyond the glare of public exposure, and beyond the immediate pressures of democratic accountability." In terms of earlier terminology, intergovernmentalism generates "democracy deficits." However, short of restructuring our central institutions (e.g., creating a triple-E Senate) or attempting to centralize the federation, both of which appear to be unachievable if not undesirable, co-determination represents the most obvious and viable way to internalize interdependencies. The challenge thus becomes one of opening up the process of intergovernmentalism to the glare of public exposure. Intriguingly, the APCs (Annual Premiers' Conferences) are moving in this direction. With a fixed meeting date each year, with plenty of lead time both to place issues on the agenda and to prepare substantive position papers on the agenda items, and with APC leadership rotating annually among premiers, each of whom is intent on advancing the common agenda, the APCs represent a creative new governing instrument. Now only if the FMCs would follow suit...

In line with the above analysis, the focus now shifts to two new governing instrumentalities that have been delivered by and embody intergovernmentalism: The *Agreement on Internal Trade* (AIT) and *A Framework to Improve the Social Union of Canada*, commonly referred to as the Social Union Framework Agreement, or SUFA.

Managing Economic Interdependence: The AIT

In the early '90s With the FTA up and running and NAFTA negotiations in full swing, federal and provincial first ministers and officials embarked on a process designed to preserve and promote the internal economic union. Foremost among the rationales driving this initiative was the realization that with international trade becoming freer under the FTA and, soon, NAFTA, it was embarrassing, let alone costly, that goods, services, labour and capital could not flow freely across provincial boundaries.

In terms of the "embarrassment" factor, countless commentators dutifully noted that selected flows of goods, services and capital were subject to fewer impediments across national boundaries in Europe than across provincial boundaries in Canada. While this was true, and in several areas probably remains true, one should exercise caution here. *Europe 1992,* which generated the single European market, is an *economic blueprint* explicitly designed to liberalize internal EU trade and to be monitored and adjudicated by *administrative* law. In contrast, federal constitutions, and in particular the *Constitution Act, 1982* (and subsequent amendments), are *political blueprints* monitored and adjudicated, in the first instance at least, by the *political system*. Thus, it should not come as a surprise that in certain areas Europe's internal markets are freer than Canada's internal markets, especially since Canada falls into the decentralized, legislative-federalism camp. On the other hand, Canada is far more integrated in terms of socio-economic policies and institutions than the EU is and, indeed, is ever likely to be. Nonetheless, the essential point is that preserving and promoting the cross-border aspects of the internal socio-economic union requires creative and collaborative political will and instrumentalities.

On the "cost" side, the Canadian business community played a catalytic role in the introduction of AIT by emphasizing the annual cost of provincial barriers and impediments amounted to nearly $7 billion. Moreover, there was a genuine fear that with increased decentralization the provinces might be enticed to become more active in mounting discriminatory barriers to trade and factor flows.

Accordingly, on July 18, 1994, Canada's First Ministers signed on to the *Agreement on Internal Trade* to eliminate barriers to trade, investment and mobility within Canada. In terms of creating an open, integrated domestic market, AIT is structured along the following five lines:

- General rules which prevent governments from erecting new trade barriers and which require the reduction of existing ones in areas covered under the Agreement.
- Specific obligations in 10 economic sectors — such as government purchasing, labour mobility and investment — which cover a significant amount of economic activity in Canada.
- Streamlining and harmonization of regulations and standards (e.g., transportation, consumer protection).
- A formal dispute resolution mechanism that is accessible to individuals and businesses as well as governments.
- Commitments to further liberalize trade through continuing negotiations and specified work programs.

Table 3 contains a more detailed tabular overview of the Agreement.

While it is difficult to be against freer internal markets, critics of the AIT abound. There is concern that it is only a "best-efforts" document with no teeth and no deadlines, for example. Moreover, the dispute resolution mechanism is not binding on the parties. My own criticism of AIT is that, despite the fourth bullet above, ordinary citizens cannot, in the first instance at least, trigger the dispute resolution process without government approval. And on and on.

In typical Canadian fashion however, the best often becomes the enemy of the good. Rather than offer a personal assessment of the pros and cons of AIT, I shall defer to the excellent and balanced (although generally favourable) overview by Patrick Monahan:

> Despite some not trivial shortcomings — both in the institutional provisions and elsewhere — the Agreement on Internal Trade nevertheless holds the potential to significantly reduce existing barriers to internal free trade in Canada. This potential lies not so much in any particular provision of the agreement, but in the recognition that internal trade in Canada ought to be subject to a set of binding norms. For the first time, governments in Canada have committed themselves to resolving trade disputes through a set of generally acceptable and enforceable rules. International experience with the General Agreement on Tariffs and Trade has shown that this commitment to a rules-based regime represents the fundamental breakthrough in promoting

Overview of the 1994
Internal
Trade Agreement

Preamble

General
- Operating Principles
- General Definitions

Constitutional Authorities
- Reaffirmation of Constitutional Powers and Responsibilities

General Rules
- Reciprocal Non-Discrimination
- Right of Entry and Exit
- No Obstacles
- Legitimate Objectives
- Reconciliation
- Transparency

Sectoral Chapters
- Procurement
- Investment
- Labour Mobility
- Consumer-Related Measures and Standards
- Agricultural and Food Goods
- Alcoholic Beverages
- Natural Resources Processing
- Energy (to be completed by June 30, 1995)
- Communications
- Transportation
- Environmental Protection

Institutional Provisions and Dispute Resolution Procedures
- Institutional Provisions
- Dispute Resolution Procedures

Other Provisions
- Trade Enhancement Arrangements
- Relationship to International Agreements
- Future Negotiations
- General Exceptions (e.g., National Security, Aboriginal Peoples, Cultures, Regional Economic Development)

freer trade. Once a rules-based regime has been established — even if the substantive requirements of the rules are initially quite modest — a foundation has been laid for future construction.

This is the promise and the potential of the Agreement on Internal Trade. Shot through with exceptions, caveats and reservations, it nevertheless commits governments to a set of norms for resolving trade disputes. It establishes a new set of political understandings about the extent to which governments should be allowed to discriminate against other Canadians in order to favour local or regional interests. In this relatively modest way, the agreement has the potential to counteract centrifugal political forces that pose a continuing challenge to Canadian unity. The agreement reflects a belief, however tentative, in the primacy of Canadian citizenship and identity over local attachments. Because the obligations set out in the agreement are reciprocal and are to be enforced through a process that is transparent and fair, it represents one of the few politically acceptable avenues by which Canadian attachments can be permitted to prevail over local or provincial ones. In a country as fractious as Canada, that is no small achievement. (Monahan 1995: 217)

In terms of addressing the interface between markets and governments under GIR, the AIT represents a creative instrumentality.[15] It addresses the challenges posed by GIR and decentralization. It is inherently intergovernmental, both interprovincial and federal-provincial. In short, it is an important initiative in managing economic interdependencies. Perhaps most important of all, it provided both the process and structure that eventually led to what I view as a much more important intergovernmental initiative — the agreement on the social union.

Managing Social Interdependence: The Social Union Framework Agreement

The rationale for SUFA mirrored somewhat that for AIT. The combination of decentralization and north-south trade held the potential for an Americanization of the Canadian social envelope and/or erosion of the pan-Canadian aspects (e.g., portability) of provincial social programs. Beyond this, the huge CHST cuts to the provinces and the passing of these cuts through to some provincial social programs generated enormous concern with respect to the future of social Canada. Perhaps anticipating such a reaction, Finance Minister Paul Martin (in his 1995 budget which introduced both the CHST and the associated transfer cuts) invited the provinces to join with Ottawa in developing "mutual consent" principles to underpin the CHST and other social programs. What followed is among the most fascinating and important exercises in

Canadian federal governance: The provinces, acting in a true (even if historically unusual) pan-Canadian fashion, donned the mantle of social policy architects and triggered not only the 1999 social union framework but, along the
way, the creative Canada Child Tax Benefit (CCTB) program. This process merits elaboration.

Within a year of Paul Martin's invitation, the provincial/territorial
Ministerial Council on Social Policy Renewal and Reforms issued their impressive
Report To Premiers (1996). Included in this Report, and compiled in Table 4,
were 15 social policy principles organized around these four general themes:
Social programs must

- be accessible and serve the basic needs of Canadians;
- reflect individual and collective responsibility;
- be affordable, effective and accountable; and
- be flexible, responsive and reasonably comparable across Canada.

The 15 principles are as close as Canada has come to a social policy charter, as it were. Intriguingly, included in the text of the Report (but not among the
15 principles) was the proposal for "the possible consolidation of income support for children into a single national program, jointly managed by both orders
of government, with options for either federal or provincial/territorial delivery of
benefits (Report To Premiers 1996: 14)." This proposal was then endorsed at the
June, 1996 First Ministers' Conference and, in turn, led to the CCTB in Paul
Martin's 1997 budget. Under the CCTB, Ottawa increased its payments to low-
income children and the provinces were allowed to convert the component of
the benefits going to families on welfare to programs relating to child support
for low-income/working-poor families. *This is creative co-determination.* The
overarching goals are mutually agreed upon, but the implementation can and
does reflect provincial priorities. An earlier precedent might be the CPP/QPP
negotiations in the mid-1960s. But what is unique about the CCTB is that it was,
first, a provincial initiative.

The provinces did not stop here. Facilitated, perhaps, by my 1996 "ACCESS"
paper (A Convention on the Canadian Economic and Social Systems) the Jasper APC
(August 1996) endorsed the Report To Premiers and directed the Ministerial Council
to design mechanisms and processes to develop and promote adherence to national
principles and standards. These mechanisms surfaced at the 1997 St. Andrew's APC
and were further honed and ratified at the 1998 Saskatoon APC. By this time, it had

Table 4 92

Principles to Guide Social Policy Reform and Renewal

Social Programs Must Be Accessible and Serve the Basic Needs of All Canadians	1. Social policy must assure reasonable access to health, education and training, income support and social services that meet Canadians' basic needs. 2. Social policy must support and protect Canadians most in need. 3. Social policy must promote social and economic conditions which enhance self-sufficiency and well-being, to assist all Canadians to actively participate in economic and social life. 4. Social policy must promote active development of an individuals' skills and capabilities as the foundation for social and economic development. 5. Social policy must promote the well-being of children and families, as children are our future. It must ensure the protection and development of children and youth in a healthy, safe and nurturing environment.
Social Programs Must Reflect Our Individual and Collective Responsibility	6. Social policy must reflect our individual and collective responsibility for health, education and social security, and reinforce the commitment of Canadians to the dignity and independence of the individual. 7. Partnerships among governments, communities, social organizations, business, labour, families and individuals are essential to the continued strength of our social system. 8. There is a continuing and important role, to be defined, for both orders of government in the establishment, maintenance and interpretation of national principles for social programs.
Social Programs Must Be Affordable, Effective and Accountable	9. The ability to fund social programs must be protected. Social programs must be affordable, sustainable, and designed to achieve intended and measurable results. 10. The long-term benefits of prevention and early intervention must be reflected in the design of social programs. 11. Federal constitutional, fiduciary, treaty and other historic responsibilities for assurance of Aboriginal health, income support, social services, housing, training and educational opportunities must be fulfilled. The federal government must recognize its financial responsibilities for Aboriginal Canadians, both on and off reserve. 12. Governments must coordinate and integrate social programming and funding in order to ensure efficient and effective program delivery, and to reduce waste and duplication.
Social Programs Must Be Flexible, Responsive and Reasonably Comparable Across Canada	13. Social policy must be flexible and responsive to changing social and economic conditions, regional/local priorities and individual circumstances. 14. Governments must ensure that all Canadians have access to reasonably comparable basic social programming throughout Canada, and ensure that Canadians are treated with fairness and equity. 15. Social policy must recognize and take into account the differential impact social programming can have on men and women.

Source: Report To Premiers (1996).

become increasingly clear that the initiative and momentum for social policy reform had shifted to the provinces. Moreover, Canadians were beginning to endorse these provincial initiatives. Not surprisingly therefore, shortly after the Saskatoon APC the federal government joined the process and, together with the provinces (except Quebec), they drove home the social union agreement on February 4, 1999 (*A Framework to Improve the Social Union for Canadians*).

Before focusing on some of the substance of SUFA, it is instructive to backtrack a bit to address the underlying rationale. Figure 5 presents five archetypes for the design and implementation of a social union. The upper right component of the horseshoe-like picture is labelled "unilateral federalism." This was the traditional Canadian approach to the social union. It was top-down, i.e., federally imposed and monitored. It was also highly arbitrary, as evidenced by the numerous unilateral caps, freezes and cuts to federal-provincial transfers from 1981 onward. In the terminology of the literature on integration, this was an exercise in "negative integration," a series of thou-shalt-nots (e.g., thou shalt not impose residency requirements for welfare) supported by the presence, and potential withdrawal, of federal transfers. However, as the social envelope became more complex, negative integration proved inadequate. What is also needed is "positive integration," a pro-active meshing of provincial and federal-provincial systems. This requires the full cooperation and participation of the provinces. In terms of Figure 5, this means moving leftward toward cooperative and collaborative processes and even, for selected areas where the provinces are constitutionally responsible, what Figure 5 labels as "provincial federalism" (i.e., the provinces take the lead role). Note that the left tip of the horseshoe (EU confederalism) is also "top-down" in the following sense: The nation-states of the EU design the policies (e.g., the hundreds of EU "directives") and them impose them on themselves via administrative law. This option is neither possible nor desirable in Canada: Ottawa cannot be sidelined because its influence in the social arena remains both too pervasive and too important.

In terms of substance, SUFA is designed along the following lines:

◆ A set of social policy principles (many adopted from the Report To Premiers).

◆ A section designed to maximize "social mobility," including a long-overdue commitment to ensure mutual recognition of occupational qualifications across provinces. [Note that mutual recognition was also an

Figure 5 94

Five Archetypes for
the Social Union

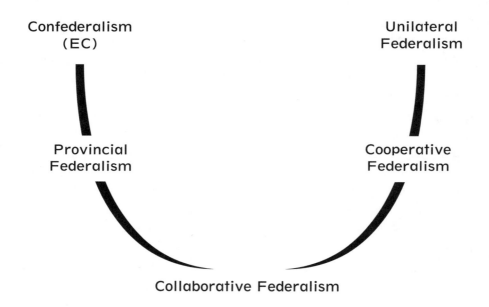

Confederalism
(EC)

Unilateral
Federalism

Provincial
Federalism

Cooperative
Federalism

Collaborative Federalism

Source: Margaret Biggs (1996).

integral component of AIT, but it became incorporated in the social union framework in order to heighten its importance and to press for implementation, TJC.]

♦ A section on ensuring and monitoring accountability and transparency, including "effective mechanisms for Canadians to participate in developing social programs and reviewing outcomes." This is intriguing, since the result of "behind-closed-doors" executive federalism was to bring citizens more fully and more formally into the future evolution of SUFA. (see Mendelsohn and McLean 2000)

♦ A commitment to a cooperative and collaborative partnership on information, planning, and implementation of new initiatives.

♦ Creative ways to allow the exercise of the federal spending power in areas of provincial jurisdiction while at the same time providing the provinces with a significant role in policy design and considerable room to manoeuvre in implementation.

♦ A Dispute Avoidance and Resolution Procedure (which would include disputes relating to the CHST) that would allow for third-party fact-finding.

This list omits one key area. Specifically, the agreement also recognizes the legitimacy of the exercise of the federal spending power as it relates to *individual Canadians* and *organizations* in order to promote equality of opportunity, mobility and other Canada-wide objectives. Presumably, the existence of this clause was a large part of the reason why Quebec did not sign the social union agreement. While this is unfortunate, it is instructive to note that this clause reflects the *status quo ante*. Moreover, as Ron Watts (1999) points out, most other federations make much more use of the spending power than Canada does. While this means there is no formal constraint on how Ottawa enacts policies with respect to its citizens, this power will nonetheless have to be filtered through the political arena.

In any event, SUFA is a watershed agreement. It preserves and promotes an east-west social Canada in precisely the period when trade is veering north-south. Moreover, it ensures, via mutual recognition, that skilled Canadians can ply their trades anywhere in Canada, an essential ingredient for a human capital era. Most important of all, it is significant because it signals and embodies the essence of appropriate policy for a GIR era: Develop creative instruments and governing instrumentalities that serve domestic priorities while being fully consistent with the challenges of globalization and the knowledge/information revolution.

Corporate Governance[16]

C ORPORATE GOVERNANCE HAS FOR TOO LONG BEEN IGNORED IN POLICY DISCUSSIONS involving the interface between governments and markets. One can and should distinguish between at least two concepts of corporate governance. At one end of the spectrum, corporate governance refers to the structure of corporate oversight, with attention addressed to issues such as the appropriate role of the board of directors, the role for outside directors and more specific issues such as whether the CEO should be allowed to be chair of the board of directors. At the opposite end of the spectrum, corporate governance relates to the general manner in which corporations conduct their activities within a society.

One must also recognize that corporate governance structures do not arise out of the blue. Rather, they are embedded in, influenced by, and in turn influence the larger societal values of which they are an integral part. For example, the nature of societal property rights are profoundly different between Japan and continental Europe on the one hand, and Canada and the United States (and Anglo-American societies generally) on the other. In turn, national approaches to corporate governance are inextricably linked to these underlying societal values, with feedback going in both directions. Indeed, it probably could not be otherwise.

Thurow's (1992) comparison between "communitarian" capitalism (continental European) and "individualist" capitalism (Anglo-Saxon) provides an instructive example. In general, the Anglo-Saxon world largely views markets as "impersonal" coordinating mechanisms; in communitarian capitalism, markets and their associated institutions are more embedded in the underlying social milieu. I have argued that these differing national approaches relate to more fundamental attributes of their respective societies (Courchene 1995-96: 205-6). Foremost among these is the prevailing legal system and framework. Anglo-Saxon law is premised on English common law, whereas continental Europe adheres to the more collectivist civil law (typically, variants of the Napoleonic Code). Indeed, I do not think it is accidental that Quebec, a jurisdiction that operates under civil law rather than common law, is the one jurisdiction in North America where aspects of communitarian capitalism have taken hold.

Markets under communitarian-capitalist, civil-law regimes are, as noted, often viewed as part of the societal social fabric. For example, institutions are viewed as much more enduring and important than is the case under Anglo-Saxon capitalism. Thus, the leveraged buyout frenzy of the 1980s in the US did not spread to continental Europe. Part of the reason for this is that if you attempt a takeover of a major German company you may first have to buy out Deutschebank and Dresdner bank, given the pervasive financial-commercial linkages in Europe. These linkages tend to be prohibited under individualist capitalism. But it is likely the case that these policies toward financial-commercial linkages are themselves a reflection of more fundamental societal values. Because institutions are part of the underlying societal glue, corporate governance arrangements reflect this, including the myriad cross-ownership relations between banking and commerce and, for Germany, labour co-determination on corporate boards of directors. This may be a large part of the explanation for the later observation (Chapter 7) that Western Europe's 25 largest companies in 1998 were also large in 1960.

This leads to several observations. First, regardless of the variant of capitalism, effective corporate governance with respect to issues like accountability and transparency is emerging as an essential ingredient of GIR-compatible "software." Arguably, the lack of transparency and accountability in East Asian countries played a major role in their recent currency crises. Second, while Canada's approach to corporate governance will remain in the Anglo-Saxon framework (with Quebec going its own way on some aspects), it is important to recognize that corporate governance is far from being value free. Third, there is nonetheless considerable room to manoeuvre on the corporate governance front, even in the GIR era. Chapter 14, dealing with Canadian competitiveness, will illustrate this in the context of Canada's approach to the governance of our chartered banks and, in particular, to levering off their strengths to foster home-based multinationals.

Turning now to the narrower concept of corporate governance, namely how corporations govern themselves, this too has been evolving, and generally, if slowly, in appropriate directions. To be sure, major corporations will not become environmentalists or social advocates *per se*, but their shareholders are coming to the realization that the financial well-being of their investments depends on creating and maintaining an appealing "brand name" across the globe. Moreover, the requirement for "outside directors" and the extension of a company's liability to members of the board of directors provides powerful internal incentives to maintain a "clean" corporate image. As noted earlier, a single e-mail message spread widely enough and documenting a corporation's environmental degradation or inappropriate labour practices can do untold financial harm to an MNE. Accordingly, many forward-looking corporations are instituting a series of internal governance directives related to areas like labour standards, environmental issues and, in areas like resource extraction, directives geared to accommodating the legitimate needs and aspirations of indigenous peoples. In many cases, these internal "social" policies of corporations are more developed than the legislated policies of the host countries.

Additionally, publicly traded companies are under the watchful eye of securities analysts of major brokerage houses. This serves to open their financial operations to the public, especially the investing public. Moreover, corporations currently *pay* bond-rating agencies to assess their credit rating. This, too, increases the financial transparency of their operations. I foresee the Electronic Citizen-Democracy Herd moving in the direction of rating MNEs on a variety of sensitive societal values — labour standards, environmental policies, respect for host-country values etc. — a social performance assessment, or global, electronic consumers' report, as it were. If and when this initiative takes hold, MNEs will likely be willing to pay for the "privilege" of having their company so assessed, in much the same way as they now pay for having the bond-rating agencies provide them with a credit rating. Should this happen, and I am convinced it will, shareholders will insist their corporations participate: Maximizing long-term MNE profits will dictate this. Apart from noting this is just one more area where information-empowered citizens will be able to countervail corporate excesses, the underlying message is that corporate governance (both in terms of government policy toward corporations and internal corporate governance structures) is a much neglected area in terms of how nations and societies and citizens can address the pervasive forces of GIR.

The Citizen-Market
Interface

T HE ROLE OF THIS CHAPTER IS TO DIRECT ATTENTION TO SELECTED WAYS IN WHICH THE relationship between citizens and markets is evolving in response to the new global order. The first of these is the citizen-market "disconnect," that is, the manner in which the links between citizens and labor markets are becoming much less secure. The section entitled *The "Internationalization" of the Elites* contrasts the implications of GIR for mobile knowledge workers and for relatively immobile unskilled workers. Since not all Canadians can aspire to become knowledge workers, the first section of this chapter devotes attention to the training imperative in the context of GIR.

The Citizen-Market
Disconnect

I N A VERY INSIGHTFUL AND FORWARD-LOOKING PAPER, CARNOY AND CASTELLS FOCUS on one of the most troubling challenges of GIR for civil society, namely the citizen-market disconnect:

> Even without a unified global labour market or a global labour force, there is a global labour dependence in the new economy...The new model of global production and management is tantamount to the *simultaneous integration of work and disintegration of workers as a collective.* (Carnoy and Castells 1996: 15, emphasis added)

What emerges is the vision of an extraordinarily dynamic, flexible, productive economy alongside an unstable, fragile society, and an increasingly insecure individual (92).

The symptoms are easily identifiable. Beyond those noted earlier — polarization of market incomes, outsourcing of routine work — these would include:

- The erosion of the traditional middle class, often in low-skilled jobs but heretofore privileged by protective barriers provided under the "old" paradigm;
- The elimination of traditional "career ladders," largely because there are precious few "careers" in the new order;
- The shift toward a "core" labour force and a "contingent" labour force where the latter has "no benefits, no job security, and no career" and which accounted for, in the US in 1992, about 25 percent of the labour force (Carnoy and Castells 1996: 19);
- The rise of non-standard work;
- The rise of the self-employed (which, in and of itself, may well have a very positive influence but is, nonetheless, a symptom of GIR); and
- The emergence of underclasses (e.g., young, unskilled males).

While these symptoms are generic in that they are present everywhere, the differing market institutions in various countries imply quite different responses to these pressures. In continental Europe, and Germany in particular, where unions remain strong, market polarization has been held at bay. However, the result has been very high unemployment rates. (However, if the unemployed are included in the data and assigned zero market income, then market polarization clearly exists in Germany as well.) In contrast, the US has maintained high employment largely because it is characterized by "flexible" markets — part of which is low wages for the unskilled — and is therefore characterized by significant market-income polarization. Canada is somewhere in between, in terms of both the flexibility of labour markets and unemployment rates.

It is important to note the US-European comparison should not end here. Specifically, the flexibility of US markets carries over to a dynamic and flexible entrepreneurial culture. Eight of the 25 biggest US companies in 1998 did not exist or were very small in 1960, for example. And of the 12 largest companies in the US in 1900, only General Electric (a firm legendary for its ability to "reinvent" itself) was still around to greet the millennium. On the other hand, all of Western Europe's 25 largest corporations in 1998 were also large in 1960. Europe has been generally unable to grow new companies into big companies in the last 40 years and, consequently, is way behind in terms of leadership in the information revolution (Thurow 1999: 93). If Schumpeter's process of "creative destruction" is an integral part of success in the new economic order, as it surely must be, this message has not yet got through to some European nations.

This caveat aside, underlying the above symptoms are some profound changes in the relationship between citizens and markets. One is the decline in the socialization of work and the socialization of production that characterized the Fordist era. Under GIR, this is giving way to an information-based production system with decentralized management, customized markets, just-in-time processes, outsourcing and contingent labour. This is serving to "individualize" work and, in the process, undermine one of the key social institutions in peoples' lives — the workplace (Carnoy and Castells 1996: 29). Another change is that national unions are, in many areas, proving to be no match for mobile international capital: "The fact that a transnational company can move its plant...while a worker cannot move to another country has robbed labour unions in industrialized countries of their power" (Strange 1988: 213). And in Canada at least, the erosion of the role of the workplace as a key component of social interaction and the similar erosion of unions (at least in the private sector) in their erstwhile role of generating middle class Canadians is complicated by the perception, if not the reality, that the social policy support network is simultaneously being downsized. However, in a sense, these are also in the nature of symptoms. The fundamental issue relates to the pervasive influence of GIR on labour markets everywhere — what economists would refer to as the full workings of the factor-price-equalization theorem. No one has expressed this better than Lester Thurow:

> In the past, first world workers with third world skills could earn premium wages simply because they lived in the first world. There they worked with more equipment, better technology and more skilled co-workers than those with third world skills who worked in the third world. These complementary factors effectively raised their productivity and their wages above what they would have been if they had been working in the third world. But that premium is gone. Today they will be paid based on their own skills — not based on the skills of their neighbours. Put bluntly, in the economy of the future those with third world skills will earn third world wages even if they live in the first world. Unskilled labour will simply be bought wherever in the world it is the cheapest. (Thurow 1995: 75)

The obvious corollary for Canada, which merely reiterates an early quotation from Thurow, is that in order to enhance wage levels for the lower half of our workforce we have to make the transition to a human capital society and economy. Phrased differently, we must buy into the human capital dictates of GIR if we want to maintain a high-wage, high-productivity economy and society. Moreover, the available evidence is that high-wage economies are generally more egalitarian societies; so on this score as well, the transition to a human capital future is imperative if Canadians wish to maintain their European-style social contract.

There is also a "pure" globalization effect that is complicating market-income polarization. When economies were largely closed, wages mattered to producers since much of their product was sold domestically. With the internationalization of markets, particularly for an economy with a small domestic market, the domestic wage bill is no longer a dominant factor in terms of corporate sales. We may not like this implication, but it goes hand in hand with the new global order, especially as it relates to small, open economies.

This citizen-market disconnect, and particularly the changing nature of labour markets (especially for the unskilled) leads to another key issue: Should access to social benefits be associated with an individual's employment status, or should access accompany citizenship. The US is clearly an outlier here, with many important benefits (healthcare coverage, access to social security) linked to employment — typically "good" employment — rather than with citizenship. We Canadians have largely taken the other and, I think, much preferable route: Medicare and access to OAS/GIS retirement benefits, for example, are citizen-based entitlements, not employment based. An important issue here is whether we should go further in terms of converting the existing employment-based benefits to a citizen basis. For example, access to maternity benefits is EI-related and many childcare subsidies are employment related. Given the human capital thrust of this analysis, let alone the later importance given to equality of access to human capital formation for all Canadian children, one has to question whether this employment basis for the above entitlements is appropriate.

Leaving this caveat for readers to ponder, we turn to another form of income-distributional disconnect triggered by GIR: the international networking of "symbolic analysts."

The "Internationalization" of the Elites

ROBERT REICH ARGUES IN WORK OF NATIONS (1991) THAT THE WELL-BEING OF Americans depends on the value they add to the global economy through their skills and insights. But not all Americans are equal in this regard. Reich focuses on three types of workers or jobs: routine production services; in-person services; and symbolic-analyst services, which he associates with problem solving, problem identifying and strategic-brokering services. Reich's thesis is that in this era of increasing ease and speed of global communication, the economic star of these "symbolic analysts" is rising dramatically while it is falling for the other two groups, particularly for routine workers as their jobs are replaced by cheaper labour elsewhere. Nothing novel here. However, Reich then adds that these symbolic analysts tend to congregate geographically (e.g., Silicon Valley and Route 128), the result being not only a widening income gap but also a geographic magnification of rich and poor areas. In effect, he suggests these symbolic analysts are "seceding" from America and linking themselves to the global economy, i.e., their social and political bonds to America will tend to unravel as their economic bonds unravel. Lasch refers to this as the "revolt of the elites," in contrast to José Ortega y Gasset's 1930 classic, *Revolt of the Masses*:

> The elites possess most of the wealth. They are becoming increasingly independent from crumbling industrial cities and crumbling public services because they have their own private schools, private health care, private security etc. Their market is international and their loyalties are international rather than regional, national or local. (Lasch 1994: 47)

The growing chasm between wealth and poverty is not so much the problem here. Rather, it is the declining influence of the middle class: "Whatever its faults, middle-class nationalism provided a common ground, common standards, a common frame of reference without which society dissolves into nothing more than contending factions" (49). Similarly, Vincent Cable (1995: 43) offers the following perspective: "We thus have one, potentially large, disadvantaged, alienated, and powerless element in society and another which is flourishing but has less of a stake in the success of any particular country."

It would be an enormous mistake on the part of Canadians to assume this is only a US problem. It isn't. It is alive and well in Canada too. Not only are Canada's economic elites powerful and eloquent, but their policy interests (smaller government, lower taxes, less regulation) are often diametrically opposed to the interests of those who fall in the category of immobile "routine workers." Indeed, the interests of the economic elites are closely aligned with mobile capital, again not surprising since they are (human) capital and they have the exit option. But because they are essential to our productivity, to our ability to attract head offices and to our general well-being, we cannot afford to have them exit. Clearly, again following Reich, the challenge is to find ways to minimize the cleavage between them and their fellow Canadians and to design policies in a manner that ensures their own economic futures depend on the well-being of their fellow citizens. This, too, is largely an instrument challenge, albeit a daunting one.

Thus far, the message arising from the citizen-market interface is a sobering one — the erosion of societal cohesion both in terms of citizens' relationships to the market and in terms of who wins and who loses in the GIR sweepstakes. The policy challenge itself is straightforward: Restore solidarity across citizens and design institutions and networks that will re-link citizens, not so much to the old-style workplace but to the emerging nature of work in the new economic order. Delivering on this challenge obviously is not as straightforward, particularly since one must address, simultaneously, the wider range of economic/competitive imperatives associated with GIR. Thankfully, however, the interactive manner in which GIR affects economies and societies suggests there are many potential levers that can be applied to this challenge. Accommodating policies and/or initiatives in other policy areas can have a salutary effect on social cohesion.

On a personal note, I suspect I am far from alone in having spent a good deal of my policy life arguing that our social policies and associated institutions must be incentive-compatible with ensuring that we are successful on the competitive and productivity fronts. This remains true, and undoubtedly more so under GIR. However, the difference now, especially since knowledge is at the cutting edge of competitiveness, *is the converse is becoming more and more important.* When we choose among alternative policies and instruments for enhancing productivity and economic well-being, there will be some room to manoeuvre to tilt these choices in directions that will serve to enhance the social and human capital aspirations and goals of Canadians. This must become an integral part of the interactive framework for socio-economic decision making in the new global order. Indeed, it cannot be otherwise since human capital is now the wellspring of competitiveness.

Training and the Marketplace

SINCE NOT ALL CANADIANS CAN ASPIRE TO BE "SYMBOLIC ANALYSTS," THE KNOWLEDGE era will have to encompass a training society as well as a (professional) human capital society. Presumably, the new middle class, as distinct from the elites, in a knowledge era will become "information technologists" of various sorts. In one sense, we appear to be world leaders here since we have a larger proportion than almost any country of the relevant age cohort attending non-university professional institutions (CEGEPs, community colleges etc.). Yet in another sense, Canada arguably remains a "professional" society — we have few para-legals, para-medicals, para-engineers or para-anythings. It is one thing not to have in place adequate skills-training or apprenticeship programs; it is quite another not even to recognize the valuable roles technologists play for Canadian society, let alone for individuals. Here, the contrast between Canada and continental Europe is particularly striking.

As Thurow has noted, some of this is the result of the different sorts of institutions that link citizens with enterprise or, probably more correctly, the result of the different concepts of capitalism — individualist Anglo-Saxon capitalism on the one hand vs. communitarian continental-European capitalism on the other:

> In the Anglo-Saxon variant of capitalism...since shareholders want income to maximize their lifetime consumption...firms must be profit maximizers. For profit-maximizing firms, customer and employee relationships are merely a means to the end of higher profits for the shareholders. Wages are to be beaten down where possible and, when not needed, employees are to be laid off...Job switching, voluntary or involuntary, is almost a synonym for efficiency.
> The communitarian business firm has a very different set of stakeholders who must be consulted when its strategies are being set. In Japanese business firms employees are seen as the number one stakeholder, customers number two, and the shareholders a distant number three. Since the employee is the prime stakeholder, higher employee wages are a central goal of the firm in

Japan. Profits will be sacrificed to maintain either wages or employment. Dividend payouts to the shareholders are low.

Communitarian societies expect companies to invest in the skills of their work forces. In the United States and Great Britain, skills are an individual responsibility...Labour is not a member of the team. It is just another factor of production to be rented when it is needed, and laid off when it is not. (Thurow 1992: 32-3)

Thus during the heyday of the Fordist era, the Europeans were enhancing citizen upward mobility in terms of skills enhancement and an industrial system geared to high-value-added production. They were "competing" as it were with their productive middle class, whereas the Americans are "competing" with a very highly paid and highly educated/skilled upper end alongside a poorly paid and unskilled lower end. Arguably, these approaches resonated well with their related immigration policies. The German focus was on unskilled foreign (or guest) workers, thereby increasing the wage grid and providing a substantial incentive for Germans to increase their human capital. The US has always been open to the best and brightest from everywhere in the world, with their own unskilled citizens playing the role of the German "guest workers."

While the new global order is blurring the distinction between the communitarian and individualist approaches to capitalism, some of the above observations still ring true. If anything, the wage grid has significantly widened in the US. I believe the US is only one good recession away from revealing that its approach to its unskilled citizens is the Achilles heel of the individualist-capitalist model, especially since recent American policy has curtailed access to welfare/unemployment benefits.

In any event, in the increasingly competitive environment, training is now emerging into a "you train, I'll hire" syndrome (Thurow 1999: 269). In other words, every employer wants a free ride from the training system, which compounds the training challenge. One approach to the challenge is to ensure that there are incentives in place that encourage firms to undertake more training. Thurow (1999: 270) points to France's refundable training tax, set at one percent of sales. If firms spend one percent of their sales on training, they pay no taxes, i.e., training becomes a free good. On the policy side, more generally, building the skills and expertise of Canadians must become a societal commitment, and one that will begin to channel much of the billions of dollars we now spend on income support toward improving citizens prospects for earning acceptable market incomes. Among the various measures proffered will be a much closer integration between universities and community colleges, incentives for firms to become partners in training and, more fundamentally, devoting more attention and funding to early childhood development along the lines advocated by Fraser Mustard.

By way of a summary, these observations about the citizen-market disconnect and the implications for the production and distribution of human capital across citizens will be pivotal in terms of informing policy design in the information era. Enhancing citizens' skills and human capital is paramount in a knowledge economy. Ensuring equality of access to information-empowerment is essential to enabling Canadians to become meaningful citizens in an information and Internet age. Building an effective human capital pyramid is one of the keys to forging a societal bond between symbolic analysts and their fellow citizens. And a societal commitment to an effective transition from a resource-based culture to a skills- and human-capital-based culture is an essential ingredient in rebuilding our middle class and, in the process, reconnecting citizens to the altered marketplaces and to society generally.

While a human capital future is a necessary precondition for success in the new global order, it is not sufficient. Societies also need social capital and cohesion. I focus on these concepts in Appendix A and will examine them in greater depth in Chapter 13.

I now turn to the final cell of the Figure 1 schema — the citizen-government interface.

The Citizen-
Government
Interface

A DDRESSING THE ALTERED CITIZEN-GOVERNMENT OR CITIZEN-STATE RELATIONSHIP begins by recalling the Chapter 2 focus on the declining role of government in our lives. This leads naturally to an analysis of the voluntary (or non-profit, or third) sector as a creative societal response to a downsized public sector. The underlying issues of this section are extremely important to the analysis since the voluntary sector holds part of the key to whether we adapt to the new global order or we reconstitute the last paradigm's vision of government in the new guise of voluntarism or the third sector. We then turn to the changing nature of *direct* relationship between citizens and governments, i.e., e-government. The chapter, and indeed Part II, concludes by focusing on the changing nature of the political market in the new paradigm. Briefly put, without any formal change in the Constitution, the electoral politics in the wake of GIR is serving to turn the original BNA Act on its head, setting the stage for a prolonged jurisdictional conflict between Ottawa and the provinces.

The Downsized
Public Sector

G OVERNMENT PROGRAM SPENDING HAS, AS NOTED EARLIER, FALLEN DRAMATICALLY as a percent of GDP. It peaked at 36 percent in 1994 and fell to roughly 26 percent by century's end, decreasing to 11 percent from 17 percent at the federal level and to 15 percent from 19 percent at the provincial level. Part of this reduction has come from a downsized civil service and a reduction of transfers to various institutions and to citizens. Part also has come from various forms of deregulation — privatization and contracting out. This represents a watershed in the evolution of the citizen-state relationship, especially for Canadians who have always held a more benign view of the role of government, and of government intervention in our economy and our lives, than have Americans, for example.

Not surprisingly, the response to a scaled-down government sector has been met with widely differing degrees of acceptance. At one end of the spectrum, some analysts celebrate the liberalizing of the individual in the information era — see Davidson and Mogg's *The Sovereign Individual: How to Survive and Thrive During the Collapse of the Welfare State* (1997). Others merely recognize that the new era will require that individuals rely more on themselves for their societal futures — the "Me Inc." vision in Sherry Cooper's *The Cooper Files* (1999).

At the other extreme are a goodly number of Canadians who not only fear for the future of the social envelope but also view the decline in government as signalling a societal turn toward the "Life, Liberty and Pursuit of Happiness" rhetoric and policies of the American Creed. I trust it is not too much of a misrepresentation of the views of this group to suggest their first preference would be to use the emerging budget surpluses (at both levels of government) to restore the erstwhile role of government in our lives. And, to the degree that this is not in the cards, their second preference would likely be for a revitalization and extension of the role of the voluntary, or third or nonprofit, sector.

With the demise of Canada's 20th-century initial "chosen instrument," i.e., the commercial Crown Corporation, Hall and Banting (2000: 1-2) note "the nonprofit sector appears to be arising as a chosen instrument of collective action in a new century." Not surprisingly, perhaps, the nonprofit sector is now the focus of increasing societal interest, let alone research. In what follows, I shall address those aspects of nonprofits or the third sector that appear to be most relevant to the citizen-state (and, indeed, citizen-market) interfaces in the new order.

The Rise of
the Third Sector

Size and Scope

T HE FIRST POINT TO NOTE ABOUT THE THIRD SECTOR IS JUST HOW LARGE AND PERVASIVE it is. Table 5 presents 1994 data relating to those nonprofits that qualify as charities. Note that this is less than half of the legally incorporated nonprofits (Quarter 1992) so that Table 5 presents only a partial overview of the size and scope of the nonprofit sector. Nonetheless, the evidence in the table indicates that the nonprofits are a major component of the Canadian economy and society. Moreover, the nonprofit sector has access to significant resources — $90.5 billion — as indicated in Table 5.

The Terminology Challenge

Given the pervasiveness of nonprofits, it would arguably advance their position and prestige had they a better label. Hall and Banting reflect on the three most-often-used labels as follows:

> Generally speaking the term "nonprofit" is the language of economists, and is derived from a model of market economics that views nonprofit organizations as a residual category of organizations in an economy that otherwise has only two actors, market-driven producers and government…
>
> The term "voluntary sector" has its origins in the work of sociological studies of voluntary associations and appears to be predominant in the British literature. It draws attention to the donations of time and money associated with these organizations; voluntary organizations can be distinguished by the fact that members of their governing boards serve without pay and that these organizations often benefit from the contributions of large numbers of individual volunteers. Without denying the importance of the voluntary impulse to the nonprofit sector, however, some critics object that the term might imply that these organizations are run entirely by volunteers, contrary to current realities.
>
> The term "third sector" and the less used "independent sector" have their origins in political science. The third sector attempts to highlight the distinction between government and the private or business sector by focusing on its independence from government and its differences from the private sector. In this framework, government is the first sector, business organizations comprise the second sector and the rest of organizational life occurs in the third sector. One of the objections to the use of this term is that it might seem to imply that third sector organizations are less important than other types of organizations. (Hall and Banting 2000: 4-5)

Table 5 112

Types of Charities and Distribution of Revenues

Type of Charity	Number	% of All Charities	Total Revenue ($ billion)	% Total Revenue
Arts and Culture	3,187	4.5	2.0	2.2
Community Benefit (e.g., humane societies, John Howard Society, Meals-on-Wheels)	5,238	7.3	2.5	2.8
Education (e.g., organizations supporting schools and education)	4,158	5.8	3.5	3.9
Health (e.g., organizations supporting medical research, public health)	3,180	4.5	6.4	7.1
Hospitals	978	1.4	27.4	30.4
Libraries	1,615	2.3	1.3	1.4
Places of Worship (e.g., churches, synagogues, mosques, etc.)	25,458	35.6	5.3	5.9
Private Foundations (organizations disbursing private funds)	3,356	4.7	1.5	1.6
Public Foundations (e.g., United Way, Centraide, hospital foundations)	3,466	4.9	4.7	5.2
Recreation	2,753	3.9	0.7	0.7
Religion (e.g., convents, monasteries, missionary organizations)	3,978	5.6	2.8	3.1
Social Services (child, youth, family and disabled welfare and services, international assistance, relief, etc.)	10,317	14.4	8.8	9.7
Teaching Institutions (universities and colleges)	2,642	3.7	23.5	25.9
Other (e.g., service clubs, employee charitable trusts)	1,087	1.5	0.1	0.1
Total	71,413	100.0	90.5	100.0

Source: Hall and Macpherson (1997).
Reproduced from Banting (2000), 12.

Hall and Banting (5) note that an alternative term, "non-governmental organization" (NGO), is frequently used in Quebec and in continental Europe but in the English-speaking world NGO is typically restricted to institutions operating in the international arena.

As is typical with many of the developments associated with the new order, Peter Drucker is an important player in the analysis of the third sector. And in terms of the appropriate name for these institutions, he offers the following insight:

> Non-profit, non-business, non-governmental are all negatives. One cannot define anything by what it is not. What then do these institutions do? They all have in common — and this is a recent realization — that their purpose is to change human beings. The product of the hospital is a cured patient. The product for a church is a changed life...[The list goes on. TJC].
> "Human-change Institutions" would be the right name (Drucker 1989: 198-99).

Drucker adds that while every developed country discharges most of these functions, in most of them they are discharged through governmental, centralized agencies. What makes the US distinct, he asserts, is that these functions are being discharged in and by the local community and, in the great majority of cases, by autonomous, self-governing local organizations. What has occurred over the decade since Drucker penned these words is that many countries, Canada included, have increasingly resorted to nonprofits as part of the process of government downsizing and deregulating these erstwhile "governmental centralized agencies." Nonetheless, there remains an important difference between Canadian and US nonprofits. As Table 6 reveals, the US nonprofits receive 70 percent of their revenues from either earnings or private giving, while Canadian nonprofits receive 60 percent of their revenues from governments.

Now that the term "human change institutions" has been broached, it is appropriate to address the manner in which these organizations are altering the citizen-government and citizen-market relationships.

An Analytical Perspective

These nonprofits or human-change institutions are superimposed both between citizens and governments and between citizen and markets. In terms of the former, they can be viewed as an alternative way to carry forward selected government imperatives, hence the frequently used term "alternative service delivery mechanisms." In terms of the latter, they represent an alternative to market provision of

Table 6   114

Sources of Revenue for Nonprofit
Organizations: Selected Countries

Country	Government (%)	Earned Income (fees, charges) (%)	Private Giving (%)
Canada[1]	60	26	14
United Kingdom	47	45	9
France	58	35	7
Australia	31	62	6
United States	30	57	13

Note: 1 Canadian data for registered charities only.
Source: Hall and Macpherson (1997); Salamon,
Anheier and Associates (1998).
Reproduced from Banting (2000), 17.

selected goods and services. However, in both dimensions, they represent new ways for citizens to embrace governmental and market activity:

> Third sector institutions are rapidly becoming creators of new bonds of com-munity...Increasingly, they create a sphere of effective citizenship. One hears a good deal these days about disintegration of community, the family, for instance, or the community of the small town. Traditional communities in all developed countries are weakening...but in the third-sector institutions, new bonds of community are being forged.
>
> Now that the size and complexity of government make direct participation all but impossible, it is the human-change institution of the third sector that is offering its volunteers a sphere of personal achievement in which the individ-ual exercises influence, discharges responsibility, and makes decisions. And, increasingly, executives in business, especially people in middle management, are expected to serve in decision-making positions as board members of non-profit institutions. In the political culture of mainstream society, individuals, no matter how well educated, how successful, how achieving or how wealthy, can only vote and pay taxes. They can only react, can only be passive. In the coun-terculture of the third sector, they are active citizens. This may be the most important contribution of the third sector. (Drucker 1989: 204-5)

Beyond this reflection on the citizen enhancement and participation role of the nonprofits, they play a critical mediating role in terms of the societal impli-cations arising from the forces of GIR. Not to put too fine a point on this, they are actively engaged in a process of "embedding GIR" domestically. That is, they are part and parcel of the process to ensure that international economic integration does not lead to domestic social disintegration. This is partly because they have a number of features that make them an attractive alternative to market-driven enterprises and/or state agencies. As Hall and Banting (2000: 3) note, "the lack of a primary profit motive strengthens the sense that they are more trustworthy than for-profit commercial firms in the delivery of sensitive public services." And in contrast to government, they are closer to people and are often viewed as "more flexible than government because they operate on a smaller scale, and they are able to attract voluntary contributions of time and money in a way that govern-ment and business cannot" (3).

More generally, Table 7, reproduced from a June 1999 Canada West Foundation research bulletin, tabulates the desired characteristics of "ideal non-profit" organizations as seen from "insiders." Specifically, the table reports on sur-vey data collected from 72 nonprofit social service agencies. If these "ideal" features were to characterize nonprofits, then they clearly would fully live up to their potential, i.e., "that nonprofit service delivery is *less* expensive than government delivery or that nonprofit social service agencies are *more* committed to helping people in need than for-profit businesses offering the same services" (Canada West Foundation 2000: 3, emphasis original).

However, nonprofits do not always live up to these Table 7 ideals. After focusing on some of the real-world shortcomings of nonprofits, the Canada West Foundation article draws, in summary fashion, on the four-fold critique of non-profits by Lester Salamon (1987): philanthropic insufficiency, philanthropic particularism, philanthropic paternalism and philanthropic amateurism. In more detail,

> *Insufficiency* refers to the inability of nonprofits to raise resources adequate enough and reliable enough to cope with the human-service problems of an advanced industrial society. *Particularism* describes the tendency of nonprofits to serve those groups that fall within their declared mandates instead of providing or redistributing resources equally throughout the population. *Paternalism* occurs when community needs are defined by those in command of the charitable resources. *Amateurism* refers to the tendency of some non-profit organizations to be unprofessional and nonsystematic in their modes of operation. (Canada West Foundation 2000: 5, emphasis original)

These pros and cons of nonprofits aside, the important reality is that they are now being thrust into a new and exciting role — key bridging and mediating institutions that have significant potential for the Chapter 7 challenge of reconnecting citizens to markets as well as for providing an alternative to the severing of the citizen-government relationship that would flow from outright privatization. In other words, they have significant potential for advancing societal cohesion in a GIR era.

To conclude this discussion of the third sector and its potential for a solution to aspects of both "market failure" and "government failure" in terms of service delivery, I now focus on a few key challenges that will confront the nonprofit sector.

Whither the Third Sector?

Given the increasing importance of the third sector, it is typically Canadian that we should approach the third sector from a government perspective. Toward this end, several task forces have been struck. One of these was the Panel on Accountability and Governance in the Voluntary Sector (PAGVS), chaired by Ed Broadbent, which reported in 1999. While the PAGVS was triggered by the national voluntary organizations, a second task force emanated from the federal government: Ottawa created the Voluntary Sector Task Force (VSTF) in the Privy Council Office to follow

Characteristics of Ideal Nonprofits

The characteristics of the ideal non-profit social service organization mentioned most often by executive directors fall into four main categories:

Community Relations	• responsive to clients and community • focused on serving clients (non-bureaucratic) • grassroots support (including volunteers) • involved in partnerships with local non-profits and for-profits
Flexibility and Innovation	• flexible approach to internal operations and service delivery • willing to take risks and try new things • creative and resourceful
Accountability	• responsible managers • accountable to clients, the community, governments, and donors • sound fiscal management
Prerequisites of Effectiveness	• strong values and clear goals • good governance (effective board, knowledge of business practices) • stable funding • significant degree of autonomy • quality staff and the resources to pay them properly

Source: 1998 ASDP Survey (N=72). This list is not an exhaustive account of all responses, but a summary based on recurring themes.
Reproduced from Canada West Foundation (2000).

up on the Broadbent Report. Ottawa also established a series of Joint Tables to consider, among other things, the building of a new government/third-sector relationship and the strengthening of the third sector's capacity, including improving the regulatory environment. Readers are referred to a comprehensive and timely summary survey (Brock 2000) of the underlying issues and recommendations emanating from these task forces. Here, we will cover only one area: the relationship of these third-sector service delivery agencies to governments.

In terms of the analysis in the earlier chapters, if the third sector is to be in the forefront of adapting to the new global order, this necessarily implies a premium on flexibility, independence, and responsiveness to citizens. This imperative does not sit well with my understanding (perhaps, perception is more appropriate) of one of the underlying thrusts of these reports, namely to find appropriate niches or leverage-points for governments (and especially the federal government) to assert their influence, if not prominence, in the operations of the third sector, typically replete with a new layer of bureaucracy. If we are not careful here, we will be resurrecting the essence of the previous paradigm's vision of government, albeit in a new guise. For reasons elaborated earlier, the new paradigm requires a vibrant third sector, but it must respond to the needs of information-empowered citizens and not be handcuffed by the visible hand of government. In this regard it is significant to note that in the Canada West Foundation survey (2000: 12), the "ideal" nonprofit was repeatedly described as "independent of government values" and at "arms length from government." In other words, "a good working relationship with the state...must be combined with a significant degree of autonomy and independence" (12). Sorting out where this balance lies across the various third-sector agencies will emerge as one of the important challenges facing a successful third sector.

Another challenge relates to the role of the voluntary sector in areas where commercial enterprises can also deliver the goods and services. Here, there is a huge philosophical divide across citizens. At one extreme are those who view the third sector as a way of maintaining and extending old-style government — monitored national standards, a unionized labour force and a prohibition of for-profit enterprise. At the other extreme are those who believe this ought to be the domain for private enterprise, albeit with governmental regulatory oversight. In those areas where Ottawa holds sway constitutionally, the former approach may well be viable politically. But in those areas where the goods or services fall into the provincial domain, it is virtually certain that selected provinces will *not* allow nonprofits to maintain a monopoly. This is an ideological minefield, so one has to tread carefully, if at all. However, I feel secure in stating that the tumultuous nature of the changes ushered in by GIR necessarily requires a highly flexible third sector to respond to the new order. Unless the mandate of a third-sector monopoly allows adequate scope for creative citizen-driven responses to their new environment, then for-profit competitors should be encouraged. Indeed, they probably merit a competitive place in any event.

A final challenge to the third sector emanates from the dramatic change in the nature of competitiveness in the new global order. Some traditional third-sector functions, such as post-secondary institutions and the generalized health sector no longer fall only in the realm of social institutions. These functions are increasingly critical to the production (universities) and employment (the health sector) of human capital and, as such, are essential to Canadian competitiveness in the new global era, both in their own right and in terms of how they relate to the larger Canadian competitive thrust. The funding they are likely to obtain from being viewed primarily as "social institutions" will be woefully inadequate in terms of the role they must play in creating and employing Canadian human capital. In other words, they no longer fall solely within the purview of social institutions — they are among the premier economic launching pads of 21st-century competitiveness. If they are to remain in the third sector, then they must have a degree of autonomy in operation and in resource access roughly equivalent to what they would have if they were in the private sector.

The above assessment of the voluntary or third sector has been long but necessary. This sector is emerging as one of the essential instrumentalities in responding to the forces of globalization and the information revolution. It possesses many attributes: It enhances citizen participation in an era where other linkages between citizens and the society at large are fraying, if not eroding; it provides delivery systems alternative to either government or the private sector; and it has the potential for creative adaptation to emerging needs since it is not (in principle) encumbered by either the profit motive or government directives. However, its potential strategic importance also implies that it is ripe for co-opting in the interplay of competing market, government and citizen interests. The key message here is that this sector must become a central focus of policy analysts, no matter what their ideological persuasion.

Citizens and
e-Government

C HAPTER 2 BROACHED THE CONCEPT OF AN INFORMATION-EMPOWERED "SOVEREIGN
citizen" no longer hindered by a territorially bound relationship to his or
her nation-state. Relatedly, Elkins (1995) notes that the traditional Westphalian
state typically presented citizens with a single "bundle" of identities and loyalties,
whereas in the emerging order these loyalties are effectively "unbundled." In
Elkins' terms, citizen identity is no longer along the lines of a nation-state pre-
scribed *table d'hôte*, but more along a citizen-determined *à la carte* choice. In a
recent paper, Segal (1999) views this multiple loyalty and multiple identity concept of citizenship in terms of a series of progressively internationalizing concen-
tric circles within which citizens can and will freely choose to situate themselves.
This is part of the erosion of the nation-state from "below." In this section, the
focus is on a quite different aspect of the altering citizen-state relationship, namely the advent of e-government and the shift in the manner in which citizens and
states/governments communicate with each other.

Canada is well along the four-point path to e-government highlighted in
"The Next Revolution":

1) Establish one-way communication sites.
2) Convert these into two-way communications and allow citizens to provide information about themselves, even if it is only a change of address,
for example.
3) Move toward web sites that allow for a quantifiable exchange of value
to take place, such as renewing a driver's license, or filing a tax return.
4) Develop portals that integrate the complete range of government services on the basis of function rather than department. (*The Economist*
2000a)

Several important implications flow from this. First, unlike the delivery of
much of governmental activities, there will be substantial pressure in this area,
even international pressure, for governments to replicate the "state of the art" in
terms of e-government. The fact that *The Economist* survey has highlighted
Singapore's integrated Web site as leading-edge will stimulate all governments to
follow suit. And in the Canadian context, a demonstrably superior Web site in
one province will surely trigger imitation in other provinces. Second, and

relatedly, by its very nature this process is leading in the direction of "respecting" the citizenry, making the Web sites increasingly user-friendly in myriad operational and functional ways. Moreover, along earlier lines that "receptors" rather than "transmitters" are increasingly in the driver's seats, this means that citizens, by "voting with their hits," will further alter the nature of the interactive citizen-government e-relationship. The bottom line here is that this is a process that views citizens as customers or clients rather than as "subjects."

A final observation here is that governments, by their very nature, have to view *all* citizens as their "customers," not only a select group. Perforce, this implies that governments cannot tolerate a "digital divide" across citizens. Hence, in line with developing an effective "e-the-people" relationship, this will be accompanied by a concerted effort to ensure Web-site access to all citizens. In the process, Leviathan will, to a degree at least, be tamed: The bureaucracy will be forced away from being civil masters and toward being civil servants.

The Evolving Political Marketplace

THE FINAL SECTION OF THE CITIZEN-MARKET INTERFACE ADDRESSES THE PROFOUND changes in the political marketplace — the market for votes and voters — triggered by the GIR forces. With powers passing upward and downward from central governments of nation-states, central governments everywhere, especially in decentralized federations like Canada, are literally scrambling to find a new political salience and currency. The electoral currency of the old paradigm — resource-based economic development — is no longer the "stuff" of nation building, let alone economic competitiveness. So one may as well pass these down to the provinces, as Ottawa has for substantial aspects of mining, forestry, energy etc. Moreover, trade policy is now circumscribed via NAFTA and the WTO, monetary policy is driven by price stability, and the tax component of fiscal policy is increasingly under the influence of the "kids in red suspenders" (the international capital markets).

So where does Ottawa turn in order to regain its political and electoral relevance? The answer, I think, is clear: It turns to many of the areas the Constitution assigns to the provinces! In other words, electoral salience as well as the essence of nation building now rests with addressing citizens' issues as they relate to information-empowerment, human capital development and redressing the income-distributional fallout of the GIR environment. But responsibility for these areas falls largely within provincial jurisdiction. Nonetheless, the very nature of politics will ensure that federal politicians will be unable to keep themselves from invading provincial jurisdiction. Moreover, armed with significant and growing budget surpluses, they are well-positioned to do so. Welcome to the evolving federal-provincial battle royal.

Ottawa can mount a reasonable case (on policy grounds if not on constitutional grounds) for becoming more involved in some of these areas. For example, few would deny central governments everywhere strive to increase the competitiveness of their respective economies. And with knowledge as the new cutting edge of competitiveness, Ottawa *will* be a player in the human capital future of Canadians. Moreover, there is a clear infrastructure role for the federal government here: The Internet and related information systems are to the GIR paradigm what the railroad was to the earlier paradigm. With research chairs, millennium fellows and the like, however, Ottawa is going much further.

Indeed, the entire social arena is increasingly attracting Ottawa's interest, frequently with encouragement from citizens if not from various provinces. Given that different countries embody widely varying approaches to who-should-do-what in social policy, there is no obvious solution to this jurisdictional tug-of-war, although the later policy sections will provide some principles and guidelines. In anticipation of this later analysis, one might note that if the provinces continue the trend toward becoming wealth-creating "region-states," then Ottawa might find, almost by default, that it has to become a more important player on the income-distribution front. Indeed, with the CCTB, it already has.

The analysis thus far has focused on the various forces of the GIR paradigm shift: They are pervasive, they are highly interactive and they are not likely to be reversed. Indeed, we are arguably only in the infancy of the information/knowledge revolution.

While the preceding analysis of the profound influence of GIR on citizens, markets and governments (and their respective interfaces) is presumably of interest in its own right, its larger role is as the requisite backdrop to inform the design and implementation of governance and policy for 21st-century Canada. This is the purpose of the remainder of the book and, indeed, the *raison d'être* of the entire exercise.

part III

Bridging Paradigms: From Boards and Mortar to Mortarboards

Framing Policy in
an Information Era

T HE REMAINDER OF THE ANALYSIS IS DEVOTED TO ARTICULATING A POLICY AND
governance response to the challenges arising from globalization and the
knowledge/information revolution. Most of the detailed policy prescriptions
and recommendations will appear in Part IV, *A Human Capital Future for
Canadians*, which focuses on economic, social and institutional imperatives
designed to promote both competitiveness and cohesion in the new paradigm.
The purpose of the three chapters in Part III is, as the title indicates, to "bridge
the paradigms" or to provide the backdrop, framework and principles to
inform the ensuing policy prescriptions and recommendations.

Toward this end, the present chapter focuses on the differing nature of the
policy challenge relating to private-sector and public-sector adjustment. In effect,
private-sector adjustment will largely be externally driven while public-sector
adjustment must be domestically driven. This is then followed by a general discussion of goals, instruments, principles and strategies and the manner in which
they relate to policy formation.

Chapter 10 highlights two examples of recent blueprints for the Canadian
economy that reflect the "winds of change" ushered in by GIR. Specifically, both
the BCNI and Ontario economic visions are rooted within a skills and human
capital framework.

In tandem, these chapters prelude the core purpose of Part III, articulating
a human capital mission statement for 21st-century Canada. This is the purpose
of Chapter 11.

GIR and the
Adjustment Imperative

G IR IS CREATING AN INCREASING DIVIDE IN TERMS OF THE NATURE OF THE ADJUSTMENT pressures and forces relating to the private and public sectors. One important difference relates to the ease of "by-pass." The private sector is increasingly international and competitive while the public sector (with some important caveats dealt with later) is inherently national and non-competitive, even monopolistic.

An example may be in order. In my role as a consumer of goods and services, I am absolutely confident that I will have access to state-of-the-art banking and telecommunications services for the indefinite future — the internationalization of financial markets ensures this will be so. What I do not know is whether these services will be imported or domestically produced and, if the latter, whether these producers will be domestically owned or foreign operated. However, as a consumer of government services, I have no such guarantee that five years from now I will be able to access state-of-the-art public services. Rather, I will have little choice but to consume the brand of education or health care or EI or welfare provided by the relevant governments.

In other words, there is no meaningful scope for "by-pass" in the public sector.[17] It is this key difference between the underlying environments — competitive vs. monopolistic — that merits attention in terms of the approaches to framing policy. I shall deal with each in turn, beginning with some recommendations for addressing or managing market adjustment under GIR.

Principles Relating
To Private-Sector
Adjustment

C ONTINUING WITH THE EARLIER ANALOGY, SINCE I CANNOT BE DENIED STATE-OF-THE-art banking, telecommunications and the like in an increasingly integrated global economy, it then becomes patently foolish for Canadian policy not to attempt to ensure that, wherever possible, Canadian enterprise plays a key role in providing these services. In effect, this constitutes a GIR-triggered, paradigmatic shift in the public policy environment as it relates to private-sector adjustment.

Thus, the first principle pertaining to public policy toward enterprise is that all governments should engage in creating "untraded interdependencies," or positive and attractive locational advantages, to ensure that Canadian enterprises and foreign-owned enterprises with a meaningful presence in Canada are at least on a level playing field with their international competition in providing these services to Canadians. I hasten to add this is not intended to be "code" for subsidies. Rather, à la Friedman (1999), the challenge is to provide GIR-consistent "software" such as appropriate tax policies, macro-management, transparent and accountable corporate governance, regulatory regimes etc. However, in the later context of balancing competitiveness and cohesion, it must mean more than this. Given that there are alternative ways to generate GIR-compatible "software," other things being equal, we should always tilt the specific policy choices in the direction of accommodating the underlying human capital imperative that will be central to the mission statement articulated in Chapter 11.

The second feature of market adjustment is that market agents, left to themselves, *will* adjust and are adjusting. Unlike the situation in the last generation's behind-protective-walls paradigm, GIR sharply enhances the Schumpeterian process of "creative destruction," and both citizens and markets/enterprise are, in general, capitalizing on these new opportunities. Intriguingly, the policy challenge here is that these adjustments may well be taking place too quickly, not too slowly.

How should government policy react to these private-sector adjustments? My answer is along the following lines: *Government should adopt as a principle the presumption that any private-sector initiative is permissible unless it can be demonstrated to be contrary to the public interest.*[18] On the surface, this seems to be a harmless reworking of our traditional approach to change and innovation: Is the new innovation/adjustment in the public interest? But the critical difference is *where* it places the burden of proof. Should the innovators have to demonstrate their activities are not contrary to the public interest, or should those espousing the status quo be required to show that the innovation/adjustment in question runs counter to the public interest? As the principle indicates, it must surely be the latter — *the status quo must be on the defensive, not the innovators.*

Society at large would of course still be assigned the role of defining the "public interest." Thus, the above adjustment principle must be viewed as operating within this societal framework. Nonetheless, shifting the burden of proof to the status quo will lead to a much more flexible and dynamic economy. This, too, is part of generating an appealing set of untraded interdependencies.

The third evolving feature of private sector adjustment is that GIR affects the relevant market size when it comes to competition policy. Whether a given firm has too much "market share" is a quite different issue when the relevant market is Canada than when the relevant market is North America or the international arena, generally. And this must be an anticipatory assessment in terms of what the nature of the market will be in the foreseeable future, not what currently passes as the prevailing wisdom with respect to the status quo. One example will suffice. Far too readily, we have adopted the rhetoric that big is bad and small is beautiful. To be sure, small firms are critically important. They are dynamic, flexible and innovative, which is especially important for the emerging technologies. But in the process, we tend to underplay the role of big companies. Thurow provides the requisite balance:

- Small new companies usually start as spin-offs of big old companies...Big companies are where managers of the new companies learn the management skills (make mistakes with other people's money) that allow them to start up their own companies with fewer mistakes...

- Usually the initial markets for small companies are components used by big companies...

- Big companies are the big exporters that every country needs. Exporting requires a detailed knowledge of foreign markets that small companies don't have and aren't going to get because it's too expensive for them to acquire it.

- Big companies provide most of the economy's good, well-paying jobs with career ladders. Remaining an employee in a small company that is going to remain small means that the prospects for high wages are bleak.

- *Small is not beautiful. What is beautiful is a small firm that rapidly grows into a big firm.* (Thurow 1999: 233-4, emphasis added)

We are making some progress toward accepting a big-can-be-beautiful vision of enterprise. We all applaud to achievements of Nortel, JDS Uniphase and the international reach of Bombardier and SNC-Lavalin, among others. Yet we do not accept these precepts as they apply, for example, to the banking sector, where the individual institutions are actually small global players. The reality of GIR is that, increasingly, there is only one market — the global market. And if we don't allow our institutions the opportunity to be meaningful players in this global market, then, increasingly, global enterprises based elsewhere will become important players in our domestic market.

Finally, and relatedly, Canadian policy should not only foster an environment conducive to the growth of larger institutions but also provide the incentives for them to incubate and "grow" associated, smaller firms. This will be a much easier policy position to adopt under GIR, since, as noted, failure to do so will likely mean that Canadians will then have to deal with large foreign enterprises.

Principles Relating To Public-Sector Adjustment

T HE DESIGN AND IMPLEMENTATION OF OUR SOCIAL POLICY INFRASTRUCTURE (E.G., education, health, training, welfare, EI, and the transitions from school-to-work and from welfare-to-work) is emerging as *the* critical policy challenge for a GIR era. There are several reasons for this. The first is that the nature of our social institutions in the next century will effectively define who we are and desire to be as a society in the upper half of North America. As already noted, "national human capital markets are essential for the productivity of economic units located in a national territory" (Castells 1997: 307), and this requires, perforce, an effective and appropriate social infrastructure. Arguably, no other policy area will be as important in this regard. This provides the primary rationale for why public-sector evolution is essential for success in the millennium.

The second reason relates to the fact that it is enormously difficult to effect adjustment in the public sector. Part of this has to do with the fact that, as already noted, there are no (or few) avenues for "by-pass" and, therefore, no direct pressures *within* the system to emulate best-practice elsewhere in the world. Another aspect is that the private-sector processes of creative destruction and cumulative feedbacks do not carry over into the political market.

This last point merits elaboration. Creative destruction is difficult to short-circuit in an open-borders environment. Whom do the concerned citizens (or other affected private-sector agents) finger as the culprit? Is it the inefficiency of the pre-existing firms, whether in the form of inadequate management or over-demanding unions? Or is it the result, for example, of international by-pass reflected in consumers opting for alternative products or services produced off-shore? Thus, it is difficult for citizens to know where, or against whom, to vent their anger and frustration. But matters are very different when it comes to public-sector adjustment: Citizens know precisely whom to blame, or whom to punish at the next election (as occurred with the Liberals in Atlantic Canada in the 1997 election in connection with EI reforms). Yet the problem goes deeper than this. Sylvia Ostry captured this wonderfully well in a recent Queen's University, John Deutsch Institute Conference when, in response to a question from the audience, she noted while governments may be no better or no worse than anyone else when it comes to picking winners, losers are incredibly adept at picking governments! In a word, governments find it difficult to *exit*. Yet exit is a key ingredient in any adjustment process.

There is a further challenge to adjustment in the government sector. Expenditures and transfers tend, by their very nature, to privilege certain interests. In the private sector, adjustment to a disequilibrium such as a new product innovation tends to generate positive feedbacks that propel the adjustment forward. In the public sector, the initial response is more likely to take the form of defensive "rent seeking" or, more appropriately "rent maintenance": The political system is used to attempt to convert the existing privileges into quasi property rights or, better yet, full-blown entitlements. This process tends to be facilitated by virtue of the fact that the adjustment costs are typically concentrated on the special interests whereas the associated benefits tend to be diffused in small doses across the rest of the citizenry. Phrased differently, there may well be more votes by retaining the status quo.[19]

There is no fail-safe way to avoid this problem, but there are some preferable strategies. For example, any new programs should avoid, wherever possible, creating special-interest or "clientele" effects. One way to do this is to ensure that all similarly situated citizens are treated similarly by the new policy. Tilting the benefits to privilege selected subsets of similarly situated Canadians (e.g., on the basis of location) is usually a surefire way to generate entitlement-type benefits that then become very difficult to change. Another approach is to ensure that all transfers to people have similar definitions with respect to family, income and tax status etc. This makes the transfers fungible — they can more easily be reallocated across programs. If, however, some benefits are taxable and some are not, then fungibility is impaired because the non-taxed benefits become more highly valued. In effect, they become entitlements. (This is currently the case for workers' compensation benefits, which are not taxable, in comparison with other benefits, which typically are subject to tax.) Ideally, new programs should embody a built-in ability to change or evolve from within, as circumstances change or evolve. Admittedly, this is much easier said than done.

Harry Arthurs' earlier-enunciated concern about increasing juridification (i.e., allowing or encouraging the courts to play a more important role in policy formation) is also relevant here, but in a somewhat different context. Specifically, the Charter of Rights and Freedoms is ensuring that our social programs measure up to the equality provision and other provisions of the Charter. This is as it should be. However, the "feedbacks" here may not be what GIR would call for:

> In general, my position is that the courts are largely constrained to seek redress within the existing social order. For example, were the courts' decisions to have the impact of expanding social envelope spending by, say, $3 billion annually, these funds inevitably would relate to enhancing spending with respect to some existing programs that fall short of the equality provisions of the Charter. This is not an attempt to downplay equity or Charter issues; rather, it is a straightforward observation that this extra $3 billion of spending may have little relationship to our emerging social policy needs. Effectively, the courts generally grant entitlements with respect to the existing social policy framework, not with respect to a conception of the overall social envelope that is more appropriate to globalization and an information society. In terms of the new growth theory, the feedbacks are all in the direction of entrenching the status quo, albeit with a nod toward equality here and there. (Courchene 1994: 205)

I hasten to repeat that this is not meant to downplay the role of the Charter: The provisions of the Charter ought to pervade our approaches to public policy. Rather, it is meant to underscore the fact that many of the incentives and feedbacks in the system serve to refine (or, in the Charter's case render more equal etc.) the *existing* social infrastructure and, in the process, may make fundamental change more difficult.

The bottom line is that social infrastructure evolution is difficult for all governments. Nonetheless, Canada has, in many areas, shown considerable ability to adjust. It is an impressive accomplishment to have been successful in tilting many of our income-support transfers in the direction of income testing, either directly or via the transformation of benefits under the income tax system from a deduction approach to a credit approach, and even a refundable-credit approach in some areas. This and other examples notwithstanding, the shift toward a GIR-compatible approach to social infrastructure remains a tall order. It is in this sense that a mission statement may be important. Specifically, reallocation of the social envelope, or of government spending generally, may become more acceptable if these initiatives are embedded in an overall framework that credibly commits overall societal evolution in directions that embrace values and goals that have the support of the majority of Canadians.

Public-Sector Adjustment: Competitive Governments

THE ABOVE ANALYSIS OF ADJUSTMENT IN THE PUBLIC SECTOR DOES NOT APPLY OR, more correctly, does not apply as fully to subnational governments that *are* subject to a degree of both by-pass and competition. This is the genius of federalism, especially in a federation as decentralized as Canada. By-pass now exists, in two forms.

First, residents of any given province need not become economic or social captives of the socio-economic infrastructure of their province: They can move elsewhere in Canada, thereby acquiring access to a different and presumably preferable bundle of provincial goods and services. In turn, this ability of citizens to exit will put pressure on all provinces to design and deliver an appropriate social infrastructure. Second, and equally if not more importantly, provinces will differ in their approaches to socio-economic infrastructure design. Some of this may be related to their differing needs on the economic and social fronts. For example, the way in which a Pacific Rim economy like BC will design its education/training/apprenticeship sub-system may differ considerably from that of a Great Lakes economy like Ontario. But some of this innovation will relate to alternative design and delivery mechanisms for programs that are common to all provinces. In this fiscally constrained era where all provinces are wrestling with the problem of how to make social policy delivery systems more effective, "winning" approaches will surely be copied in other provinces. In the federalism literature, this is referred to as the process of "competitive federalism," although a preferable term might be "dynamic social learning." This introduces aspects of market flexibility and innovation into the operations of the public sector.

Appropriately, there is concern that this competition could lead to a "race to the bottom" on either, or both, the economic policy or social policy front. An oft-cited example of this dysfunctional behaviour was the competitive erosion of succession duties on the part of the provinces. The lesson from this example is at least twofold: First, not all taxes or expenditures are suitable candidates for decentralization; second, mechanisms need to be put in place to prevent such races to the bottom. One of the key rationales for AIT and SUFA is precisely to address this latter issue, namely to provide the pan-Canadian frameworks for the economic and social union that embody principles and processes within which dynamic provincial socio-economic learning can proceed. An appealing way to view all of this is that it represents a Canadian version of the post-war compromise of embedded liberalism. Indeed, in a recent paper, Kenichi Ohmae (2000) refers to federalism and its inherent social-learning dynamic as the most "cyber-compatible" form of governance for the emerging global era.

With good reason, the most-often-cited exercise in competitive federalism is Saskatchewan's series of innovations in the medical and hospital areas which, when coupled with creative shared-cost programs from Ottawa, eventually led to Canada's healthcare system. But this was nearly 40 years ago. We need a fresh infusion of competitive federalism to generate the social infrastructure for a human capital era. On this score, the prospects are looking excellent indeed, given the incredible array and diversity in terms of creative social policy approaches in the various provinces:

- Quebec has the lead in family policy, replete with a novel day-care plan.
- Ontario has just released the results of a task force on early childhood development.
- As a result of the co-determination approach to the CCTB, the provinces are experimenting in creative ways in terms of designing child-support delivery systems for working-poor families.
- On the health front, all provinces are engaged in rethinking and reworking their systems in terms of a broad range of issues: payment systems, decentralizing control, addressing the home care / hospital care linkage, and integrating the sickness and wellness components of the healthcare spectrum.

- On the tax side, competitive federalism has shifted into high gear now that the tax system has shifted from a tax-on-tax system to one where the provinces have the flexibility to mount their own rate and bracket structure. Alberta is leading the way here with its 10.5 percent single-rate or flat tax.
- The list goes on.

Critics of competitive federalism will surely emphasize that the system now appears in disarray, with provinces mounting a bewildering array of alternative policy approaches. But this is a necessary part of the process, and as long as AIT and SUFA provide the overarching frameworks, the system will begin to converge on winning strategies. What is needed to facilitate this is an information gathering and sharing mechanism that initially compiles and describes the variety of approaches and then begins to evaluate them. Perhaps this is an appropriate role for the Annual Premiers' Conferences — to provide a focal point for documenting and assessing the differing provincial social infrastructure strategies. This would be the social policy counterpart to the valuable service that the Canadian Tax Foundation provides in documenting the evolution of provincial tax changes. Without the existence of an equivalent agency on the social side to collect and disseminate information relating to the range of provincial policies, institutions and delivery systems, Canada will not reap the full benefits of the provincial approaches to dynamic social learning.

Goals and Instruments

THE FOCUS OF THE CHAPTER THUS FAR HAS BEEN THE ARTICULATION OF SETS OF principles related to both private sector and public sector adjustment. The remainder of the analysis will deal in turn with the goals-instruments trade off and with policy strategies.

A recurring theme in the preceding chapters is that the impact of GIR need not affect the overarching goals we set for ourselves in the upper half of North America, but it will certainly alter the nature of the instruments we deploy to achieve these goals. For example, we could as a nation still opt, relative to the US, to be a high-wage, high-tax, high-transfer economy. But we could never achieve this goal without a wholesale reworking of our existing set of policy strategies and instruments. In broad terms, achieving the high-wage component would require a dramatic shift in our social infrastructure toward human capital creation; maintaining the high-transfer component would require the reorientation of our inter-regional redistributive system in the direction of emphasizing "people prosperity" over "place prosperity"; and maintaining a high-tax economy relative to the Americans would require a significant shift in taxes away from mobile factors (human capital and corporations) and toward residence-based and export-neutral taxes such as the GST. Beyond this, the policy instruments would have to be GATT/WTO and FTA/NAFTA consistent.

Many Canadians, perhaps a majority, would opt for a high-wage, high-transfer, high-tax economy. Indeed, this is probably an apt description of "the way we were" in the former resource-based paradigm. However, to carry this goal over to the emerging GIR/human capital paradigm requires, as noted, a complete revamping of policy instruments. But here is where a huge disconnect exists: I have yet to see social activists amongst us embrace the shift in instruments needed to achieve the goal of a high-wage, high-transfer, high-tax economy. Specifically, I have yet to see a prominent social group embrace the notion that the export-import neutral value-added tax (the GST) represents one of the key instruments in maintaining a high-tax, high-transfer economy. Yet, it clearly is. And since Canada ought to retain important aspects of its "sharing community" commitment which, in turn, implies a higher overall tax rate than that in the US, I will (in Chapter 14) have no qualms about recommending a shift in taxation away from income and toward (export-import neutral) consumption. Readers may well disagree with whatever philosophical bias I may bring to the policy imperatives facing Canada, but I trust they will agree with the underlying proposition that GIR has fundamentally altered the avenues and instruments by which we Canadians can achieve our societal goals.

One can probably go further here and make a convincing case that in some spheres GIR actually expands our choice of goals. Because of information-empowerment, Canadians have already achieved quantum leaps as consumers and, with appropriate infrastructure and creative instrumentation, we can aspire to become more meaningful players in our roles as citizens, both nationally and internationally.

Two other aspects of the goals-instruments nexus merit highlight. The first relates to our tendency to view instruments as goals; the second relates to the manner in which goals/instruments interact with considerations relating to sovereignty or global interdependence.

Instruments as Goals

Some instruments become so enmeshed with our values and/or identity they become elevated to the status of goals. In the current time frame, medicare surely falls into this category, and to a degree, so does our flexible exchange rate (i.e., monetary sovereignty). But at base, these are *instruments* for delivering ultimate goals: arguably, universally accessible, tax-financed health care in the case of medicare, and a growing, prosperous and stable economy that enhances the well-being of Canadians in the case of flexible rates or monetary sovereignty. To view these as *immutable* instruments (i.e., *as goals* in and of themselves) may, in a dynamic, changing socio-economic order, place the ultimate goals in the balance. For example, the 100 percent public funding for medicare-covered activities and the more or less zero percent public funding for non-covered items such as home care and chronic care may progressively run afoul with the equality of access to essential health services. The European approach — more comprehensive coverage, but with income-tested co-payments throughout — may resonate better with the underlying goals, especially as the non-covered components loom larger in terms of population health. Likewise, in the face of enhanced trade-flows and increasing currency integration elsewhere in the system, a fixed exchange rate may become a preferable instrument to deliver on the overall goals of monetary policy.

These reflections are not to be interpreted as arguments against either medicare or flexible exchange rates. Rather, they are a reminder that while the underlying goals of a society tend to be enduring across paradigms, the instruments tend to be paradigm- or environment-specific. In effect, they are the means toward achieving the underlying ends or goals, and we must be willing to rethink their relevance as the overall parameters of the system evolve.

Sovereignty

Not surprisingly, there is a natural tension between embarking on creative instruments to accommodate GIR and the potential erosion of national sovereignty. In a growing number of policy arenas, however, this is a false dichotomy. To see this, it is important to recognize that the mutual interdependencies that can arise under GIR are in some cases converting key policy areas to a "global commons."

The environment is an excellent example of such a global commons. What does national sovereignty mean in this context? At one level, we Canadians could withdraw from all international environmental agreements. This would surely enhance our sovereignty and national independence (in the traditional definition of these terms), since we would then be free to implement *any* environmental policy we wished. Because this would be true for all other nations as well, the result here would almost surely be a reduction in our ability to exercise control over aspects of the environment and, therefore, in any meaningful definition of Canadian sovereignty. Thus, in the face of a "global commons" reality, sovereignty is best interpreted as the ability of Canadians to ensure that the global environment is being preserved and that we have some input into the process. We do this by entering into international agreements that admittedly constrain our decision making but, more importantly, also constrain the independence of all other signatories. In effect, we engage with others in creating "property rights" to the global environmental commons to ensure that it will not be "overgrazed," to fall back on the traditional "tragedy of the commons" analogy. It may well be that the resulting international agreements on the environment are not as comprehensive or as binding as we Canadians might like, but this is another matter. This analogy applies to the many other "environments" created by GIR.

As the earlier quotes from Kymlicka (Chapter 3) argue, the "political" accommodation to enhanced integration need not also imply a reduction in sovereignty *per se*, if any resulting international agreements are the result of a conscious decision by citizens (e.g., via a referendum or an election): "Choosing to accept globalization is not necessarily a denial of people's national identity or autonomy, but instead may be an affirmation of their desired identity, and a deliberate exercise of their national autonomy" (Kymlicka 1997: 316). As long as we are focusing on self-imposed constraints, arguably no initiative, domestic or international, constrains parliamentary sovereignty to the degree that attends the Canadian Charter of Rights and Freedoms. Yet we typically do not refer to this constraint on our parliaments as reducing our sovereignty or compromising our identity. Quite the opposite. Likewise, the decision of the eleven European countries to join together in the creation of the supranational Euro certainly *does* constrain each nations' room to manoeuvre on the monetary policy and exchange-rate front (although there may have been precious little meaningful "independence" associated with the former national monetary regimes).

Presumably, however, the cost-benefit calculus in terms of embracing this new "instrument" had to do with whether the Euro would advance the more important national goals of socio-economic well-being, for example, and, perhaps, an end to recurring European conflict. Revealed preference suggests that it has.

Policy Strategies: Anticipation, Incrementalism, Multi-Dimensionality

To round out this "framing policy" chapter, we need to discuss a few strategy/process dimensions that become more important in the face of GIR. As noted, there is no single best overarching strategy or set of policies to address the GIR challenges, especially since the information revolution is far from over. To be sure, this represents a veritable nightmare for policy analysts and politicians alike. My preferred approach to this unavoidable policy uncertainty is to articulate a societal mission statement that captures the essence of the GIR revolution. This is the role of Chapter 11. Here, I offer three further perspectives relating to policy formation that may provide a way out of this dilemma.

First, policy formation should become more anticipatory. In too many areas, perhaps, Canadian policy is mired in a reactive mode. We await the next external or internal crisis, then swing into action. Even if we are highly adept at reacting, or at damage control, this is ultimately a losing strategy in the fast-paced GIR era. We need to remind ourselves of the oft-cited dictum of the philosopher of summer, Yogi Berra: "If you don't know where you're going you may end up somewhere else!"

Hence, we need to "catch the wave" or get on top of the GIR revolution. Policy and, particularly, policy thinking must become anticipatory rather than reactive. This is not inherently as difficult a challenge as one might at first imagine: While ultimately unknowable in terms of its final destination, the GIR revolution embodies some easily identifiable and irreversible trends. What makes this challenge difficult on the political front is that the very nature of responsible government and cabinet solidarity means that our political leaders are not as free to engage in "blue skying" as are US politicians within their system of checks and balances, for example. Relatedly, the enormous reservoir of policy intelligence that resides in our various civil services has to be filtered through the operations of responsible government and, therefore, is not readily available to society at large. This being the unfortunate reality, we have to rely on other sources to ensure that the policy process can anticipate the evolution of the domestic and international socio-economic orders. Canada's think tanks play a very important role in this process but, with some notable exceptions, they are increasingly ideologically or special-interest based. The media also have a key role to play here, and the presence of an additional national newspaper certainly has served to widen the policy discussion. But more is needed. Particularly, parliamentary committees, especially the less-partisan nature of Senate committees, need to play a more important role. For example, for the six months prior to the WTO ruling on Canada's approach to the Auto Pact, the Ottawa corridors of power knew we were going to lose this challenge. Why didn't the House or Senate embark on hearings to address the consequences, including the possibility of moving toward a customs union with the Americans? Why isn't the Senate engaged in rethinking Canada's tax system in light of pressures on the status quo emanating from GIR? Or more forward-looking still, what will the challenges facing Canada and Canadians look like in, say, 2010, if the current GIR trends are maintained?

The bottom line here is that Canada does have room to manoeuvre in the face of GIR, but if we rest on our laurels and adopt a reactive stance, even if we are highly adept at reacting, we may well end up "somewhere else" than where we ought to be.

The second perspective is that while an anticipatory approach to the GIR revolution is essential, it is also important that policy remains "incremental." Incremental in this sense is not meant to preclude bold initiatives. Rather, I am using the word in the sense that policy should not make irreversible plunges into new areas, unless the related trends it is responding to are likewise irreversible. Policy in a rapidly changing GIR era must be capable of continuous evolution. It must be capable of changing from "within," as it were, to accommodate further change.

This leads to the last imperative: Policy in the GIR era has to be multidimensional. This follows directly from the foregoing analysis of the implications of GIR, where the impacts were pervasive and interactive across citizens, markets and governments. For example, there is no one policy that can address the income-distribution challenges of GIR, because the challenges arise from a variety of forces and influences, many of which transcend the traditional approaches such as enriching the various income-supplementation programs. Thus, addressing Canada's income-distribution challenges requires a multi-dimensional approach that reflects the variety of ways in which GIR impinges upon the income-earning capacities of Canadians.

Missing from the analysis thus far is the articulation of a more comprehensive set of principles to guide public policy: accountability, transparency, and recognition of the duality inherent in Canada, among many others. These transcend paradigms and are implicitly assumed applicable in the above analysis. Readers wishing a reasonably comprehensive list of these government precepts in a Canadian context can consult Courchene (1996), among other sources.

While this chapter has focused on some principles of governance relating to the "bridging paradigms" theme, the following chapter directs attention to two recent economic initiatives that embrace the necessary transition from boards and mortar to mortarboards.

Winds of Change

A S THE FINAL STEPPING STONE OF THE PATH TOWARD ARTICULATING A HUMAN CAPITAL mission statement for Canada, it is appropriate to recognize that many societal actors are already embracing processes and policies that resonate well with the dictates of a progressively economically integrated, knowledge society. In terms of the process dimension, Chapter 6 focused on AIT and SUFA, two creative governance instruments designed to address the economic and social dimensions, respectively, of the GIR challenge. AIT ensures that in the face of increased north-south trade and increased decentralization Canada remains an east-west economic union without internal impediments to the free flow of goods, services and capital across provincial borders. SUFA's role is to ensure that Canada not only remains an east-west social union but, in the process, also establishes values and principles that ensure Canada's more generous distributional and transfer systems do not fall prey to American values. An integral component of SUFA is the mutual recognition of Canadian's skills and accreditation across provinces, so that SUFA also makes significant strides in the direction of creating an east-west human capital union.

This chapter focuses on two economic blueprints that explicitly recognize the new GIR realities and, particularly, the shift toward a human capital future. The first of these is the Canada Global Leadership Initiative (CGLI) launched by the BCNI; the second is Ontario's economic mission statement, prepared by the Ontario Jobs and Information Board (OJIB).

At the outset, it is very important to realize that focusing on these blueprints is not in any way meant as an endorsement of either the BCNI, the province of Ontario or their positions. Readers may well be of the view that, based on my previous writings, I may be sympathetic to either or both Ontario or the BCNI. Perhaps. But irrelevant, because the purpose here is to show that the pervasiveness of the influences of GIR is such that even market-oriented agencies and governments have to tilt their prescriptions toward knowledge and human capital. It is this observation — or reality — that serves as a catalyst for the Chapter 11 mission statement.

The BCNI's Canada Global Leadership Initiative (CGLI) [20]

T HE CGLI IS A YEARLONG RESEARCH AND CONSULTATION PROCESS LAUNCHED IN April 1999 that culminated with a series of final reports and a National Economic Summit in May 2000. This is the most comprehensive research undertaking ever launched by the BCNI. While the BCNI initiative focuses initially on what it calls some "unfinished business" relating to Canada's economic performance (e.g., high debt, a depreciating currency), what is of interest for present purposes is its vision of Canada's "new challenges." It describes these challenges as follows:

- ◆ Global economic turmoil and the "prosperity gap" are resulting in a backlash against globalization and free markets.
- ◆ Electronic commerce and the Internet are profoundly changing economic fundamentals and the nature of competition between firms and between countries.
- ◆ Global competition and the need for improved financial accountability are demanding more effective corporate governance practices worldwide.
- ◆ Global integration of commerce means that countries must develop strong "country brands" to attract investment.
- ◆ Rapid industrialization in emerging markets creates stronger pressure for sustainable development worldwide. (BCNI 1999: 4)

In light of the analysis in Part II, there is really little that is either novel or controversial in these challenges, except that they represent a rather narrow vision of the overall range of GIR implications for the Canadian economy and society.

With this as backdrop, the BCNI proceeds to articulate its "new agenda for action" and, in particular, the five areas where it will focus its research and consultation. These five areas are:

◆ competing for leading-edge political governance;
◆ competing for global market shares and influence;
◆ competing for ideas;
◆ competing for human capital; and
◆ competing for financial capital.

The detailed research agenda relating to these five challenges appears as Table 8.

In perusing Table 8, one is struck (or at least I am struck) by the fact that the BCNI's detailed concerns extend well beyond what one would expect from a "business agenda." There is recognition of not only the critical importance of education, training and human capital, but also the important role of Canada's social infrastructure. And in terms of internal political governance, the focus is on the economic union, the social union and creative ways that federalism can contribute to national competitiveness. Were I to summarize the social dimensions in Table 8, they would run along the lines of designing policies that would improve Canada's ability to develop and retain its human capital. Given that corporate Canada must respond to the interests of its shareholders, it is quite remarkable that this BCNI research agenda transcends a narrow business perspective and embraces challenges that are also of major concern to all Canadians. To be sure, this reflects that fact that in the new GIR environment, human capital policy is becoming indistinguishable from economic policy. Nonetheless, it would be hard to find a recent time when the concerns of corporate Canada have gone this far in terms of embracing many of the concerns of Canadian society. Thus, there is clearly a "window of opportunity" to devise some version of a "common front" to address our joint challenges.

Before so doing, I direct focus to the Ontario economic mission statement produced by OJIB, the chair of which is Premier Harris. To the best of my knowledge, no other subnational government, anywhere, anytime, has produced anything equivalent to this forward-looking and GIR-compatible approach to the challenges of the millennium.

Table 8   144

The BCNI Research Agenda

Competing for Leading-edge Political Governance
- The economic union — which barriers to interprovincial mobility of people, capital, goods and services must be removed without further delay?
- The social union — how can federal-provincial co-operation be improved so as to deliver optimum efficiency in the delivery of social programs?
- National competitiveness — how can federal-provincial co-operation be improved so as to benefit national competitiveness?

Competing for Global Market Share and Influence
- The Canada-United States border — what further barriers to Canada-United States trans-border commerce can realistically be removed?
- World trade rules — how can government and business maximize Canada's influence in shaping the next round of global trade negotiations?
- Priority markets — how can government and business ensure a more concentrated focus of energy and resources in the development of priority markets?
- Outward orientation — what can be done to more effectively encourage the outward orientation of Canada's SMEs?

Competing for Ideas
- Research and development — why is Canada's generous tax treatment not enough, and how can we improve the odds of attracting more R&D work to Canadian locations?
- The innovation gaps — what are the barriers to the more rapid adoption and diffusion of new technologies by Canadian companies, especially SMEs? Given that Canada's patent application rate is the poorest in the G-7, what can we do about it?
- Electronic commerce and the Internet — how rapidly are our enterprises and institutions embracing 21st-century winning technologies?
- Capital gains and corporate taxes — lower capital gains and corporate tax rates will spur innovation — how can government resistance to this fact be overcome?
- Best practices in innovation — what examples of Canadian success can be used as lessons for others?

Competing for Human Capital
- Education and training — what can business do to improve the quality of education and access to lifelong learning?
- Personal taxation — what tax changes would be most effective in improving incentives for work and investment and in attracting and retaining highly skilled employees?
- Leading lights — what measures would help make Canada the home of choice for leading-edge work and the brightest minds in any field of endeavour?
- Social infrastructure — what changes to programs and policies in areas such as health care, income support or immigration would be most effective in improving Canada's ability to attract and retain skilled workers?

Competing for Financial Capital
- Equity markets — why do Canadian stocks and multiples lag?
- Currency risk — how much of a penalty do Canadian companies pay for operating with a depreciating dollar?
- Corporate taxation — what aspects are most damaging to investment and job growth?
- Foreign direct investment — what can be done to reverse deterioration in Canada's share of inward-bound foreign direct investment?
- Rules and regulations — how much damage is done by the accounting rules restricting pooling of interests in acquisitions and mergers?

Ontario's Economic
Mission Statement

"I skate to where the puck is going to be, not where it's been."
—Wayne Gretzky

A *Road Map To Prosperity: An Economic Plan for Jobs for the 21st Century* (OJIB 1999) begins with the above quotation from Wayne Gretzky. As will become clear, this is a wholly appropriate quote because Ontario's economic mission statement is indeed anticipatory or forward-looking. Involving the input of 2,500 Ontarians and more than 300 organizations, OJIB (67) notes that "never before has a discussion about our collective economic future reached out and engaged so many Ontarians."

Table 9 presents the overview of the economic mission statement. Both the vision, "Ontario is the best jurisdiction in North America to live, work, invest and raise a family," and the mission, "Ontario will achieve sustainable economic prosperity with the best performing economy and highest quality of life in North America over the next 10 years," suggest that Ontario may well have donned the mantle of a North American region-state (Courchene and Telmer 1998). This observation aside, the core of the economic mission is the five-pronged set of goals/strategies: knowledge and skills, innovation culture, strong global orientation, industry and regional strengths, and favourable investment climate. It seems to me that these goals and strategies resonate well with the dictates coming from the new global order.

But the mission statement goes well beyond this. In Table 10, these five goals/strategies appear as the leftmost column of the matrix; the matrix itself focuses on what these goals imply for the roles and responsibilities relating to individuals (citizens), businesses, governments and educational institutions. Intriguingly, this framework is remarkably similar to the one I have adopted in the foregoing analysis, indeed, embarrassingly so since I thought my framework was novel! There are some important differences, however. Whereas the foregoing analysis was largely diagnostic — identifying challenges — the Ontario mission statement tends to be prescriptive as well. In this important sense, it represents a valuable bridge or transition to the prescriptive approach in Part IV of this monograph. In addition, the Table 10 matrix, under the "Governments" column, attempts to assign responsibility to the various levels of government: M, P,

Table 9

Ontario's Economic Mission Statement

Vision

Ontario is the best jurisdiction in North America to live, work, invest and raise a family

Mission

Ontario will achieve sustainable economic prosperity with the best performing economy and highest quality of life in North America over the next 10 years

Implementation Goals and Strategies

Knowledge and Skills	Innovation Culture	Strong Global Orientation	Industry and Regional Strengths	Favourable Investment Climate
1 Ensure that Ontario's education and training system is high quality and market responsive. 2 Promote strong employment skills and a commitment to lifelong learning. 3 Facilitate smooth school-to-work and job-to-job transitions.	1 Build innovation capacity throughout the economy. 2 Provide an appropriate incentive structure to create an innovation culture. 3 Invest in research and development and new ideas.	1 Aggressively market Ontario internationally as an attractive place to invest. 2 Expand Ontario's trade with the world. 3 Develop world-class infrastructure to connect Ontario to the global marketplace. 4 Promote global citizenship and position Ontario as the preferred home for the world's best and brightest.	1 Encourage more effective local governance to support local economic development leadership. 2 Capitalize on the economic development potential of the GTA and other large urban centres. 3 Build on strengths, capabilities and potential of rural and Northern Ontario. 4 Strengthen industry sectors and economic clusters.	1 Ensure sound fiscal management 2 Provide the right climate for growth and investment and reward entrepreneurship 3 Remove barriers to business activity.

Source: Ontario Jobs and Investment Board (1999), 15.
Full details at www.ontario-canada.com/jobgrow.

F and A, for Municipal, Provincial, Federal and All levels, respectively. Wrestling with the appropriate division of powers in terms of the GIR challenges will also be a feature of the Part IV analysis.

In terms of the substance of Table 10, several comments are in order. First, the framework itself is as important as the substance. Specifically, it is highly interactive: On the one hand, individuals have, appropriately, a role/responsibility in terms of achieving all five goals; on the other hand, the pursuit of any given goal requires, again appropriately, the cooperation and collaboration of individuals, governments, businesses and educational institutions.

Second, while this is explicitly designated as an *economic* mission statement, it nonetheless embodies a wider range of goals relating to social cohesion, democracy etc. Above all, the human capital imperative is front and centre, even to the degree of incorporating "educational and other institutions" as one of the four essential "players" in the process. Relatedly, there is a close link between the Ontario mission statement and the BCNI agenda in the sense that they are both concerned not only with creating and enhancing human capital but also in employing this human capital in Canada or Ontario, as the case may be.

Third, there is of course a strong dose of ideology permeating Tables 9 and 10 — the emphasis is on excelling economically within the North American geo-economic space. Thus, many readers might prefer to fill in the cells of the Table 10 matrix with a very different set of roles and responsibilities. Fair enough, especially since this framework is intended as an economic mission statement, not a social mission statement. Nonetheless, the framework itself represents a creative and novel initiative in terms of articulating and designing an overall policy strategy.

Alberta is probably in the lead in terms of addressing accountability and transparency issues in its government operations and in articulating "business plans" across departments; Quebec is probably the leader in coordinating its social infrastructure around the primacy of the family; New Brunswick was probably the first to implement a new-paradigm approach to its economic future. But it is Ontario's forward-looking human capital/economic vision for the 21st century that is probably the most comprehensive and integrated vision.

An important caveat is in order. Ontario's economic mission statement is a framework — *it is not policy*. It is one thing to formulate a GIR-consistent framework; it is quite another to follow through on its implementation. My focus here has been on the former. Indeed in *From Heartland to North American Region State*

Roles and Responsibilities Pursuant to Ontario's Economic Mission Statement

Table 10

Roles and Responsibilities in Achieving the Plan

Strategic Goals		Individuals	Businesses
Knowledge for Skills and Prosperity	Ontario will be recognized as a model jurisdiction known for its high quality and adaptable workforce. Ontarians will have the knowledge and skills — emphasizing creativity and entrepreneurship — to provide a strong foundation for sustained prosperity.	• Commit to lifelong learning through continuous upgrading of skills and knowledge. • Make sound, informed decisions about what you need to learn. • Acquire skills you need for employment. • Adopt the entrepreneurial spirit required to achieve your goals.	• Re-invest a greater portion of earnings into workforce skills upgrading and training. • Identify the future skills your business will need. • Invest in equipping your employees with necessary skills. • Provide youth with work experience, career counselling, mentoring, and job opportunities.
Innovation Culture	Ontario will be a leader among North American jurisdictions within the next ten years in building "innovation capacity" throughout the economy and in translating ideas and research into commercial success.	• Take initiative, be creative, take risks and be confident about doing things in new ways. • Learn to use new technologies and become better at dealing with change. • Acquire teamwork, communication and problem-solving skills.	• Sponsor and champion risk-taking and idea generation. • Examine processes, practices, policies and structures for improvements to strengthen innovation capacity. • Invest in more innovative and productive business concepts and technology applications. • Provide attractive research and career development opportunities to retain and attract people with talent and skills.

Strategic Goals

Strong Global Orientation	By the end of the next decade, Ontario will be one of the best international jurisdictions in terms of: export and international trade performance; infrastructure to support the movement of people, goods, services and information; global citizenship and cosmopolitan outlook; preferred home for the world's "best and brightest." Toronto will be ranked as one of the leading international city-regions for business and quality of life.	• Think globally. • Acquire international business and language skills and work experience. • Promote Ontario as a place to live, invest and visit when you travel.	• Adopt globally oriented strategies. • Act as pro-Ontario "ambassadors" to market Ontario. • Invest in retaining and attracting the "best and brightest."
Building on our Industry and Regional Strengths	All regions of Ontario will realize their full economic development potential and will be home to globally competitive, thriving business, industry sectors and communities within 10 years.	• Actively engage in the economic development in your community. • Be a local "champion" and provide leadership in your community. • Promote your community and region as a place to live, invest and visit.	• Be better and faster at identifying emerging market trends and in bringing new products and solutions to market. • Be more outward looking and export-oriented. • Work with sector or economic cluster partners to identify and act on opportunities to improve competitiveness. • Play an active role in economic development at the local level.
Favourable Investment Climate	Ontario will be one of the best places in North America to invest and do business within five years.	• Take advantage of entrepreneurial opportunities. • Celebrate local successes. • Ensure that government and public institutions are accountable. • Be "demanding" consumers and taxpayers.	• Invest in new technology and training to improve productivity. • Work co-operatively with other businesses, labour and communities to build a competitive economy. • Forge partnerships to strengthen industry sectors and clusters.

Table 10 Cont'd

Roles and Responsibilities in Achieving the Plan

Strategic Goals		Governments*	Educational and Other Institutions
Knowledge for Skills and Prosperity	Ontario will be recognized as a model jurisdiction known for its high quality and adaptable workforce. Ontarians will have the knowledge and skills — emphasizing creativity and entrepreneurship — to provide a strong foundation for sustained prosperity.	• Implement a single, simple to understand, made-in-Ontario employment and training system to eliminate duplication. P/F • Set and enforce high standards for education and training. P • Wisely invest public funds available for education and training. P/F • Ensure education and training remain accessible. P/F	• Strive for excellence. • Foster entrepreneurship and innovation. • Increase market-responsiveness by post-secondary institutions. • Expand education and training partnerships among business and government. • Professional, trade and labour associations representing individuals promote training and life-long learning.
Innovation Culture	Ontario will be a leader among North American jurisdictions within the next ten years in building "innovation capacity" throughout the economy and in translating ideas and research into commercial success.	• Review current incentive structures so that risk-taking is not penalized. A • Take a forward-looking approach to ensure regulations and standards to ensure positive impacts on competitiveness and new business opportunities are seized. A • Foster an environment in which innovation and entrepreneurship can flourish. A • Be innovative in delivery of services and programs. A	• Strive for excellence. • Adapt more quickly to change and respond to market opportunities. • Engage in more basic and applied research. • Act as catalysts in the development of new and better products, processes and technologies. • Promote the sharing and commercialization of new ideas. • Develop people-based and infrastructure networks.

Strategic Goals

Strong Global Orientation	By the end of the next decade, Ontario will be one of the best international jurisdictions in terms of: export and international trade performance; Infrastructure to support the movement of people, goods, services and information; global citizenship and cosmopolitan outlook; preferred home for the world's "best and brightest." Toronto will be ranked as one of the leading international city-regions for business and quality of life.	• Ensure Ontario offers a competitive and attractive climate for investment and jobs creation. A • Aggressively market Ontario as a place to live, invest and visit. A • Be fast, flexible and adaptable in order to meet the competitive challenges of a dynamic and ever-changing global economy. A • Promote open and fair markets, domestically and internationally. P/F	• Equip students and our workforce with the skills, global mind set and entrepreneurial spirit to do business in the global market-place. • Ensure Ontario's educational standards match or exceed the best international benchmarks for academic performance. • Encourage international student exchanges and study programs. • Attract "best and brightest" researchers and educators.
Building on our Industry and Regional Strengths	All regions of Ontario will realize their full economic development potential and will be home to globally competitive, thriving business, industry sectors and communities within 10 years.	• Invest in building research and development and idea generation capacity. • Support efforts to create accessible mechanisms to connect researchers, entrepreneurs and business to expertise and information on technology transfer, commercialization and intellectual property. A • Create positive climates for business investment. A • Respond quickly to changes in the competitive global economy. A • Develop the infrastructure and common platforms that support economic clusters and industry sectors and enable access to global markets. A	• Strengthen role as catalysts in regional economic development. • Produce graduates with world-leading business, entrepreneurial and technical skills. • Perform leading-edge, commercially viable research. • Foster and participate in private-public partnerships to support economic development.
Favourable Investment Climate	Ontario will be one of the best places in North America to invest and do business within five years.	• Ensure sound fiscal management and competitive taxes. A • Remove barriers to business activities and jobs creation. A • Strategically invest to create competitive advantages. A	• Look outward to find new links to the changing economy. • Look inward to adapt to the changing demands of the 21st century.

*M - Municipal / P - Provincial / F - Federal / A - All levels
Source: OJIB (1999).

(1998), Telmer and I argued that an effective region-state needed to privilege human capital as the capstone of its economic policy. Our view then, and my view now, is that despite the impressive rhetoric of its mission statement, Ontario has yet to deliver on this human capital agenda. Nonetheless, this does not detract from the conceptual framework underpinning the mission statement.

Considerations of balance would suggest that I also present recent examples of social policy initiatives that embody a healthy dose of concern for ensuring economic competitiveness. This would surely fall in the "redundant" category, since social policy has long been viewed as having a role to play in fostering competitiveness, with the EI program serving as the exception that proves the rule.

Conclusion

IN THEIR *CONCEPTION*, BOTH THE BCNI AND THE ONTARIO PERSPECTIVES ARE TRULY exciting initiatives. Both attempt to wrestle with the challenges and opportunities posed by GIR. While they are underpinned by economic considerations, both go a considerable distance toward integrating individual Canadians, in their human capital capacity, as leading players in our collective economic future. In the final analysis, these initiatives will of course be judged in terms of what they deliver. I do not know how they will eventually fare on this score. (The BCNI's May 2000 "national summit" was hardly a roaring success.) What I do know, however, is that they have made important strides in identifying key challenges and in providing integrative frameworks designed to address these challenges. In this important sense, they represent a valuable analytical bridge between the foregoing analysis and Part IV of this study which focuses on what all of this means for policy, for instrument choice and for the governance of our federation.

But bridges are built to be crossed and the time has come to venture fully and forcefully into the new terrain of the GIR reality. The entire foregoing analysis, including the windows of opportunity provided by the BCNI and Ontario perspectives, will now be distilled into a single-sentence, overarching, societal mission statement for 21st-century Canada.

A Human Capital
Mission Statement
for Canada

The old foundations of success are gone. For all human history, the source of
success has been the control of natural resources — land, gold, oil. Suddenly,
the answer is "knowledge." The world's wealthiest man, Bill Gates, owns nothing tangible — no land, no gold, no oil, no factories, no industrial processes,
no armies. For the first time in history the world's wealthiest man owns only
knowledge. (Thurow 1999: xv)

In a global economy where employers arbitrage the world looking for the
lowest wages, people's pay is not based on whether they live in a rich or a poor
country but upon their individual skills. The well-educated living in India
make something that looks like American wages, while the uneducated living
in America make something that looks like Indian wages. If unskilled first
world workers don't want to be in competition with equally unskilled but
lower wage third world workers, they will need much better skills. With globalization and a skill-intensive technological shift, much better skills must be
delivered to the bottom tow-thirds of the labour force in the developed world
if their wages are not to fall. (132-3)

If capital is borrowable, raw materials are buyable and technology is copyable, what are you left with if you want to run a high-wage economy? Only
skills, there isn't anything else. (Thurow 1993: 5)

A Human Capital
Future for Canadians

W HILE THE SPIRIT, IF NOT THE LETTER, OF EACH OF THE ABOVE QUOTATIONS FROM
MIT's Lester Thurow appears earlier in the analysis, together they present
a powerful and persuasive vision of a human capital and citizen-based future for
Canada and Canadians. The first quote speaks to the emergence of knowledge as

the bedrock of twenty-first century competitiveness and, in the process, it reiterates the earlier theme of the required transition from a resource-based economy and society to a human-capital- and knowledge-based economy and society. The third focuses on skills and human capital as the key to a high-wage economy. And the middle quote highlights the fact that the principal way to address income inequality and, relatedly, to forge societal cohesion, is to ensure that *all* citizens have an equal opportunity to develop their skills and human capital.

One can also approach the importance of a human capital future from another perspective. The powerful and pervasive impacts of GIR are generating both enormous opportunities and enormous anxieties for citizens and societies everywhere. Were I to isolate the two key assurances that Canadians desire most from the interplay of GIR with citizens, markets and governments, they would be that this new order generate not only economic competitiveness but also societal cohesion. From this vantage point we are presented with a historically unprecedented societal window of opportunity since a commitment to a human capital future is emerging as the principal avenue by which to succeed on both the competitiveness and the cohesion fronts.

The Mission Statement

E MBOLDENED BY THIS UNIQUE WINDOW OF OPPORTUNITY, AND DEFINING HUMAN capital to encompass citizens' skills, knowledge and information empowerment, I offer the following mission statement for Canada and Canadians in the 21st century:

> Design a sustainable, socially inclusive and internationally competitive infrastructure that ensures equal opportunity for all Canadians to develop, to enhance and to employ in Canada their skills and human capital, thereby enabling them to become full citizens in the information-era Canadian and global societies.

I submit that the letter as well as the spirit of this mission statement must be integral to what the essence of being a Canadian ought to mean in the 21st century. Anything less would be not only failing our citizens in this progressive knowledge/information era but also failing to take advantage of the opportunities presented by GIR.

The role of Part IV (*A Human Capital Future for Canadians*) is to begin the
process of implementing the mission statement and informing policy choices in
the context of achieving economic competitiveness and societal cohesion. Prior to
embarking on this endeavor, several observations relating to the mission statement are in order.

Reflections on the Mission Statement

F IRST, BY THEIR VERY NATURE, MISSION STATEMENTS TEND TO BE ARTICULATED IN AN
unconstrained manner. This is certainly the case with the above mission statement. Yet the real world is full of constraints — fiscal, political, institutional, as well
as those emanating from the international arena. This does not detract from the value
of a mission statement: Indeed, the existence of a societally accepted common goal or
beacon may well serve as the catalyst for overcoming some of the myriad constraints.

Second, the mission statement is an overarching goal toward which overall policy should strive. In some areas, the design of appropriate policy may have
little to do with the human capital imperative: It will be designed in terms of its
own analytical framework or informed by best practices elsewhere. Yet, as will
become evident in Part IV, in a surprising number of key policy areas, the human
capital imperative will be seen to inform appropriate policy. Even in terms of the
former, however, if there are degrees of freedom in designing a competitive infrastructure, this freedom should be used to tilt the policy mix toward being consistent with the human capital goals and aspirations of Canadians.

Third, and relatedly, the mission statement offers a uniquely Canadian
vision, or version, of post-war embedded liberalism, namely an approach to
embedding the pervasive openness and competitiveness of the new order within
a citizen-related social infrastructure.

Fourth, the mission statement addresses Canada's competitiveness imperative (apart from the role that human capital plays on the competitiveness front)
by virtue of its commitment to an "internationally competitive infrastructure" and
the "employ in Canada" aspect of the human capital dimension. This employ-in-
Canada aspect, for example, would resonate well with the BCNI's earlier enunciated desire "to make Canada a better place to live and work and do business" as

well as to "create a uniquely attractive home base for competitive and growing global enterprises."

Fifth, on the social cohesion front, the analysis in Appendix A emphasizes the role that the pursuit of human capital plays in developing both social capital and social cohesion. Beyond this, social cohesion is captured in "a sustainable, socially inclusive...infrastructure." In addition, the "to enhance" wording of the mission statement is a recognition of the need for lifelong learning, which is distinct from the "to develop" reference that is intended to capture kindergarten-through-university skills and human capital formation.

Finally, but hardly exhaustively, there is also a strategic or public-policy rationale for this mission statement. If we merely attempt to muddle through the challenges posed by GIR, we are likely to eventually end up with a competitive economy, but not with one that addresses the social requisites of the new order. This concern can be rephrased as follows: Canada will eventually get its economic policy in line and in tune with the American and global economies. For example, we *will* eventually end up with tax rates that are compatible/competitive with those south of the border. But if this is all we do, then we will, in the process, place social Canada in the balance. What the mission statement does, and does forcefully I trust, is embed competitiveness, up front, in a human capital and social cohesion framework. This is where our greatest challenge is in terms of accommodating the GIR forces. Moreover, if we can first commit ourselves to a human capital future for all Canadians, we may then be able to generate a "first-mover" advantage on the competitive front. If we know we will eventually have to match Americans on the tax front, surely it is much better to do this sooner rather than later, i.e., close the barn door *before* the horse leaves. But we will not be able to do this unless Canadians believe, through an upfront and transparent process, there is a credible societal commitment to social cohesion.

I recognize that the more I attempt to "read into" the above wording of the mission statement, the more it may be viewed as degenerating into a "good-feeling" sort of platitude consistent with a wide range of policy responses, perhaps even accompanying the reigning status quo. However, my view is precisely the opposite. It represents a profound and integrative rethinking and reworking of who we ought to be as a nation in the upper half of North America. More to the point, it has profound implications for the design and implementation of Canadian economic policy.

Albeit tentative and prospective, focusing on these profound implications is the purpose of the final chapters in this study — *A Human Capital Future for Canadians.*

A Human Capital Future for Canadians: Toward Competitiveness and Cohesion

Building Blocks for a
Human Capital Future

Introduction

T HE ROLE OF PART IV IS STRAIGHTFORWARD: RETHINK AND REWORK OUR
governance, infrastructure and policies in order to ensure that achieving a
human capital economy and society becomes Canada's "National Policy" for the
21st century. In pursuing this overarching goal, I shall, *inter alia*, give priority to
two operational goals — social cohesion and economic competitiveness — in line
with the above title. Toward these ends, this chapter initially focuses on generating a pan-Canadian information infrastructure. What then follows is a series of
perspectives — relating to children, to the family and to the structure of governments — that will serve to nudge underlying societal values in the direction of
bestowing pride of place to human capital.

With this as backdrop, chapters 13 and 14 will, respectively, address the
manner in which a human capital perspective (and GIR in general) impinges
upon, and alters, the range of policies on the social and economic fronts. Chapter
15 then addresses the enduring chestnut of federal-provincial relations and, within this context, "who should do what" within a human capital framework. This
final chapter will also link up with the Chapter 2 emphasis on cities and reflect
further upon their future as the leading forces in the new economy and in
Canadian federalism.

Two further introductory comments are in order. First, while the focus on
competitiveness and cohesion in terms of an overarching human capital framework broaches many of the daunting implications arising from GIR, it does not
address them all. For example, while there is implicit recognition of the importance of democratic participation, this area is not singled out for detailed

attention. To focus analytically on every one of the implications arising in Part II of the study is well beyond my ability. Moreover, apart from indefinitely extending the length of this exercise, such a comprehensive approach might undermine the dedicated focus on what I perceive to be the key message emanating from GIR — the primacy of human capital in the new order.

Second, while I believe a focus on cohesion and competitiveness within a human capital mission statement will serve to ameliorate the natural tension between social policy and economic policy, the fact remains that policy choices will remain very difficult and, over the short term at least, societally divisive. Much as one might wish, it cannot be otherwise given the profound implications arising from GIR.

Cohesion, Competitiveness and the Information Highway

T HE PAN-CANADIAN INFRASTRUCTURE RELATING TO INFORMATION, KNOWLEDGE AND human capital must become the new "railroad" in a human capital era. In terms of one essential element of this objective — making Canada the most connected country in the world (to use Industry Canada's phrase) — Canada can claim much success. We are among the most connected or "wired" countries when it comes to Internet access. Facilitated by SchoolNet, all of Canada's schools and libraries now have (or should have) Internet access, and we are well on our way to establishing 10,000 Community Access Portals, designed to provide Internet access to non-school-age Canadians. Moreover, as e-government evolves, minimizing the "digital divide" across citizens will become an even higher priority for governments since they have a responsibility to ensure that all citizens have access to public services. And this is quite apart from the dramatic take-up rate of private citizens. This is the good news and it is an essential component in facilitating Canadians' access to information and to enhancing human capital.

But there is a disturbing side to this good news: Although Canada ranks at or near the top in Internet usage by its citizens, Canadian businesses lag behind US companies in electronic commerce. Nortel's John Roth does not mince words here:

> We're on the eve of a discontinuity in business that we've never seen before.
> This really is a call to action for Canadian business, academics, the institutions,
> the governments, to make this our market. (quoted in Vardy 2000)

This harkens back to the ominous warning of the CEO of Intel (cited in Chapter 4): "In five years' time all companies will be Internet companies or they won't be companies at all." As Canada's Don Tapscott points out in his many writings, the underlying issue here is not just becoming "more efficient" as a business. Rather, the Internet is much more than a new way of doing business: It is permanently transforming the way that firms are structured, and it is the new platform for innovations in design, production and delivery. To be left out of e-commerce (or the "business web," more generally) is to have the new commercial paradigm pass one by. Were this to happen, then our costly investment in Canadians' human capital will largely be an investment in their job opportunities elsewhere on the globe. This is one implication of becoming a laggard on the e-commerce front. The other, as noted in the report of the Canadian E-Business Opportunities Roundtable (co-chaired by Nortel's John Roth and Baton Consulting Group (Canada) CEO David Pecaut) is that "we could in the future hear a huge sucking noise as imports from other countries rush to meet the demand created by high Internet use in Canada" (Vardy 2000).

Ultimately, of course, we depend on the creativity and innovativeness of Canadian businesses to catch the Internet e-commerce wave. Thankfully, we have some world-class Canadian enterprises that are more than holding their own in the Internet, e-commerce and information global sweepstakes. And, hopefully, the later recommendations with respect to policy areas such as taxation will ensure that they will remain headquartered in Canada. Actually, the relevant concern is that their valued *human capital* will choose to remain in Canada. For this to happen however, the larger challenge is to ensure that the rest of Canada's commercial pyramid joins the e-commerce revolution.

What makes this so daunting is the dynamic first-mover advantage that American business is increasingly possessing. The rash of hundred-billion-dollar mergers and acquisitions is generating "mega-portals" which, if unchecked, will lead to US domination of e-commerce in ever-more-local Canadian markets. This problem extends beyond the commercial realm. The "content" of the Internet will progressively be driven by US laws, regulations and, even, values. What is emerging is an enormous infrastructure externality, one that calls for a collective (i.e., societal) response. Not to put too fine a point on all of this, what Canada needs is a new National Policy — an informational infrastructure project to rival the 19th century railway era — "filaments of fibre" rather than "ribbons of steel" to provide the commercial infrastructure to underpin our economic competitiveness in North America.

Toward this end, the recommendations of the Canadian E-Business Opportunities Roundtable cannot be ignored:

- ◆ Establish a Canadian brand e-business.
- ◆ Make it easier for companies to invest in e-business through tax incentives and a new E-corps, a sort of Peace Corps of young people trained to help firms create a web presence.
- ◆ Improve the investment climate for emerging Internet firms, boosting the amount of available venture capital.
- ◆ Fix the tax treatment of stock options and boost Internet literacy to deepen the pool of high-tech workers in Canada.
- ◆ Make Ottawa the world leader in web commerce.
- ◆ Create a Canadian "trust seal" — a world-recognized consumer protection mark that would be enforceable through an international dispute-resolution body. (Vardy 2000)

To a degree, these recommendations are falling on sympathetic ears in Industry Canada. (As an important aside, this report no doubt was the catalyst for the introduction of US-compatible treatment of stock options in the 2000 federal budget, an issue I will address in Chapter 14.) In particular, at least as I understand it, Industry Canada is well launched on a massive project to provide Linux-based infrastructure that will allow up to 10,000 personal and commercial portals. In turn, this will allow myriad Canadian firms to access this overarching infrastructure and to become e-commerce players in spite of the dominating presence of the US mega-portals. To the extent that this facilitates an environment in which Internet users anywhere in Canada can access local as well as national and international e-commerce opportunities, then this will not only foster local enterprise but also surely provide an avenue for fruitful interaction between local educational institutions and the local commercial sector in the creative design and implementation of innovative applications of the 21st-century approach to competitiveness.

The underlying message of the above analysis is that the provision of meaningful e-commerce access to Canadian enterprises and entrepreneurs must be an integral part of our collective approach to ensuring that the 21st century also belongs to Canada. Indeed, "democratizing" both individual and commercial access to the Internet is so critical to our social and economic future that we need to consider the creation of a human capital super-ministry that would oversee the new "National Policy." More on this below.

While Internet/e-commerce access addresses the physical infrastructure dimension of the information era, it must go hand-in-hand with increasing the information empowerment and human capital of Canadians. We can take pride in the fact that Canada now ranks first among nations in terms of the percentage of relevant cohort that pursues post-secondary education. In Chapter 13, I shall focus on how to make the PSE sector even more effective. However, the immediate concern is how to ensure a human capital future for those Canadians who currently do not end up in our post-secondary institutions. If the human capital mission statement is to have any meaning at all, it has to address *access* to human capital. But this requires rethinking some fundamental societal values and perspectives, the purpose of the next section.

Embracing a Human Capital Future

A Human Capital "Bill of Rights" for Children

THE APPROPRIATE PLACE TO BEGIN IS WITH OUR CHILDREN. HOW MANY TIMES HAVE we heard or been told by our politicians that our children are our future — our most important societal asset? Disraeli was probably a latecomer in the litany when he proclaimed "The youth of a nation are the trustees of posterity." The answer is that we have heard this so often that this obvious truth has passed from the realm of substance to the realm of rhetoric. The time has come to impart some meaning to these words. Accordingly, the path toward a human capital future for all Canadians has to begin with a societal commitment to a human capital bill of rights for our children.

Among other things, this would imply buying into Fraser Mustard's crusade for a much greater emphasis on, and societal commitment to, early childhood development as a necessary precursor to the ability to acquire later skills and knowledge. One has the vision of our system of daycare centres shifting in the direction of Canada's own version of Dr. Maria Montessori's impressive model. When was the last time you or I were part of, or even aware of, a discussion about what ought to be part of a childcare or daycare curriculum? Given the importance of early childhood development, this must become an important issue in the context of a human capital bill of rights for children. What we now need is a set of instruments to deliver on this goal in a manner that embodies equality of access and affordability.

The Family as the Locus for the Production of Human Capital

Children exist in families. And families play a variety of critical roles in our society. Without intending to downplay these various roles, the time has come to also view the family as the *principal locus for the production of human capital*. This is a variant of an idea in the insightful 1996 paper by Martin Carnoy and Manuel Castells, *Sustainable Flexibility: Prospective Study on Work, Family, and Society in the Information Age*. Their take on this new role of the family as the centre of "production and reproduction" is, *inter alia*, as follows:

> Far from losing its fundamental importance to work, the family will be even more crucial as the economy shifts to flexible, knowledge-based production...Its role is already changing from a "family consumption partnership" to a "household investment and production partnership." Shifts in family organization are not new. They result from the inherently close relationship between family and work and women's changing social role. What is new — and rarely discussed in analyses of the changing work system — are the potentially ruinous implications for the development of highly competitive yet socially stable knowledge-based societies should families not emerge from the current transition restructured and healthy. (Carnoy and Castells 1996: 62)

One implication of this general approach to the family as the central hub of human capital decision making and production is that it becomes an explicit or implicit partner in a broader network that includes business, government, social organizations and civil society. As an important by-product, this "reconceived" family would play a key integrative role in fostering a new citizen-market relationship.

In terms of the implications for policy, the rhetoric we tend to associate with the old economy — investment tax credits and accelerated depreciation, among many others — would now apply to families, children and human capital generally; this would replace the "GIR-incorrect" existing terminology — transfers, subsidies and the like. Rhetoric matters! And human capital has every bit as much, and more, a claim to this rhetoric in a GIR era as do physical capital and resource capital. This is part of the rationale for viewing families (however organized) as the locus for producing and developing human capital. And with this concept of children and family, the way is far more open for creative approaches to human capital development.

Families and Child Benefits: Policy Choices

In order to breathe more reality into this conceptual approach to children and families, and what this might mean in terms of specific policy approaches, it is instructive to focus on *Taxing Canadian Families: What's Fair and What's Not,* by Carole Vincent and Frances Woolley (2000). They provide a highly useful survey of a wide range of economic and social issues surrounding the taxation of families and children. At the core of their analysis is the appropriate evolution of the two major child-related policies. The first is the Canada Child Tax Benefit (CCTB) and the associated National Child Benefit Supplement (NCBS). These are income-tested benefits that at their maximum are worth just under $2,500 per child, and which are fully taxed-back in the $66-75,000 level of earned income, depending on the number of children. Associated with this benefit is a high tax-back rate — nearly 25 percent in the $30-40,000 earned income range — which is piggy-backed on the existing marginal income tax rates. Together, these tax rates are higher than those for any other component of the working-population.

The second program is the Child Care Education Deduction (CCED) which allows daycare expenses of up to $7,000 per child for dual-earner families to be deducted from earned income. Because the CCED is a deduction rather than a credit, its value rises apace with income levels.

In rethinking these programs, Vincent and Woolley address a wide variety of alternative approaches, running the gamut from making the CCED a tax credit rather than a deduction, extending the credit to stay-at-home spouses, focusing on income-splitting as a possible complementary policy, and broaching the issue of imputing a value to household services within a family context. Their recommendation is to leave the CCED basically as is, but to convert the CCTB and the NCBS into a universal, non-taxable benefit, the cost of which would roughly double the existing $6 billion value of these two programs. The rationale here is essentially twofold: First, the universality and the non-taxable status of the CCTB/NCBS would eliminate the difficult "notch" problem (i.e., very high tax rates for families in the $30-40 thousand range); second, it would satisfy the high priority they place on *horizontal equity*, meaning that regardless of income level, families with children should pay less in terms of taxes than similarly income-situated families without children. Within their framework, this is probably the appropriate recommendation.

However, I see two problems with this framework that flow from the earlier analysis in this chapter. The first of these relates to the overall role of the personal income tax as a social instrument. As Vincent and Woolley note, it was not too long ago when we adhered to a horizontal equity vision in terms of taxing families, i.e., the era of universal, non-taxable family allowances. Gradually, however, we made a conscious societal decision to shift the social role of the income tax system away from horizontal equity concerns and toward a vertical equity approach, i.e., we converted the universal child payments first to tax credits and later to refundable and income-tested tax credits. For the same amount of public money, this allowed the targeting of much enlarged child benefits to low-income families. As noted earlier, Banting (1997) argues that it was this retreat from universality that has allowed lower-income-earning Canadians to fare much better than lower-income-earning Americans. I applauded this initiative at the time and I applaud it now. But the result does generate horizontal inequities among higher-income families with children and those without children. The CCED represents an offset, but the offset is not full.

Is this an argument for converting the now-higher family benefits (because of targeting) back into a universal entitlement, and in the process spending an additional $6 billion? My answer is no, in large measure because the income tax system is evolving along many fronts, not only in terms of child benefits. Specifically, we are in the midst of a GIR-triggered process that is reducing marginal tax rates on higher-income Canadians and this process will have to continue (see Chapter 14). To be sure this privileges all high-income earners and not only those with children. But if we then factor in the fact that the university attendance of higher-income families is much higher than it is for lower-income families, and that students, in spite of increasing tuition fees, are in effect recipients of very substantial subsidies, this provides a further offset to the horizontal equity issue. In terms of the other concern, the high tax-back rates, this can be solved by ways other than universalizing the CCTB/NCBS, i.e., an *all-in maximum* tax rate over the tax-back period.

However, this analysis is inadequately informed by the above human capital perspective. Thus, my second and overriding concern with the Vincent-Woolley analysis is that it is not GIR compatible. If we are to imbue substance to the *concept* of a human capital bill of rights for children, access to childcare/daycare should become the right of every child by virtue of Canadian citizenship, and not restricted by either income class or whether both spouses are gainfully employed. This would breathe meaning into the documented virtue of Mustard's early-childhood-development theorizing. While admittedly short on operational details, the essence of this approach[21] is that every Canadian child would be born with an *entitlement* to a daycare voucher (alternatively, a refundable tax credit from the family's point of view), and this voucher would be able to be exercised irrespective of the organizational make-up or employment status of the family — it would be a child's right. Whether the voucher is actually exercised will obviously rest with the parents/guardians.

Admittedly, many operational complications are associated with such an entitlement. What should its value be? Will parents who opt for more expensive care be allowed a deduction for the difference? How will this play in the federal-provincial arena? One might note that Quebec's $5-per-day childcare program and BC's proposals along similar lines represent alternative approaches to this challenge.

Thus, from a human capital perspective, I would reverse the Vincent-Woolley recommendations. Despite the fact that the CCTB/NCBS violates horizontal equity, I would keep it in place. And I would convert the CCED to a program that bestows on our children a universal right of access to childcare/daycare at a societally acceptable level. The rationale is straightforward. If we are ever to make a meaningful dent in the divergent human capital outcomes of Canadians, we have to break into the human capital formation process as early as possible. To me, this requires, as part of a human capital bill of rights for children, that we move boldly into bestowing a daycare/childcare entitlement on all our children so they can access the socializing and learning environment at the earliest possible age.

The State as Knowledge and Information Intermediary

Drawing again from Carnoy and Castells (1996: 75), although intimately linked with the mission statement, the rethinking of the socio-economic dimension of GIR must also extend to the state at its various levels. As the title of this monograph indicates, Canada must become a "state of minds" and, as indicated in the title of this section, governments must don the mantle of knowledge and information intermediaries. Albeit with some innovative initiatives here and there related to the requisites of GIR, the design of government still embodies, by and large, old paradigm priorities:

> Government bureaucracies organized around the previous industrial production system will...not be easy to change. That system assumed increasing employment in stable jobs, stable communities, a family where a man worked and a woman stayed home, an employed working life that lasted 40-45 years...Until government accepts the dramatic changes in the workplace, it will continue to be notoriously inflexible in responding to the disutility of old programs and the development of new ones. Shifts in programs and policies have been made doubly difficult because political constituencies have been built around the old programs, and they have joined with existing bureaucracies to resist change. (77)

Actually, the problems run deeper. In many of the existing government departments, the focus is on industrial sectors that trade internationally. Admittedly, it is important that we design and tailor our policies in these areas to suit our particular Canadian environment. But when all is said and done, all we will do in terms of internationally traded sectors is add a few innovative tweaks (as elaborated in Chapter 14) to the model the rest of the world is converging on. NAFTA and the WTO, let alone competitive forces, make this so. But this is clearly not the case for our social infrastructure. Here, we are largely on our own in designing and implementing a GIR-compatible social policy that embraces the goals we collectively set for ourselves.

Much more could be said here, but the following comment will suffice. Along mission statement lines, a commitment to provide equality of opportunity for all Canadians to develop, enhance and employ in Canada their human capital must become a societal *state of mind*. But this also requires that it become a *mind of state*. To accomplish this we must restructure our respective bureaucracies to ensure that pride of place is given to human capital formation in its social and economic roles. It is wholly inadequate to tuck concerns relating to the information economy and human capital formation somewhere under the umbrella of Industry Canada. Since knowledge is now at the cutting edge of competitiveness, the reverse is arguably the GIR-consistent approach — we ought to tuck our industrial policy initiatives within an overarching human capital super-ministry, with comparable initiatives at the provincial level. This applies to social policy as well. Without such a restructuring of the priorities of public policy, we will never be able to fully embrace the challenges and reality of the emerging information era, let alone meaningfully embrace the societal mission statement. For example, we are ever watchful that our social programs remain affordable and consistent with our ability to maintain competitiveness. But we tend to ignore the fact, noted earlier, that in the new order we must be concerned with both dimensions of this relationship: Where degrees of design freedom are available, policies oriented toward enhancing our competitiveness must also take account of our social (human capital) objectives. Overarching knowledge and human capital government agencies will ensure that this will become a two-way street.

With these infrastructure issues relating to information and human capital now in place, I direct attention in turn to rethinking our range of social and economic policies from the perspective of the human capital mission statement.

Human Capital,
Societal Cohesion
and the
Social Envelope

Introduction

THE STARTING POINT FOR ALL RETHINKING OF SOCIAL CANADA IS OUR EXISTING SOCIAL
infrastructure. Here, we can be justly proud of our achievements. In the
post-war period, Canadians collectively toiled long and hard and creatively to
marry key aspects of a continental-European social contract with an Anglo-
American approach to the economic sphere. Arguably, it is this collective achievement in generating American-style economic outcomes alongside European-style
social outcomes that perennially results in our earning top ranking in the United
Nations' Human Development Index as the most livable nation on earth.
Moreover, we distinguished ourselves from the Americans on the social policy
front in precisely the same period that we progressively integrated with them on
the economic and trade fronts.

For example, programs like medicare, which serves as a defining feature
for Canadians as well as a key competitive asset, and equalization, which breathes
vitality and equity into the functioning of our federal system, have no equivalents
south of the border. Moreover, by creative use of tax credits, especially refundable
tax credits, and by increased targeting, particularly in the area of children's and
seniors' benefits, we tilted our social envelope more in the direction of addressing inequality and poverty than have the Americans. Indeed, our policies in this
area serve as models for other federal systems — even the Americans are now
talking about refundable tax credits. And on the post-secondary-education front
we rank atop the world in terms of the percentage of the PSE-age cohort that
attends universities and community colleges (including Quebec's CEGEPS). In
other words, we proved to ourselves and to the world that we can integrate

economically with the Americans while striking our own made-in-Canada social vision. We must, and more importantly this proves *we can*, create a made-in-Canada social vision for a GIR era.

The challenge is to maintain faith in and with our demonstrated social achievements while we tilt these programs more in line with the "to develop, to enhance and to employ in Canada" imperative as it relates to the human capital of all Canadians. What is at play in redesigning our social infrastructure for a GIR era is not so much our social policy goals, except that GIR calls for shifting emphasis toward children and their human capital future. Rather, it is that the nature of the incentives embedded in these programs is too frequently designed with the characteristics of the old paradigm in mind: a tranquil international economy, a behind-tariff-walls domestic economy, a fiscal dividend arising from our rich resources endowments, an east-west trading system alongside an east-west transfer system etc. But these features no longer characterize 21st-century Canada. Thus, we have to bring our social infrastructure in line with this new information and human capital reality.

The good news, therefore, in redesigning social Canada for the millennium is that this is *not* about a wholesale rethinking of the values and objectives of our social order. Rather, it is about deploying creative new instruments and altering some of the incentives in existing instruments to ensure that the overall social infrastructure is consistent with the human capital mission statement. Moreover, in several important areas, our social envelope is already evolving in this direction.

The ensuing analysis directs attention in turn to the school-to-work transition, the PSE sector, the health sector, aspects of the welfare system, and to some reflections on the recent social union framework. Consistent with GIR and the mission statement, a key perspective in addressing these areas will be to emphasize that they are no longer only social programs: They are also leading-edge economic programs in a human capital and knowledge world and, therefore, they must be recast with this in mind.

The two following sections will provide some backdrop relating first to social cohesion and, second, to the linkages between the social and economic spheres.

Social Cohesion

While a commitment to equality of opportunity in terms of accessing Canada's human-capital-formation infrastructure is obviously a key variable in terms of the future level and distribution of market incomes as well as one of the principal thrusts serving to underpin a more societally cohesive future, this chapter is also about the more general contributions of the social envelope toward social solidarity. In this context, it is important to reference the 1999 *Final Report on Social Cohesion* produced by the Standing Senate Committee on Social Affairs, Science and Technology. As a pertinent aside, this juxtaposition of social affairs with science and technology is, arguably, a highly appropriate framework from which to view social cohesion in a progressively technological society. Table 11, reproduced from the report, presents a compendium of social cohesion concepts across a selected spectrum of countries, including the European Union. While I can easily buy into the phraseology for Canada, it clearly does not go far enough. Apart from being too narrow (the "within Canada" reference) it is environment free, as it were — there is no recognition that achieving social cohesion in the 21st century is a quite different challenge than achieving social cohesion under the former paradigm. To be sure, a definition of social cohesion should probably be an overarching concept of a societal order and, to this extent, transcend paradigms. Nonetheless, this particular definition falls short. However, the report itself eventually does attempt to wrestle with social cohesion in light of GIR. For example:

◆ The most serious challenge for policymakers in the years ahead lies in making globalization compatible with social cohesion. The challenge is to ensure that international economic integration does not contribute to domestic social disintegration. (Standing Senate Committee…1999: 10, noting in passing that the last sentence is directly from Rodrik 1997)

◆ For social cohesion the challenge is to identify policies that enable those left behind to participate in markets on more equitable terms, nationally and globally (10).

By way of addressing these challenges, the report appropriately focuses on the importance of what it refers to as *social investment*, within which it subsumes skills and human capital formation and a commitment to a learning culture in terms of objectives and new forms of collective action such as societal partnering across sectors and a commitment to breathe life into SUFA in terms of process. As part of its conclusion, the report hones in on what I believe gets much closer to the essence of the underlying issue:

Social cohesion is a societal project which transcends all the institutions in a society. It is the ultimate common property resource. We can all benefit from it if it exists, but it is far too easy to let the social fabric deteriorate as we each pursue our own short-term interest. (44)

For purposes of this chapter, social cohesion incorporates both this perspective as well as the norms and values of the various definitions in Table 11, especially the phraseology at the bottom of the table. In other words, social cohesion incorporates not only a set of shared underlying values that transcends paradigms but also a process dimension that allows these values to be interpreted and implemented in light of the prevailing paradigm. But social cohesion should be more than this: It should also be a societal commitment to a shared vision of our collective future. Were we to succeed in this dimension, then social cohesion becomes one of those intangible societal assets (or "common property resources," in the Senate's vision) that can propel a society and economy onward and upward. Without this shared commitment to a common goal, the pervasive forces of GIR may well trigger a *Me Inc.* future where, in the words of the Senate quote, the social fabric deteriorates as we each pursue our own short-term interests. We should not delude ourselves on this issue. Left unchallenged, the dictates of GIR are clearly and forcefully propelling us in this direction of effectively becoming northern Americans. And in the grand scheme of things, this is not an unattractive alternative. We can do better, however, and in particular we can ensure that Canada remains socio-economically unique in North America. But the prospects for doing this without a cohesive societal vision of where we want to be and how to get there runs the risk of being overcome by American values and, eventually, culture.

I submit that the societal mission statement articulated in Chapter 11 embodies both the essence of social cohesion and a common socio-economic future that is both GIR compatible and distinctively Canadian.

Static vs. Dynamic Approaches to Income Redistribution

While not in any way embracing the underlying tenets of US social policy, there is one aspect of their approach to income distribution that merits serious consideration in the Canadian context: their focus on dynamic or temporal mobility. By way of broaching this issue, if most Canadians are like me, they are astounded by the degree to which apparently "down and out" Americans remain committed to their system. I used to chalk this up to the more overt nationalism of the Americans and their melting-pot indoctrination of their citizenry. Along with their superpower role and their self-appointed status as guardians of global

Social Cohesion: Various Definitions

Canada	Social cohesion is the ongoing process of developing a community of shared values, shared challenges and equal opportunities within Canada, based on a sense of trust, hope and reciprocity among all Canadians.
France	Social cohesion is a set of social processes that help instill in individuals the sense of belonging to the same community and the feeling that they are recognized as members of that community.
New Zealand	Social cohesion describes a society where different groups and institutions knit together effectively despite differences. It reflects a high degree of willingness to work together, taking into account diverse needs and priorities. Social cohesion is underpinned by the four following conditions: • individual opportunities, including education, jobs, health • family well-being, including parental responsibility • strong communities, including safe and reliant communities • national identity, including history, heritage, culture and rights and entitlements of citizenship
Australia	Social cohesion is the bond between communities of people who coexist, interact and support each other with material help and by sharing group beliefs, customs and expectations.
Denmark	Social cohesion refers to a situation where everyone has access to establishing basic social relationships in society, e.g. work participation, family life, political participation and activities in civil society.
European Union	Article 2 of the Treaty of the European Union states that the tasks of the Union include: "Maintaining economic and social cohesion and solidarity between all Member States of the Union".

The objective of social cohesion implies a reconciliation of a system of organization based on market forces, freedom of opportunity and enterprise, with a commitment to the values of solidarity and mutual support which ensures open access to benefit and protection for all members of society.

Source: Standing Senate Committee on Social Affairs, Science and Technology (1999).

economic and moral principles, this may well be a large part of the answer. However, I have come to the view that there is something else at play, namely that the American notions of equity and income distribution are viewed *temporally*, not at any given point in time. The essence of the American dream is the notion of upward mobility, or the opportunity to have a better tomorrow. This feeds into other aspects we associate with the Americans. For one thing, Americans, much more than Canadians, tend to celebrate their entrepreneurs and success stories. Relatedly, and as many Canadians have noted, Americans tend to view business as a true "profession," and an honorable one, more so than do Canadians. Moreover, they work much harder at it. And most intriguing of all, the "down and out" Americans referred to earlier typically place a good deal of the blame for their current plight on themselves. Arguably, the temporal focus of "equity" and "mobility" may well be why the Americans can pursue high employment even in the context of very divergent market incomes and a weak and porous social safety net.

I hasten to note that I am not suggesting we applaud, let alone adopt, the American version of social policy. It is intended as a gross generalization of the US approach, in the same way that what follows exaggerates the Canadian approach.

By and large, Canadians are much more concerned with static or point-in-time income distribution. Indeed, we have put in place a pervasive set of incentives that literally forces our citizens to focus on a static rather than a dynamic concept of income distribution. A few examples will suffice. At the lowest end of the income spectrum, we have typically embedded confiscatory (i.e., 100 percent) tax rates in the transition from welfare to work and from EI to work. And by far the highest marginal tax rates exist for middle-income taxpayers because of myriad clawbacks associated with various income-support and child-support programs (as noted in Chapter 12). This even carries over to our equalization program. As I have elaborated elsewhere (1998), for the bulk of the equalization-receiving provinces an increase in provincial tax revenues arising from an increase in their economic base *will not yield a single penny in increased provincial revenues*, since equalization payments will decline dollar for dollar. Now it is a sign of a civil society to be concerned with the static distribution of income. But it is quite another matter to implement a system of policies such that the gains from moving up the income ladder are frequently quite minimal and, for selected groups of provinces and individuals, essentially non-existent.

I would hazard to guess there is actually much more in the way of upward mobility for low-income Canadians than there is for similarly situated Americans, despite the US rhetoric of a better tomorrow for their citizens. Indeed, in a recent article in the *International Herald Tribune*, Michael Weinstein (2000) notes that in the 1970s almost nine of ten US children in the bottom income group remained in the bottom two (of five) income groups 10 years later. This also applied for the 1980s, implying that upward mobility for the least-well-off Americans has not materialized over this 20-year period. Moreover, mobility is no higher in the United States than in Western Europe, where living standards are comparable and there is only a fraction as much inequality (Weinstein 2000). While some inequality is no doubt unavoidable in a capitalist economy, there is no evidence that US-type static inequality leads to a better tomorrow for the poorest of their population. Phrased differently, the American Dream is likely more myth than reality for low-income Americans. Thus, *static distribution does matter and so does the inclusive approach we Canadians take to our social spending programs.* We are clearly on the right course here.

Nonetheless, we do have to acknowledge that the by-words and buzzwords of the GIR era — creative destruction, technological change, innovation, self-reinforcing feedbacks etc. — all point in a dynamic or temporal direction. Without foregoing our commitment to the social justice inherent in point-in-time income distribution, we clearly have to tilt our social infrastructure in a forward-looking direction. To be sure, this is what a human capital perspective is all about. Paraphrasing the second of Thurow's frontispiece quotes to the mission-statement chapter, if we want the bottom of our labour force to have a better tomorrow, we have to provide equality of access to the keys to the GIR future, namely skills development. But the challenge goes beyond this direct human capital dimension: The social infrastructure must reward initiative and self-improvement and not embody policy-induced incentives that serve to entrench aspects of the static distribution.

Along similar lines, this issue can be placed in a historical context. As Keith Banting has noted, a key component of Canada's approach to post-war social policy was conceived against the backdrop of the Great Depression and the Second World War:

> [In Canada], the primary goal of the postwar social contract was security. Indeed, the welfare state was fundamentally rooted in a quest for security in an insecure world. The touchstone for the builders of the post-war welfare state

was the formative experiences during the depression of the 1930s, with its mass dislocation and widespread economic and social insecurity for entire populations. (Banting 1997: 265)

But with the Keynesian revolution and the development of economic stabilization, these mass dislocations have, to a significant degree, been tamed. Consequently, over the years Canadian social policy became more concerned with addressing poverty and inequality. The advent of GIR introduces a new type of insecurity into the system, one characterized, as already noted, by incredibly rapid technological change, by innovation and by dynamic creative destruction. In this new era there is no security in an economy that does not adjust. More to the point, a sustainable and secure social policy is one that is itself dynamically flexible, amenable to change and provides a bridge between the twin objectives of static and dynamic income distribution. The US focus on dynamic income distribution is one aspect we need to embrace as part of our system, albeit with made-in-Canada incentives and instrumentalities.

With these introductory sections as backdrop, the remainder of this chapter assesses selected aspects of Canada's social envelope in light of the human capital mission statement.

The School-To-Work Transition

A MONG OTHER IMPORTANT ATTRIBUTES, HIGH SCHOOLS PREPARE CITIZENS FOR THE transitions from school to PSE and from school to work. In terms of the former, they appear to be fully up to the challenge, as reflected in the earlier evidence of Canada's internationally high and arguably leading post-secondary participation rates. This does not mean that periodic curriculum reviews, designed to ensure we are state of the art in terms of the GIR reality, are not in order. The real problem appears to be that far too many Canadians fail to make a successful school-to-work transition and fall into what we tend to refer to as the "lost generation." This is a tragedy both for these individuals and for society.

Unfortunately, I have no creative approaches to address this challenge. What follows constitutes a few ideas that are "in the air," as it were:

- We Canadians are really a "professional society," when it comes to human capital. Compared to European nations we have few para-doctors, para-engineers or para-anything. This may be because our professional organizations are too strong and, therefore, wield too much influence. The larger, and no doubt related, issue is that as a society we do not accord anywhere near the recognition or prestige that, for example, the Germans accord their master tradespersons or technologists. This is a major problem because in an information age much of what will constitute the GIR middle class will be information or computer technologists or entrepreneurs of various sorts.

- One obvious solution is to forge a closer linkage between the business community/third sector and the high schools, so that students for whom the high school curriculum presents little interest can find alternative avenues for their interests and potential. Presumably, many provinces are involved in these sorts of linkages. Certainly other countries are. This is another area where the Council of Provincial Education Ministers, perhaps under the auspices of the APCs, could collect data relating to both initiatives and outcomes.

- Part of the problem with relying on the business sector for significant training and even apprenticeship programs is that this is not a key component of the Anglo-American business culture, as elaborated in Chapter 7. One way around this is for the various provinces to enlist businesses in a dedicated apprenticeship program. However, with the erosion of career ladders under the new paradigm, there is likely to be less interest (and capability) in mounting apprenticeship programs. But there are ways around this. One is the traditional route — provide tax credits to business for investing resources in the training of Canadians. Another could be for the federal government to provide EI premium relief to corporations that devote resources to apprenticeship-like training. My preferred route is quite different. Given that we endow each post-secondary-education student with a significant societal gift (to be consistent, this should be viewed as an "investment voucher") because tuition fees fall way below the full cost of tertiary education, why do we not endow those that do not go on to university with an equivalent sort of "investment voucher." Available data indicate that the draw of the "lost generation" on society's income support systems is enormous, so that even a modest success rate here would be in the interests of the public purse. In any event, the purpose of this voucher would be to "buy" one's way into the labor market as a trainee. The important point here is that we generously use public monies to accommodate those who go on to post-secondary education. Resorting to nearly any concept of equity in this regard would suggest that public support in search of training/apprenticeship should also go to those whose future income prospects are most bleak. This would make sense socially, economically and from the vantage point of the public purse if the recipients of the voucher were thereby able to avoid falling back on income-support programs.

◆ In what clearly falls in the off-the-wall category, why not experiment with allowing potential high-school dropouts to transfer to a community college for a "make-up" year or years. All of us in universities are familiar with make-up years, which are intended to bring students from (generally) unrelated programs up to the standard required for the program in question. The above recommendation would fall in this category in the sense that the make-up requisites for a technical program may well be more compatible with a student's interests than following through with a regular high school curriculum.

Having clearly exhausted my limited scope for meaningful recommendations, let me conclude with this hope: Were we to embark on a societal human capital commitment for all Canadians, much or at least some of the high school transitional challenges would be considerably ameliorated.

Along with the analysis relating to a human capital bill of rights for our children, the underlying message is that addressing the looming income-distribution implications of a human capital era requires creative reform and restructuring of the K-12 system as well as, arguably, pre-kindergarten childhood learning. The most efficient post-secondary education system in the world cannot make up for deficiencies that exist at these early childhood, primary and secondary levels. Moreover, because the returns to a remodelled pre-PSE system accrue more to society than to individuals and because such reform is a *sine qua non* for a more equitable income distribution, this area arguably has at least as much claim on our education dollars as does higher education in the context of achieving societal cohesion and a productive economy.

The Post-Secondary-
Education (PSE) Sector

A FUNNY THING HAPPENED ON THE WAY TO A KNOWLEDGE-BASED SOCIETY AND economy. While universities remain an absolutely vital institution in fostering a human capital society, they are at the same time losing their traditional position as having a natural monopoly over, or even being the principal repository of, knowledge. In the information era, the production and distribution of knowledge is verging toward the ubiquitous. As far back as 1993, *The Economist* offered the following generalizations:

♦ Today, knowledge is too important to be left to academics.

♦ Private entrepreneurs have been much better than their public sector counterparts in harnessing the information revolution...The combination of tenure and cumbersome decision making means that they [the universities] are much better at conserving old subjects than they are at extending, let alone inventing, new ones.

♦ Technical innovation means that universities have ever-less control over the dissemination of knowledge. [And this was written prior to the pervasiveness of the Internet. TJC]

♦ Soon you will be able to enjoy many of the advantages of first class education without ever setting foot on a campus. (*The Economist* 1993)

These concerns will ring even more true in the millennium.

Obviously, none of this is intended to undermine the role of post-secondary education in a progressively knowledge- and human-capital-based era. It is, however, intended to make the point that universities have no claim to *carte blanche* in the knowledge/information era: Adjustments to the evolving reality must also be their stock in trade.

The universities are, of course, well aware of the challenges they face in a knowledge/information era. In an insightful and comprehensive assessment of these challenges, Shapiro and Shapiro (1996: 105) begin with the observation that the PSE sector has in general made a successful transition "from an elite (i.e., small) to a mass (i.e., large) system of higher education". However, confronting the ongoing needs of citizens and society will require addressing a series of inter-related public policy issues related to access, size, burden sharing, diversity, quality and, finally, the role and purpose of higher education. Interested readers will surely profit from their penetrating assessment, given that in what follows I shall address only selected aspects of their analysis and that of others.

My first observation relates to heterogeneity and diversity. Specifically, the Canadian university system is arguably too homogeneous. Canadians may well view this homogeneity as a virtue: Focusing on what *Maclean's* magazine defines (non-pejoratively) as the lower tier of the university hierarchy, these lower-tier Canadian institutions clearly provide a higher quality education than is true for any definition of the American lower tier. This is an impressive achievement and the quality must be safeguarded. My concern, however, relates to the other end of the spectrum — we have too few world class universities. The Shapiros (1996: 90) argue that it is the "steeply and inherently stratified nature of the [American] mass higher education system that has made possible the relatively small number of great research universities which combine liberal and professional education with graduate education and research." They go on to note,

> It was...both the wealth and heterogeneity of this enterprise as a whole that allowed these relatively few institutions to afford the critical and costly inputs necessary for their success. To argue, however, that this rich resource base is necessary for all meaningful higher education is to take a position that is not only contradicted by the facts but is also a disservice to students, not to mention the public treasury. (90)

And, relatedly,

> Mass higher education systems are best served when there is differentiation not only among different types of institutions as, for example, among polytechnics and universities, institutional and workplace programs, or community colleges and universities, but also among institutions all of which have the same generic name. It is clear in most mass systems of higher education and in both the popular and the institutional mind that not all baccalaureate degrees are (or should be) the same and that not all baccalaureate institutions are (or should be) equivalent to each other. Moreover, assuming that access between institutions and institutional and program types is not only possible in theory but feasible (although not necessarily easy) in practice, this kind of stratification is entirely appropriate to a mass and therefore necessarily heterogeneous system, for it allows for an increasing variety of responses that can better match the increasing variety in both the needs and objectives of faculty and students. In addition, such differentiation is economically efficient. Differentiation must not only be legitimized, it must also be espoused as a matter of deliberate public policy. (89-90)

While one has to guard against the potential "downsides" of this diversity — e.g., erosion of quality control and inappropriate credentialism (91) — the underlying rationale for concentrating specialized resources in a select few leading universities relates to the "employ in Canada" tenet of the mission statement. In a progressively knowledge/information era, Canada needs a few world class research universities, institutions that can sit atop the research hierarchy and become national centres of excellence in their own right as well as become significant players in the knowledge-driven "clusters" (à la Porter) that are increasingly the dynamic motors of the new economy. It is precisely this knowledge-driven clustering and partnering that will allow us to have competitive claim to our best and brightest. With its billion-dollar-plus endowment, the University of Toronto is leading the way here. Others must follow.

My second observation also relates to the diversity dimension. We have succeeded in creating a "system" of post-secondary education, with universities and community colleges existing side-by-side. The challenge now is to forge a greater degree of integration among and between these components. They now largely exist as two solitudes — culturally and in terms of mission. To a degree, this is appropriate. But what is also appropriate is to better facilitate the commingling of the respective training and education missions for more areas and for more students. This could arise in the context of more or less formal linkages between community colleges and selected universities. At a minimum, it requires more access and more transparent transfer provisions between these sets of institutions.

The California higher education system is a potential model in this regard, comprising as it does community-college equivalents, state colleges and the University of California institutions as an integrated system. During his experience in the University of California system, York University's James Gillies noted that on more than one occasion in the 1970s the gold medal winner in several of the elite California universities was a transfer student from one of the "lower" tiers, if I can again use this term in a non-pejorative manner. Students, and perhaps especially mature students, should be able to integrate the "technical with the liberal," as it were. In this context, the recent British Columbia initiative in creating "university colleges" may well warrant replication elsewhere. The main point here is there is a need for the PSE sector to move in the direction of accommodating the changing needs of skill/knowledge accumulation in the GIR era.

Implicitly, I suppose, this is really a call on government policy to ensure that this integration does materialize. Indeed, I would be rather ruthless here — either the universities provide acceptable and transparent transfer provisions for community college students or governments should follow the British Columbia and Ryerson model of endowing these colleges with degree-granting privileges. Faced with this alternative, the universities *will* respond.

My third observation is again diversity related. Given the enormous inertial properties of a PSE system that, for the universities at least, has its roots in centuries of tradition, we need to "quick start" PSE innovation. To my mind, there is no better way to do this than to charter new "private" universities. Indeed, I would settle for *one* such institution. The information revolution and the Internet are altering forever the nature of learning. Massive traditional libraries will progressively give way to a series of Internet-accessible libraries, as old-style published information becomes increasingly available on-line and selected institutions worldwide are converting (scanning) a good deal of received knowledge and "old masters" into Internet-accessible form. Moreover, the traditional "full frontal" approach of a professor holding forth for one or two terms is an equally old paradigm in its conception, given that lectures from the worlds' best and brightest are now only a mouse-click away. It seems to me that the information-era university needs a much smaller "core" faculty, with much more reliance on bringing the most impressive minds and newest ideas via creative short-term contracting or accessing the "packaged" Internet lectures. Moreover, at least for undergraduate education, there is a need to tailor education in a much more interdisciplinary manner than is possible under the existing PSE system, as the earlier quotes from *The Economist* emphasized.

To be fair, the university sector is responding to aspects of this challenge, especially in terms of their professional programs. However, unless there is a demonstrable example of a "new" model (e.g., a new private-sector university) from *without*, as it were, there will be nowhere near the required evolution from *within* the existing system. With tuition fees on the rise, there is now scope for the emergence of creative new institutions of higher learning. Ontario appeared well on its way toward chartering a new private-sector university, but the province's enthusiasm on this score has apparently waned of late. At the very least, Ontario (or any other province) should remain open to granting a charter to any private-sector initiative in this regard.

As a prelude to this, and as a recommendation that has merit in its own right, the existing government grants to universities should be channelled through students via government vouchers. Intriguingly, this would lead to a degree of student influence on universities not unlike the case for the early origins of universities — just as federalism ought to be a form of government for citizens, and not just for governments, a voucher system ought to ensure that universities exist for students and not just for tenured faculty and administrations. And into this voucher system, one should incorporate apprenticeship or on-the-job training vouchers for those who do not access the PSE system. As noted above, both equity and public-purse considerations would be on side here. My final comment on the structure of universities and the PSE sector generally relates to the tuition fees. These fees have been rising sharply as of late. One can, of course, rationalize these increased tuition fees since graduates fare much better in the jobs and income sweepstakes, as noted in Chapter 3. The latest wrinkle here is to argue for income-contingent repayment plans to accompany tuition increases. However, in developing these schemes, two features relating to human capital as an *investment* should be kept in mind. First, the "pay-back" should be triggered only if the earnings of university graduates *exceed* that of the cohort that does not attend university and, second, the students must be able to "depreciate" their investment in the same way a mining company can depreciate any capital investment. These features are typically lacking in the various income-contingent repayment plans.

This leads to a further recommendation with respect to tuition fees. In order to encourage "access" to the PSE system, the *first year tuition* should be kept as low as possible. If students then wish to continue within the PSE system, higher tuition fees would then apply. Presumably, continuing students will be much more informed of the benefits and costs of continuing with their PSE studies. High first year fees would serve only to deter a goodly number of Canadians from initially accessing the system. This would run counter to the "access" concept implicit in the mission statement.

Finally, if we want the universities and the PSE sector generally to play their appropriate role in a knowledge-based era, then they likewise have to have access to an appropriate level of funding. Figure 6 focuses on a comparison of Ontario universities and public universities in 11 American states that are in the Ontario vicinity. The message is clear — US public universities have access to

Figure 6   186

Revenue per Student in Public Universities

Ontario and 11 American States, 1997-98

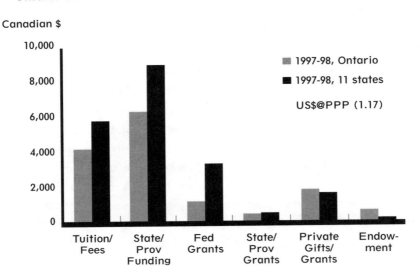

Canadian $

Legend:
- 1997-98, Ontario
- 1997-98, 11 states

US$@PPP (1.17)

Categories: Tuition/Fees, State/Prov Funding, Fed Grants, State/Prov Grants, Private Gifts/Grants, Endowment

Ontario and 11 American States, 1997-98
States Advantage over Ontario (%)

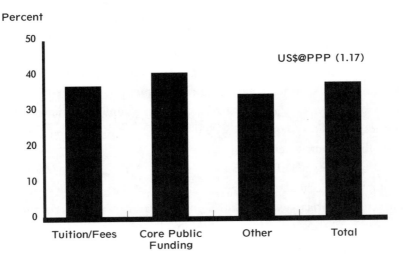

Percent

US$@PPP (1.17)

Categories: Tuition/Fees, Core Public Funding, Other, Total

Source: Davenport (2000)

a state of minds

nearly 40 percent more revenues than do Ontario universities. And these are very conservative estimates for at least two reasons. First, the comparison is made at the purchasing-power-parity exchange rates of 1.17 Canadian dollars per US dollar. At actual exchange rates (roughly 1.47 Canadian dollars per US dollar at the time of this writing), the US advantage would be significantly magnified. Second, the US universities are public universities: The Canadian advantage in the endowment category (the rightmost data bar in the upper half of Figure 6) would shift dramatically to a US advantage if US private universities were included in the sample. To be sure, some extenuating factors can be brought to bear in Canada's favour. We have a more extensive non-university PSE sector than the Americans, so some of our public dollars are spent on these institutions. Second, Ontario is among the least generous provinces in terms of university per student grants, so a comparison of the US with other provinces (e.g., Alberta) might alter the picture somewhat. Third, recent federal initiatives, such as the Millennium Scholarship Fund and the inauguration of the research chairs are not included in the data. Nonetheless, the evidence speaks for itself — we are falling behind in an area essential to our future as a human capital society. We do this at our longer-term peril to our citizens, our society and our economy!

The Healthcare Challenge

C ANADA'S SYSTEM OF MEDICARE (DEFINED GENERICALLY TO ENCOMPASS HEALTH CARE) is clearly one of the defining symbols of what it means to be Canadian:

> Polls have consistently demonstrated that medicare is by far the most popular public program in Canada...This level of public support exists not only because of the tangible benefits that medicare yields, though that is clearly an important factor. It exists also because medicare is a central part of Canadian public mythology. It has become an important element by which Canadians distinguish themselves from other nations, and particularly from the United States. During the heated and wrenching public debate over the Free Trade Agreement with the United States in 1988, politicians opposing the agreement repeatedly invoked medicare as one of the things that distinguished Canada from the United States, and alleged that it was threatened by the agreement. Public opinion polls showed that this allegation was the most effective way of galvanizing opposition to the FTA...Given the volatility of symbolic politics, it is difficult to judge how tightly the mythological status of Canadian medicare

constrains fundamental constitutional change. But it is fair to say that proposing structural change in medicare, especially in the direction of the
"American" model of managed competition now gaining increasing prominence on the policy landscape, carries great political risk. (Tuohy 1994: 207)

But medicare is more than just a national symbol: It is also a key element
of Canada's competitiveness, since publicly funded and universal access to health
care provides an important competitive advantage to Canadian enterprise. Thus,
medicare is a crucial component of achieving and maintaining both economic
competitiveness and social cohesion. And the interrelationship goes further:
Several empirical studies have shown that population health is positively related
to citizen well-being and security on the economic front.

Yet all is not well on the medicare front. Concerns relating to under-
funding (reflected in unduly long waiting periods for essential services as well
as the high-profile emergency room dysfunctions across many provinces) and
to the potential emergence of "two-tier" health care continually capture the
headlines. Diagnosing the underlying problem is anything but straightforward.
Many at the provincial level appropriately focus on the 1995 federal budget and
its cuts to CHST transfers as the principal culprit. While most of the recent
funding cuts have been restored, the federal contribution to medicare remains
in the range of 11 to 15 cents for each provincial healthcare dollar — a far cry
from 25 cents for each provincial dollar under the original 50-50 sharing[22] of
the former Established Programs Financing (EPF). Others would finger the
series of healthcare restructuring initiatives across the provinces, with particular focus on the closing and restructuring of the hospitals and hospital infrastructure, although the provinces would likely reply that much of this
restructuring was in turn triggered by federal transfer cuts. In either case, the
answer here would appear to be "more funding." However, there is also a growing view that the problems do not relate only, or even principally, to funding.
In a very courageous article, Michael Bliss (2000) argues that medicare needs
"root and branch" reform:

> Are you fed up yet with the state of Canadian health care? You should be. You
> should be mad as hell about the mess we have created in this country with
> socialized medicine.
>   Even if you're healthy now, it is an absolute certainty that your time to be
> sick will come. Then you will find yourself in the clutches of a deteriorating
> system of shortages, queues, demoralization, excuses and profound cruelty. It

is a system created without regard for principles of elementary economics, and
sustained by ideologues wildly out of touch with the real needs of Canadians.
It is desperately in need of fundamental reform; as every day passes more of
our citizens are condemned to conditions of care that are disgraceful in a rich
country in 2000. (Bliss 2000)

Part of the trigger for Bliss's critical assessment was the "Kafkaesque situation [that] is developing in the [wake of the] proposal of Toronto's University
Health Network to have cancer patients sign wavers acknowledging the inability
of Canada's largest and most prestigious cancer facility to give them the care that
they need."

From this vantage point, enhanced funding cannot be the full answer
since, under the current structure, the healthcare system can probably absorb any
and every additional dollar without contributing to the long-term sustainability
of the system. For example, Saskatchewan already devotes 40 percent of its budget to health care, with other provinces not far behind. And citizens' pressures in
all provinces are clearly in the direction of more funding.

This issue can be broached from another perspective. With health care
occupying upward of one-third of all provinces' program expenditures, the cuts
to the CHST not only put health care in jeopardy, they also placed the provinces'
fiscal positions in jeopardy. Additional healthcare dollars must now come from
expenditures elsewhere in the provincial budgets (e.g., expenditures on human
capital or infrastructure) or from raising taxes. Both options would serve to compromise the implementation of the societal mission statement for 21st-century
Canada. Hence, one must find ways to put Medicare on a more sustainable path.

I do not claim to have the answers to the healthcare challenge. What follows
is more in the nature of alternative perspectives designed to place the healthcare
issue within a context that is more amenable to thinking through some of the key
societal issues at stake. I begin by raising the issue of whether part of the challenge
relates to the fact that Medicare is now viewed as a goal rather than as an instrument.

Has Medicare Become a Goal Rather than an Instrument?

In Chapter 9, I noted that selected Canadian policy instruments have become so
intertwined with our identity that they have been raised to the position of policy
"goals." Medicare has certainly fallen into this category, as the above quotation
from Tuohy makes very evident. But Medicare is *not a goal*. It is an *instrument* for
achieving our overall societal goal for health care. For example, the World Health

Organization defined "health" as far back as 1968 as physical, social and psycho-logical well-being, and not merely the absence of disease. But medicare falls short of a goal even if the focus is on "sickness." Here the overarching goal would obvi-ously include key aspects of the status quo, such as tax-financed funding and uni-versal access, but it would go much further than the status quo to embrace the concept of an integrated "health network" — primary care, acute care, long-term care and home care. As an example, Medicare provides one hundred percent pub-lic funding for some of these areas but essentially zero percent funding for oth-ers. In contrast, Europeans tend to have more comprehensive coverage, but they link this extended coverage with some degree of private funding throughout the system. Suggestions that we might follow the European models in terms of this approach to funding typically generate a response to the effect that we will then be "Americanizing" Canadian health care. The reality is that Canada and the US tend to represent opposite poles on the healthcare system, with the rest of the world occupying the middle ground. Moving to the European model is *not* mov-ing to the American model! But it effectively becomes so, as long as Medicare is elevated to a goal, in and of itself.

But all of this relates to "old-style" health. In *Four Strong Winds:...*, Michael Decter (2000) provides important glimpses of health care in an infor-mation era — Access Health (a Sacramento company delivering health care by telephone), various forms of e-health and the increasing trend for a greater number of procedures to shift out of hospitals and into specialized institutions. This changes the ways in which health care is delivered and shifts power from providers to consumers (patients). Relatedly, in the face of rapid technological advances in health diagnoses and treatment, the notion that an unswerving commitment to an immutable version of medicare means that aging boomers will not be able to use their pensions and/or savings to address their health needs as they see fit is surely far-fetched. So is the notion that we can prevent the spread of specialized clinics that have significant cost advantages over hos-pitals as service providers.

The genius of Medicare is that it was an ideal societal instrument for addressing Canada's health challenges in the previous era. Unfortunately, the nature of the overarching health goals have changed and will continue to change as information and technology work their way into the health system. The time has come to change the instrument.

Thankfully, Canadians are rising to this instrument challenge and rethinking the healthcare system in very creative ways. As already noted, Michael Decter's *Four Strong Winds:...* assesses Canada's healthcare experience in a comparative context as well as in terms of its evolution in the direction of "Webhealth." David Gratzer's *Code Blue: Reviving Canada's Heath Care System*, which won the Donner Prize for the best book on Canadian Public Policy published in 1999, heralds "medical savings accounts" as a key component toward a revitalized and sustainable evolution for health care. Beyond these and other recent books, there are a wealth of ideas and creative proposals emanating from think tanks, health analysts, academics as well as healthcare professionals and agencies (e.g., IRPP Task Force on Health Policy, 2000).

However, in terms of building upon our achievements (i.e., working with the basic Medicare model but altering it in key ways to cope with the new challenges), the best starting point is Tom Kent.

Kent's Proposal for Rethinking Medicare

Canada's social policy architect of the Pearson era, Tom Kent, recently sent a "memo" to the Prime Minister, *What Should Be Done About Medicare* (2000). The main points of Kent's proposal are summarized here, but interested readers are encouraged to seek out his work. The essence of Kent's memo is contained in his "principal suggestions":

- ◆ Replace the H of the CHST by a continuing commitment that from this year on the federal government will reimburse each province for at least 20 percent of the cost of its agreed medicare program.
- ◆ As the basis for such partnership in medicare, issue a joint declaration by all Canadian governments that the purpose of our medicare is to make a consistent level of health care equally accessible to everyone according to his or her needs. For this purpose, agreed programs must be entirely tax-financed. The principle of care according to need rules out any muddling of public and private finance, any "second tier" of privately purchased variations to, or queue-jumping within medicare.
- ◆ Establish a joint, federal-provincial Canada Health Agency in order to provide regular consultation on health policies; to collaborate in defining the content of agreed medicare programs; to monitor the operation of the programs; to facilitate cooperation in improving the effectiveness

of medicare and containing its costs; and to express accountability to the public by regular and full reports.

◆ Assign to the Agency the priority task of creating and operating a nationwide health information system that enables all health treatments to be costed and related to the evidence of their benefits.

◆ Undertake that, as soon as the Canada Health Agency is in operation and its information system established, the federal government will increase to 21 percent its committed share of the costs of medicare.

◆ Agree to foster more awareness of medicare costs in the minds of both the providers and the recipients of care. For this purpose, provinces will provide an annual total of the costs of the medicare services received by each individual or family. A small part of the costs will then be recoverable through the tax system, on a scale that is related to income and does not deter access to needed care.

◆ Initiate consultations to define the improvements to medicare that are agreed to be desirable and potentially practicable over a period of a few years. While all the items will be agreed, each province can set its own priorities among them.

◆ Undertake that the federal government will facilitate these improvements by graduated increases in its share of each province's medicare costs, up to a ceiling of 25 percent. Timing of the changes will be determined by procedures that reconcile the provinces' freedom of selection with fairness among them and that also establish restraints on cost increases.

◆ Ensure that the federal financial contribution to the medicare partnership is made continuingly clear. This transparency is required not only for the credit of the present government but, equally, to protect the provinces against any future federal government thinking that it could cut its funding with little political penalty. (Kent 2000: 1–2)[23]

By way of elaboration, among the ways in which Kent attempts to sort out the federal-provincial dimension of health care is the creation of the Canada Health Agency, which would be a federal-provincial agency constituted fully in the spirit of SUFA. While this CHA would develop pan-Canadian principles, these principles require federal-provincial partnership and consen-

sus, not federal domination of the sort that characterizes the implementation
of the Canada Health Act principles (6). And although the provinces would
have to buy into these principles, "each province must be free to establish its
own priorities, to arrange what it thinks best for its people" (13).

Relatedly, the eventual 25 percent federal funding would not be tied to any
specific federal priority:[24]

> Recently, for example, the widespread need for more home care has led to the
> proposal that we provide special funding for it. We should not. The effect
> would soon be to over-expand home care relative to other health services, to
> waste money by distorting the allocation of resources. It would be inequitable
> as well as inefficient, because the extent to which home care is more needed
> than better community facilities, for example, varies among areas and among
> provinces. Such priorities are matters for management within each provincial
> program. Special federal funding of bits and pieces of medicare would be nei-
> ther efficient nor fair. Our partnership role is to support the program *as a
> whole*. (6, emphasis added)

What is clearly novel in terms of the existing Medicare model is Kent's proposal for the provision of a delayed user fee via the tax system, i.e., a tax clawback related to a taxpayers' use of the medicare system. Kent sets the maximum
clawback at 2.9 percent of income. Since this is a taxable benefit, it is very progressive — individuals whose income levels do not generate positive tax payments would obviously be exempt from the clawbacks.

A detour is in order here. While Kent makes the interesting claim that this
concept of healthcare use tax clawback was part and parcel of the Liberal party's
seminal Kingston Policy Conference in 1961 (which laid the groundwork for
much of the impressive social agenda of Pearson era), it was also a key recommendation of an Ontario Economic Council position paper in 1976:

> In Ontario, it would be quite feasible, with some adjustments to our current
> administrative and information system, to establish a given family's use of the
> health care system as well as a dollar measure of the benefits received. These
> benefits, subject to possible exemptions and catastrophic limits, could be sub-
> jected to a form of income taxation. This whole process would be integrated
> with the income tax returns process in a manner such that the following con-
> ditions held:
> (a) Taxation and hence financing of health care would be related to use and
>   benefits received;
> (b) the poor would avoid paying because taxation can be geared to income,
>   exemptions and other ability-to-pay criteria;
> (c) ceilings would exist on the amount of taxation, thus building a
>   catastrophic insurance feature into the system; and

(d) averaging provisions would exist to permit a smoothing out of tax payments, and so on.

Of course, whether such a system is desirable must be judged in terms of
a number of factors including ease and cost of administration and how well it
permits the achievement of the social and economic objectives of Ontario's
health policies. (Ontario Economic Council 1976: 15)

Thus, this is an idea whose time may be nigh. Kent also envisages the
provinces as levying a clawback in addition to the federal clawback. However,
since the provinces are on the hook for 75 percent of all medicare funding, my
view is *the provinces, not Ottawa,* should, if they wish, have first dibs at enacting
the entire clawback. Moreover, this should become part of the personal income
tax collection agreements, in that Ottawa should collect the clawback free of
charge to the provinces (with compensation for Quebec's collection expenses if it
adopts a similar policy).

There is one other important departure from the existing Medicare model.
Kent has no problems with the public system contracting out with privately run clinics or service-delivery agencies, as long as these clinics or agencies work within the
system, i.e., have open access and do not allow private money beyond the system's
fee for service. What Kent is against is the commingling of private and public financing within the overarching public system. He has no problem with first dollar, private health care. His analogy is interesting: "Those who do not like the tax-financed
school system are free, if they can afford, to send their offspring to Upper Canada
College or whatever" (Kent 2000: 8-9). The same would be true for private health.

Finally, underlying Kent's proposal, always implicit and at times explicit, is
a call for statecraft on the part of the Prime Minister — break through the federal-
provincial quagmire that is medicare and mount a 21st-century healthcare system
that will be the Prime Minister's enduring legacy.

This proposal will not satisfy everyone. For example, many of the
provinces will be wary of yet another shared-cost program from which Ottawa
can exit sometime in the future: These provinces would much prefer the more
secure route of a further tax-point transfer. Some other potential concerns, such
as the lack of effective "internal markets" in the healthcare system, are not really
problems with the Kent proposal since there is nothing to prevent such innovations within his general scheme.

While it is quite exciting, from a policy perspective, to have one of the
original architects of Medicare reflect on how it might be updated for the 21st

century and while I agree with the general thrusts of the new vision as far as it
goes, my concern is that it does not go far enough. Specifically, reworking health
care will fall short of Canadians' needs and expectations unless this reworking
takes account of the realities of GIR and, in particular, the implications of the
human capital mission statement. To this I now turn.

A Human Capital Perspective of Canada's Healthcare System

Earlier in this section, reference was made to the fact that publicly funded
health care provides a significant leg up for Canadian enterprise. Indeed,
former Chrysler president Lee Iacocca once lamented that his American operations spent more on health care than on steel. This is an important *indirect*
economic benefit of our healthcare system. However, a human capital perspective with respect to health would also focus on the *direct* economic benefits. In the new knowledge/information era, health is emerging as one of the
leading-edge economic sectors for research, innovation and exports, as well as
for employing the high-level human capital and talent of Canadians. In a pre-
budget submission to the Standing Committee on Finance, the Ontario
Hospital Association (OHA) reflected on the economic role of the health sector as follows:

> Knowledge is a fundamental factor behind the effectiveness of our health-care
> system. During a time of major change, it is the expertise, skills and commit-
> ment of our knowledge workers that will keep the system together and will
> create the necessary conditions for improved health care in the future (OHA
> 1999: 13)....
> The advantage of creating world-class organizations in a growing market
> such as health care is that there are significant opportunities to share our
> wealth of knowledge. This creates new high-skilled employment opportunities
> for Canadians and generates alternative revenue sources for Canadian health-
> care providers.
> A recent example of global recognition of Canada's expertise is the suc-
> cessful bid of Toronto-based InterHealth Canada, which won a $1.1 billion
> contract to operate a 335-bed hospital in the United Arab Emirates.
> Not only is health care an essential service, it is also a major engine of eco-
> nomic growth that leads to new high-skilled jobs and investment. Therefore,
> the sharing of health-care expertise, goods and services should continue to be
> part of the government's international trade strategy. (17)

According to Industry Canada estimates, the market in biotechnology in
2005 will be more than double that in 1995 — $50 billion vs. $20 billion. A
recent IRPP Task Force on Health Policy (2000: 41) recommended strategies to

develop the export of healthcare services and management and to expand the production of goods and services that stem from the health sector. The relevant promising industrial subsectors would include information technology, healthcare delivery services, healthcare management, knowledge management systems (including data collection and software development) and imaging systems, among others. There is much more at stake here than merely missing out on a major export platform in the information area: Failure to be in the forefront of these remarkable diagnostic, treatment and service delivery innovations will mean we will never have access to state-of-the-art health care.

The underlying problem is straightforward. We tend to view the healthcare system as falling entirely within the "social" envelope. Moreover, our collective approach to health care is to emphasize cost containment, subject to some national concept of an "acceptable" or appropriate standard of services (which we appear willing to have decline over time). The reality is that in a GIR era, the healthcare sector needs a massive infusion of physical, intellectual and financial capital to enable it to become a dynamic engine of economic growth with multitudes of spin-offs in other new technology sectors. Viewing the health sector solely as a social policy sector will guarantee that it will never receive the requisite infusion of capital.

One can be fairly confident that the future on the health front will be characterized by a rapid growth of specialized diagnostic and treatment centers which will be cost-effective, innovative and separate from, although possibly linked to, the hospital sector. Thus, the real challenge is not how to keep the private sector out of health; rather, it is how to bring it in! Kent's proposal does allow for the integration of these private clinics into the overarching public sector, but the model needs to be much more creative, especially in terms of the transition of such agencies from the private to the public sector. Perhaps we need a different model entirely. If we fail in this challenge, the prospects are for Canadians to insist that foreign-based diagnostic and delivery systems become an integral part of Canadian health care.

The essential point is that in the 21st century, maintaining state-of-the-art health care for Canadians requires that we view the health sector as a dynamic economic sector as well as an essential social institution. We cannot allow the last paradigm's notion of medicare to prevent the health sector from emerging as a pivotal player in our society, in line with both the economic opportunities generated by the new knowledge/information era and with the pressing health-care needs of Canadians.

I now turn to the final section dealing with the social envelope — income-support and training, where the common bond between the two is one of enhancing the citizen-market interface.

Income Redistribution
and Training

More on the CCTB

C HAPTER 12 DEALT WITH THE CCTB AND THE DAYCARE DEDUCTION IN THE GENERAL context of the taxation of families with and without children. The emphasis here is different, namely on the creative role the CCTB has played both in federal-provincial relations and in terms of facilitating the transition from welfare to the marketplace. As noted, the CCTB had its origins in the 1996 *Report To Premiers*, prepared by the provincial Ministerial Council on Social Policy Renewal and Reform. Ottawa bought fully into this provincial recommendation, the result of which was that the federal government initiated, and over time has progressively enriched, the CCTB.

The CCTB is a prime example of innovative federalism. Since the CCTB puts more money in the pockets of families on welfare as well as lower-income working families, the agreed-upon federal-provincial arrangements are that the provinces can reduce the child component of welfare payments in line with the increase in the CCTB, provided they re-deploy these "savings" in terms of related programs for low-income working families with children. This not only respects provincial flexibility (as it should since this is in an area of provincial jurisdiction) but also serves to facilitate the transition from welfare to work. This is so because the CCTB is an income-tested benefit, i.e., it remains in place even if the family moves off welfare and into the work force. Moreover, because the provinces are required to re-deploy these funds for working-poor families, the transition becomes easier still, in the sense that the effective rates of taxation from welfare to work are reduced even further. Compared to the situation as recent as a decade ago, where families typically lost *all* welfare benefits if they engaged in work, this represents a remarkable development, one that we should celebrate. Indeed, it can be viewed as a necessary step in the direction of developing a comprehensive package relating to early childhood development and a human capital approach to children.

The corollary to this federal-provincial "creative entanglement" with respect to the CCTB is that the provinces now have much more flexibility in terms of formulating labour-market strategies for their working-age populations. For example, it becomes much easier, in the transition from welfare to work, to implement income-tested wage subsidies, or even the US version of earned-income tax credits. This is especially the case under the new tax-on-income approach to the shared personal income tax since the provinces can have their own rate and bracket structures replete with income-tested clawbacks. All of this assumes the provinces *will* begin to adopt policies that will ease the transition from welfare to work. I am optimistic here, because the income-tested CCTB provides a valuable beacon in the direction of a more general approach to what economists call a negative income tax, or an income-tested guaranteed annual income. Although not in the league of comprehensive policies directed to develop and enhance the human capital of Canadians, these new programs for low-income Canadians clearly move in the direction of addressing both point-in-time and dynamic income-distribution concerns, as highlighted earlier.

EI and Human Capital

In terms of the overall mission statement, there is no question that Employment Insurance or EI is the social program that is most offside with a human capital future for Canadians. Among the defects in EI (then UI) noted by the Newfoundland Royal Commission on Employment and Unemployment (1986: 406-10) were the following:

- ◆ The system undermines the intrinsic value of work.
- ◆ The system undermines good working habits and discipline.
- ◆ The system undermines the importance of education.
- ◆ UI is a disincentive to work.
- ◆ The system is vulnerable to manipulation [including the 12-week work syndrome].

The Royal Commission elaborates on these and other defects of the then-existing UI system. Importantly, but probably not surprisingly, the Royal Commission recommended scrapping UI and replacing it by an income-tested guaranteed annual income. The Macdonald Commission report recommended much the same.

However, Canada's approach to EI has been to progressively "tighten" the system over time, increasing the "entrance" requirements and reducing the "generosity" of the system.[25] Unfortunately, in the process, many of the disincentives within the system have remained in place, albeit scaled down. (A detailed assessment of these disincentives as well as a menu of reform options appears in Chapter 10 of Courchene (1994).) For present purposes, I focus on only one problem area: the inappropriate tax-back rates associated with EI. Specifically, an EI claimant is able to earn a portion of his/her benefits tax-free — up to 25 percent of benefits. Beyond this, there is a dollar-for-dollar offset that serves both to "trap" the individual in the EI system and to provide a huge incentive for underground economic activity. To ensure that EI becomes a trampoline rather than a hammock, the incentives for EI-to-labour-market transition must embody much more in the way of income testing. At an even more fundamental level, it would be preferable to split EI into its two components: social insurance, which should be run on strict insurance principles, and social assistance (or income support), which should be folded into existing social assistance programs. It is noteworthy that an egalitarian society like Australia does not even have an equivalent to EI. Unless our EI system becomes much more in tune with the imperative of developing and enhancing Canadians' human capital, we should not have an EI program either. It is exciting to imagine what the billions of dollars of EI benefits could do if they were put in the service of delivering a human capital future for Canadians.

EI and Maternity Benefits

In the 2000 federal budget the maternity provisions relating to EI were substantially enhanced — on the order of an additional $900 million annually. It is also important to note that this is really an income-tested benefit. Maternity-leave benefits are largely taxed back for high-income, EI eligible families. Given this, it is appropriate to raise the rather fundamental issue of whether this should be an *employment-related benefit* or a *citizen-related benefit*. Presumably, one of the rationales for an employment-related (or EI-related) benefit is that this enhances the labour-force attachment of women, and more generally families, since either spouse can access aspects of the benefit. However, the changing nature of work, including the quite dramatic rise in the self-employed, means many "working"

Canadian families are not eligible for EI maternity benefits. A further rationale may be that these benefits are "insured benefits" and, therefore, they are "earned." But the cross-subsidization here is surely substantial.

My counter argument could be constructed as follows: Along lines associated with early childhood development and a human capital bill of rights for children etc., might not this benefit be made *universal*, i.e., on a *citizen-eligible* basis rather than an *EI-eligible* basis? Since EI benefits are in effect income-tested, so too would these citizen benefits. Perhaps one could argue that we have alternative programs in place for low-income families who do not qualify for EI maternity benefits. Yet my concern is that addressing social cohesion in the context of quite dramatic changes in the citizen/labor-market nexus should mean equality of access to a broad range of programs relating to children and families. We frequently rail against the American social policy approach where full social entitlements (e.g., for health care) tend to apply only to those who hold good jobs. We must be careful that we do not fall into this same trap, where benefits differ markedly depending on whether one has an EI-eligible job.

EI and the Federal-Provincial Quagmire

Thanks to a constitutional amendment, EI falls under federal jurisdiction. But federal control over EI is increasingly offside *vis-à-vis* the *de facto* division of powers in our federation. In particular, it rests uncomfortably not only with the on-going trend in provincial policy to assert greater control over subsystems relating to working-age Canadians (e.g., welfare-to-work, school-to-work) but also with the recent devolution of training to the provinces.

Even prior to these developments, UI or EI created federal-provincial havoc for both individuals and labour markets. Stories still abound of provincial programs whose principal goal is to employ *provincial* welfare recipients for periods just long enough to qualify them for *federal* EI. Presumably, these provincial schemes are somewhat less prevalent with the recent scaling down of EI. But they still exist. It is hardly the mark of a civil society or of a society devoted to developing citizens' human capital to treat economically disadvantaged Canadians as mere pawns that can be shunted across programs to further the financial interests of governments. Shame on us!

Part of the problem here, as noted above, is that EI departs from insurance principles in terms of rewarding short-term labour-force attachment with inordinate benefits. This is the EI feature that has led to the very serious distortion of regional and, indeed, provincial labour markets because of the "12-week work syndrome." How does a provincial labour ministry devise a comprehensive labour-market strategy for its citizens when these perverse EI incentives dominate key aspects of the citizen/labour-market interface? It is important to recognize that individual citizens are acting in a wholly rational manner: *The problem lies in the incentives embedded in EI.* Actually, the challenges facing these same labour ministries in several provinces have, arguably, become exacerbated with the recent tightening of the EI provisions. In the event, what effectively transpired was that the new EI changes "off-loaded" some individuals from EI to provincial welfare during precisely the same period in which Ottawa abandoned 50-50 cost sharing for provincial welfare.

It is time to halt this intergovernmental gaming.

Training and EI
Finally, the focus shifts to the training dimension of EI in the context of the earlier theme that the provinces are exerting greater policy control over the social infrastructure subsystems relating to their working-age populations. With federal-provincial agreements devolving key aspects of training to the provinces, some unfortunate and inappropriate asymmetries have arisen. The general point is the following: The devolution agreements are generating two classes of citizens when it comes to training — those who are deemed to have access to EI-eligible programs and services and those who are not, where the latter can access only provincial programs. Again, the issue relates to equal access for all citizens. To be sure, equality of access would be guaranteed if the provinces, in their own programs, *matched* the EI-eligible programs and services. But this would hardly be consistent with the *devolution* of the responsibility for training to the provinces. Alternatively, Ottawa could allow these monies to be "block funded" to the provinces and used for training all of their citizens. But this would hardly be consistent with the contributory nature of EI. An alternative would be to designate a portion of the existing *employer* EI contribution to be in the nature of a general training fund that could be used for training all Canadians, i.e., this would be an employer-, not employee, financed general training fund accessible to all citizens. Admittedly, one must be careful to ensure that the best does not become the enemy of the good. The training-devolution initiative is an improvement on the

status quo. What is required now is a more flexible arrangement so that the provinces are better able to integrate these EI training dollars into their own training and apprenticeship programs. Indeed, this is in the way of an apt conclusion for this entire discussion of EI. The logic of the recent series of developments — CHST block funding, devolution of training to the provinces, the enhanced role of the federal government in income support for children thereby freeing up the provinces to focus their attention on the working-age population — points in the direction of much more federal-provincial cooperation in terms of the operations of the Employment Insurance program.

A final word is in order. EI does not sit well with the thrust of the human capital mission statement. Indeed, even in its present reincarnation, it runs counter to the dictates of GIR. Unlike the other social programs, it really has outrun its usefulness. Thus, rendering EI consistent with the human capital mission statement requires some dramatic changes. For example, we could rework the program in ways that would return it to insurance principles, rewarding long-term labor-force attachment. Or, we could abolish it and fold the existing income-support component of EI into existing welfare systems, moving in the direction of generating a full-blown, income-tested guaranteed annual income for Canadians. The fact that the Chrétien Liberals have, for electoral gain, recently rolled back some of the hard-won EI reforms is clear evidence that we have a long way to go before we are ready to adopt a human capital future for Canadians.

Citizens, SUFA, and Mutual Recognition of Skills

T HE FEBRUARY 4, 1999, SOCIAL UNION FRAMEWORK AGREEMENT (SUFA) embodied a provision, carried over from the earlier *Agreement on Internal Trade*, for mutual recognition of provincial skills and occupational accreditation. Mutual recognition of provincial accreditation is an essential feature of any meaningful east-west social union and it is equally essential for economic competitiveness. Pursuant to SUFA, countless backroom negotiations are ongoing to reconcile the various provincial occupational and accreditation standards. While this is a commendable approach to mutual recognition, it is nonetheless the *wrong* way to proceed. Rather, we must take a page out of the Australian approach to mutual recognition: Convert the transferability of skills and accreditation into a right that is inherent in citizenship.

Accordingly, I suggest the following approach to mutual recognition. Suppose, for illustrative purposes, an individual with Nova Scotia accreditation as a marine technologist moves to Ontario and applies for an advertised position for a marine technologist. Consistent with mutual recognition as a right of citizenship, the individual's credentials *would be deemed equivalent unless proven to the contrary*. The operational process could proceed along the following lines. If the Ontario authorities challenge his/her credentials, the citizen should be able to appeal to the SUFA dispute resolution board or panel. If the individual does not receive a response from the panel within a meaningful period, say six weeks, *the accreditation will be deemed equivalent*. However, if the panel challenges the credentials, then the individual must be informed of the specific ways in which his/her credentials can be made equivalent. This approach harkens back to the burden-of-proof issue raised in Chapter 9. In the existing Canadian context, the burden of proof rests with the citizen. This is surely wrong in terms of any meaningful approach to mutual recognition. The burden of proof must be on governments, i.e., on SUFA. In short, a citizen's credentials should be deemed to be mutually recognized unless SUFA provides evidence to the contrary.

The implications of this operational process are entirely salutary. If the SUFA panel refuses to grant mutual recognition, then the citizen in question will clearly bring pressure to bear on the Nova Scotia government (or on the professional regulatory body) to introduce provisions that will make these skills transferable to Ontario. This is a far superior operating procedure than the current system, which tries to negotiate equivalencies across all provinces. Among other things, the current negotiation process could take years, in spite of the existing deadlines.

The general point is that while SUFA is an agreement among governments, the social union itself has to be an agreement *for citizens, not for governments*. Assigning the burden of proof with respect to mutual recognition disputes on SUFA, rather than on citizens, is a necessary and critical step in the direction of ensuring that in the final analysis SUFA is about privileging citizens' access to, and rights within, the Canadian social union.

SUFA, Training and the Canadian Armed Forces

The Canadian Armed Forces are by far the most dedicated institution in terms of training and apprenticeship. They are also among the most important institutions for upward mobility in the country. Most of the occupational training undertaken in civilian Canada has a military equivalent. This leads to two observations relating to the interaction between civilian and military training as it relates to SUFA and mutual recognition.

The first and most obvious is that the Armed Forces, directly or via the federal government, must be fully incorporated into SUFA and, in particular, into the mutual recognition process. Some significant progress has already been made. For example, the military now recognizes many occupational training programs of our community colleges. This means the military can "buy" their required skills rather than "build" them internally, where this is appropriate. The converse is less true. We need to ensure that the training and apprenticeships acquired in the military are given civilian accreditation so those who leave the military can more easily apply their skills and human capital in civilian positions. Indeed, we should go further and formally recognize that one or two terms of service in the military are, for many Canadians, an ideal avenue by which to develop and enhance their skills and human capital.

This leads to the second observation, one that falls in the category of "levering off our strengths." Given that the military has, arguably, the most dedicated training and apprenticeship culture in the land, we are wasting an extremely valuable asset if civilian Canada does not take greater advantage of the military's broad range of training and training facilities. This is especially true in the context of the recent downsizing of our armed forces. Temporarily, this means that many of these training facilities remain underutilized. Allowing civilians to access this training benefits both parties. The advantage to the military is that their training facilities and instructors can, as a result, maintain state-of-the-art standards.[26] I welcome the recent agreement among Canadian Forces Base Kingston, Queen's University and St. Lawrence College, among others, to utilize their combined expertise to mount training activities in the general electronics area.

This, too, is in the nature of resorting to creative new instruments that can serve to privilege Canadians and Canada in terms of achieving both economic competitiveness and social cohesion.

Conclusion

T HIS SELECTIVE OVERVIEW OF CANADA'S SOCIAL ENVELOPE AND HOW IT CAN BE
rendered more consistent with the dictates of the new global order has, in
some areas, emphasized the role new instruments can play in increasing access to
the human capital objective of the mission statement. In other areas of the social
envelope, the role of the knowledge/information explosion has been to propel social
programs into becoming essential economic and competitive platforms. These programs can no longer be constrained by limiting our vision of them solely to their
social roles: They have also become leading-edge human capital and competitive
institutions in a progressive GIR era. If we view them as such, we will make important strides toward developing, enhancing and employing in Canada the human
capital of our citizens. The exciting news is that by so contributing to the emerging
new-economy opportunities, these programs will also be much better positioned to
address the social needs of all Canadians in the new global order. Most important
of all, this revitalized approach to social Canada will serve to advance a reinvigorated vision of social cohesiveness which will be absolutely vital to complement
the many difficult decisions we will have to make on the economic front.

As a bridge to the following chapter dealing with economic policy, it is
instructive to recall that GIR has created a symbiotic relationship between the social
and economic spheres. For example, it is rather axiomatic that, other things equal,
the best social policy *at any given point in time* is an economy that is running flat out
on all cylinders, i.e., a rising tide lifts all boats. Relatedly, the best social policy, *over
time*, is an innovative and productive economy, since raising Canadians' living standards is all about increasing productivity. Phrased differently, there is little future for
a successful, societally cohesive, human-capital-based social envelope in the context of a failing or faltering national economy. And there is no prospect for a prosperous economic future unless we succeed on the human capital front.

Human Capital and
Canadian
Competitiveness

Introduction

WITH THE CANADIAN ECONOMY CURRENTLY RUNNING FLAT OUT, THE NOTION THAT Canada faces a severe competitive challenge because of the interplay of the forces associated with GIR may well fall on deaf ears. Indeed, the advocates of an all-is-well view can muster an impressive array of indicators to buttress their position. Inflation is running at post-war lows and is lower than that in the US. Canada was the first OECD country to tame its federal deficit and we are now in the third year of budget surpluses. Our exports to the US have literally mushroomed, which hardly heralds an uncompetitive Canadian economy. And our unemployment rate has fallen by half over the last six years. While it is true the unemployment rate remains stubbornly higher than that in the US, the evidence is that this relates more to structural issues than to competitiveness, *per se*. Where, then, is the problem or challenge on the economic/competitiveness front?

My response is two-fold. First, GIR is ushering in a new economic era that has the potential for both enormous opportunities and significant economic costs unless our economic policies become GIR-compatible. From this perspective, the challenge is future-oriented — *new policies and new instruments for a new global order*. A few examples are in order. We tend to downplay the fact that Canadian productivity lags the US by noting that the significant lag occurs only in two related industries — computers and information-related areas. *But this is the new economy!* Likewise, we tend to downplay the migration of Canadian "talent" to the US by noting that this high-profile "brain-drain" is more than offset by the "brain-gain" from immigration. Relatedly, we tend to ignore the reality that, at existing exchange rates (i.e., bargain-basement prices), innovative Canadian start-ups are easy prey for the Americans, frequently resulting in the transfer south of human capital, jobs and technology. Thus, the forward-looking perspective would recognize our ongoing achievements on the economic front. However, it would highlight the need to design policies in the face of the rapidly changing economic reality to ensure that Canada becomes a more attractive location for growing new economy firms into export platforms or home-based multinationals that would, in turn, allow us to employ in Canada our human capital and talent. Much of the ensuing analysis will focus on this forward-looking challenge.

The second concern would, beyond buying into the above perspective, emphasize that the very positive economic indicators referenced above paint far too rosy a picture of the Canadian economy in 2000. In particular, they mask a rather dramatic collapse in our standard of living relative to the Americans. Figure 7 shows the real purchasing power of adult Canadians, relative to adult Americans, reached a peak of near 84 percent in the late 1970s. By 1998, purchasing power had tumbled to a low of almost 70 percent. Figure 8 presents a 1998 snapshot of this standard of living gap. Canadian per capita income was $29,357. The comparable US per capita income (expressed in purchasing-power-parity Canadian dollars) was $36,840. And at the existing average exchange rate in 1998, the Americans enjoyed a per capita income (in Canadian dollars) of $46,712 — a $16,000+ difference! As this chapter was in the final editing stages, Industry Canada (2000) issued a study, *A Regional Perspective on the Canada-US Standard of Living Comparison*, which compares Canadian provinces and US states over the 1992-97 period. The results are sobering:

> A third of the states had a standard of living more than 25 percent higher than the Canadian average. In particularly high-income states, such as Delaware or Connecticut, the wealth gap was 50 percent...the best Canadian performer, Alberta, ranks 18th...while Ontario is in 37th place...British Columbia ranked 49th while Saskatchewan was 51st and Quebec 52nd. All other Canadian provinces ranked below Mississippi, the state with the lowest standard of living. (Toulin 2000)

Figure 9 contains the full regional picture in both countries (where the Purchasing Power Parity (PPP) exchange rate used to make the comparisons is 123 Canadian cents per US dollar).

Purchasing Power of
Total Real National Income per Adult,
Canada as a Percentage of
the United States, 1970-1998

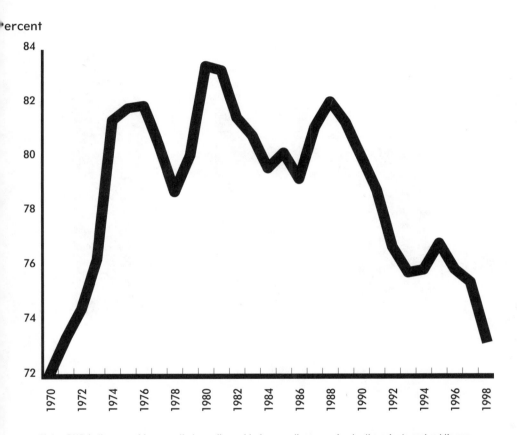

Note: GNP is the sum of incomes that are disposable for spending or saving by the private and public sectors after net payments to foreigners have been made — which is why it is called gross *national* product instead of gross *domestic* (territorial) product. It is deflated by the total domestic spending price index (TSPI), which is the average price Canadians pay for all the private and public consumption and investment goods and services they buy.

In national accounts terminology, the TSPI is the implicit price index for C+I+G, sometimes called the absorption price index. As in Figure 2 [in Fortin (1999)], based on Statistics Canada's bilateral comparisons of purchasing power, the ratio between Canadian and US real GNP per adult assumes that in 1992 it cost C$123 in Canada to purchase a representative basket of private and public consumption and investment goods worth US$100 in the United States.

Source: Statistics Canada, *National Income and Expenditure Accounts*, cat no. 13-201, various issues; United States, Department of Commerce, *Survey of Current Business*, various issues.

Reproduced from Fortin (1999), Figure 3.

Figure 8   210

The Standard of Living Gap

**Income per Capita in Canadian Dollars, 1998
US Conversion at Purchasing Power Parity
and at the Exchange Rate**

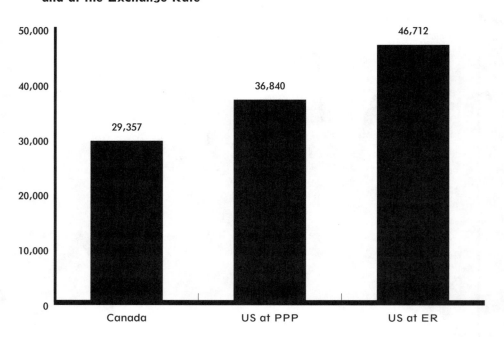

Source: Davenport (2000).

Figure 9

Standard of Living

Canadian Provinces, 1995-97
Canada = 100

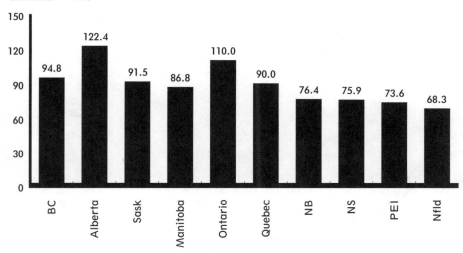

Source: Statistics Canada.

US Regions, 1995-97 Average
Canada = 100

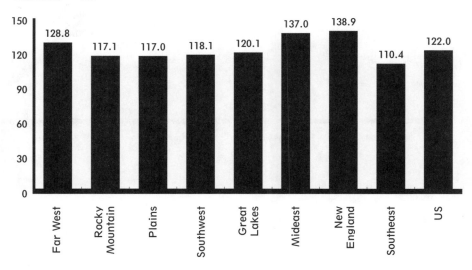

Source: Bureau of Economic Analysis, Bureau of
Labour Statistics and Statistics Canada.
Létourneau and Lajoie (2000), reproduced from
Industry Canada (2000, 5).

Figure 10 212

Canada's Share of Inward FDI Stock in North American 1985-1998*

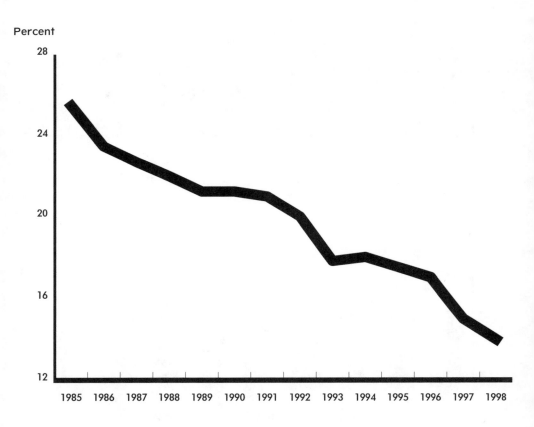

Percent

*   1997 and 1998 data for Mexico, adding flows to
    1996 stocks.

Source: World Investment Report 1999, Statistics
Canada, BEA, SCOFI

Reproduced from Sulzenko (2000).

Another way to look at the performance of the Canadian economy over the last decade or so is to focus on Canada's share of the inward flow of North American FDI (foreign direct investment). From Figure 10, our share has fallen from roughly 27 percent of total FDI in 1985 to 15 percent in 1998. Although we still receive a share of FDI larger than our GDP share, this is nonetheless a startling and troublesome graph, even if some of the downward trend represents the emergence of Mexico as a more favourable investment location.

These data ought to set off alarm bells in the corridors of economic policy decision making. It is not just that we significantly lag the US in terms of income levels, but our relative position is declining. And from the trend line in Figure 10, the prospects for the future are very worrisome. While these income differences are associated with the brain drain and productivity differences, they are beginning to show up in other ways as well. For example, Figure 11 reveals that the American public sector, on a purchasing power parity basis, now spends more per capita on health care than does the Canadian public sector. If we fail to narrow these gaps, the prospects are for a declining capacity to compete with the US on a variety of fronts, social policy included.

Why did this occur? The most convincing answer is that provided by Pierre Fortin in his seminal 1999 C.D. Howe Benefactor's Lecture, *The Canadian Standard of Living: Is There a Way Up?* Drawing from a copious body of evidence, Fortin mounts a persuasive case that we Canadians, relative to the Americans, are *underemployed*, *overtaxed* and *underproductive*. If these were problems associated with our past economic performance, they loom much larger in the GIR era. More to the point, they do not bode well for an effective implementation of the human capital mission statement.

Accordingly, the purpose of this chapter is to rethink Canada's economic policy to bring it onside with the innovation and dynamic requisites of the new global economic realities. The focus initially will be on the traditional macro policy indicators/instruments — fiscal policy, monetary policy and the exchange rate. This is followed by a brief set of principles designed to inform the remainder of the economic policy arsenal — trade, regulatory and industrial policy. By way of backdrop, I now direct attention to the manner in which GIR has influenced, and continues to influence, the underlying structure of the economy as it relates to growth, productivity and inflation.

Figure 11 214

Public Health Spending per Person
Is Higher in the US,
and the Gap Is Widening
(PPP data)

Public Sector Health Care Expenditures

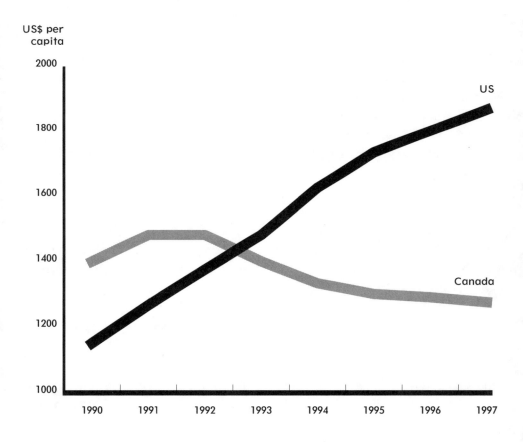

US$ per
capita

Source: OECD Health Data, 1999.
Supplied by Industry Canada.

GIR and the Economy: Let the Good Times Roll!

A S THE KNOWLEDGE/INFORMATION REVOLUTION PROGRESSIVELY SPREADS THROUGH the economy, the good news is that some of the traditional economic trade-offs (e.g., inflation vs. unemployment) will be significantly ameliorated, and the prospects are for a prolonged increase in productivity and growth. The potential downside is that those economies that do not "catch the GIR wave" will be subject to increasing competitive pressures from those economies that do. This important caveat aside, what are the nature of the structural changes in the underlying economic parameters (apart from those highlighted in Part II) that are being ushered in by GIR?

While the existing economics and policy literature abounds with insights relating to GIR-triggered changes in the economy, the most comprehensive overview is the March 2000 edition of Goldman Sachs' CEO newsletter, *Technology and the New Global Economy*. In what follows, I shall refer to this as "GS" (Goldman Sachs).

The first GS observation is that the taming of deficits everywhere and the shift toward an inflation-control strategy on the part of central banks have, in tandem, reduced the risk of having supply shocks derail economic performance. This can be phrased differently: We now have adequate flexibility on both the fiscal and monetary fronts to address these supply shocks. Either way, we are in a period of a new business cycle, one that will "reduce the variability of the economic cycle, while leaving both the long-run level of GDP — and its rate of growth — unchanged" (GS: 3).

The second GS observation relates to the labour market and, in particular, to NAIRU (the Non-Accelerating Inflation Rate of Unemployment) or, more colloquially, to the equilibrium rate of unemployment that is consistent with stable inflation. In a word, the advent of an information economy and the resulting greater labour-market flexibility has facilitated a decline in the NAIRU. This leads to "a permanently higher level of GDP, but only a temporarily higher growth rate for GDP" (GS: 3) as NAIRU shifts to its new value. While the precondition exists for a fall in NAIRU, this will not fully materialize if governments maintain policies that serve to rigidify labour markets.

While the reduction in the variability of business cycles and a permanently higher level of GDP are most welcome, the really exciting news in terms of future living standards arises from the third of the GS observations, namely the prospect for long-term productivity gains as the revolution in information technology takes hold across the economy. In effect, the information revolution has become what growth theorists refer to as a "general purpose technology" (GPT), which begins to transform production and distribution across the economy (Helpman 1998).

The last observation drawn from the GS newsletter relates to the role of the Internet on B2B (business-to-business) commerce. GS predicts that B2B commerce in the US "will rise from $39 billion in 1998 to $1,500 billion in 2004 — an annual growth rate of 84 percent" (GS: 5). This will be a "positive" supply shock since it will considerably reduce the price of business inputs (in line with the GPT transformation referred to in the previous paragraph). There is, of course, a danger that this could lead to deflation. However, if monetary authorities react by maintaining low and stable inflation, the result "should boost long-run GDP by almost five percent in industrialized countries" (GS: 5). All in all, tremendous potential news on the economic front.

However, it is worth emphasizing that the GS view is that thus far only the US economy is well positioned to take advantage of these dramatic opportunities. How does Canada ensure that it catches this wave? I shall deal in turn with the implications for tax policy, debt reduction, monetary policy and the exchange rate.

Taxation and GIR

THE IMPLICATIONS FLOWING FROM GIR FOR TAXATION ARE STRAIGHTFORWARD economically, although difficult politically. Taxes on mobile factors of production must be reduced at least to rates comparable to those which characterize those of our major trading partners, particularly the US, and reduced below those levels for areas like corporate income taxes if we wish to establish a first-mover advantage. To a degree, this is not a particularly novel recommendation: Key aspects of Canada's tax policy have long been influenced by American rates and levels. However, GIR has altered this traditional relationship in two distinct ways.

First, the definition of which factors are "mobile" increasingly includes the upper echelons of *human* capital, especially given the easy access to TN (Trade-NAFTA) temporary visas under NAFTA. In other words, as the prospects for "exit" (by enterprises or human capital) and for "by-pass" (by shifting profits of a multinational toward low-tax countries) become not only more available but also more commonplace, high tax rates on mobile factors become increasingly problematic.

The second development is that country after country is reacting to GIR by cutting taxes. Yet over the recent past, Canada has, if anything, gone the other way. One example will suffice. The Saskatchewan Personal Income Tax Review Committee's (1999) Final Report noted that had there been full indexing for inflation from 1988 onward, the value of the various thresholds/deductions in 1999 would have been as follows (with the actual values in parenthesis): basic exemption, $8,072 ($6,794); spousal exemption, $7,399 ($5,718); 26 percent threshold, $36,990 ($26,590); and 29 percent threshold, $73,981 ($59,180). Hence, the result of this inflation-related "bracket creep" has been quite dramatic. Specifically, the 2000 federal budget (which reinstated indexation and essentially adopted the values suggested in the Saskatchewan Report) puts tax saving for citizens for year 2004-05 at over $6 billion. In other words, this lack of indexation was effectively equivalent to significant *increases in tax rates* on real (after-inflation) income. On this count, then, taxes have been rising in Canada, not falling. This is part and parcel of Fortin's claim that Canadians are "overtaxed" and, as a result, their after-tax incomes are falling relative to similarly situated Americans.

An important aside is in order here. To prevent a "race to the bottom" in terms of the taxation of highly mobile factors, interest has grown in many quarters for a minimum "global" corporate tax.[27] Indeed, as part of Rodrik's approach to ensure that international economic integration does not lead to domestic social disintegration, his first proposal related to the introduction of a global tax on mobile factors (see Chapter 6). Similarly, Breton (1990) noted that while Margaret Thatcher's interest in a single European market was presumably related to the gains from trade, François Mitterrand was probably more interested in the existence of a pan-European authority that could then levy a tax on capital. Thus, the income distribution implications of a global minimum tax on mobile factors would be such as to ameliorate the tendency for the costs of GIR to be borne largely by immobile factors. Since this is, thus far at least, beyond our reach, we need to pursue other ways that ensure the costs of GIR are borne more equally across citizens. And in the present context, it means that Canada cannot avoid being influenced by US tax rates on mobile factors.

Continuing with some specifics relating to the taxation of mobile factors, two further caveats are in order. First, it is important to distinguish between the *tax rate* issue on the one hand and the *tax mix* or *tax structure* issue on the other. As already noted, much of what follows will argue that tax rates on mobile factors need to be reduced. I refer to this as the *tax-rate* issue. Without compensating changes, this will likely lead to a fall in the overall level of taxation. But it need not, since compensating tax rate increases could be levied on *other* tax bases. This is the *tax-mix* issue. Phrased differently, a reduction in the tax rates on mobile factors need not imply an overall decline in tax revenues or, by extension, a decline in public services. In general, the message emanating from the dictates of GIR is that tax rates on income should fall relative to tax rates on consumption.

This reference to increasing taxes on consumption leads to the second caveat. In a GIR era, the most appropriate tax is one that is export and import neutral. This characteristic is clearly associated with a VAT (value-added-tax), Canada's version being the GST. Exports are exempt from the GST and we apply the GST to all imports, thereby guaranteeing both export and import neutrality. (It is important to note that we should also apply the GST to cross-border shopping since it is a domestic tax, not a tariff.) If we want a larger government sector than the Americans, and we clearly do, then the GST is an ideal tax in an increasingly competitive world. Surprisingly, however, the GST has not found favour with Canada's social policy advocates. To be fair to them, their concern is largely focused on the regressivity of the GST. Some, but not all, of this concern can be addressed via a larger GST tax credit as well as the many other tax provisions which have lightened the tax load on the lower-income classes, or via increased deductions and credits that have progressively moved more lower-income Canadians off the PIT rolls. Nonetheless, the general message is that the GST is the most GIR-compatible tax. And the specific message to the provinces is to follow the lead of Quebec and three of the four Atlantic provinces in integrating their Provincial Sales Taxes into a VAT or GST framework.

In addressing the taxation issue, I shall mingle analytical perspectives with the policy initiatives contained in the 2000 federal budget. This 2000 federal budget is an important bellwether: It was the first budget directly geared to the

era of surpluses, and it had as its goal the reform of the income tax system, both
personal and corporate.

Business Taxation[28]

Since capital is by far the most mobile of factors, the initial priority needs to
be directed to Canada's corporate income tax system. Table 12, reproduced
from Mintz (1999) presents clear and stark evidence that Canada is way offside our trading partners in terms of our corporate tax rates. Of the 16 countries in the table, only Japan has a higher corporate tax rate than does Canada,
48 percent vs. 43.3 percent, where the Canadian figures include the average
provincial corporate income tax. Table 13, also reproduced from Mintz, provides a breakdown for manufacturing and services (the focus here is on effective tax rates, as distinct from the statutory rates in Table 12). For
manufacturing, the above observation still holds — only Japan has a higher
manufacturing corporate tax rate than does Canada, among G-7 countries. For
services industries, however, which account for most of the recent employment growth, Canada's corporate rates are the highest in the G-7, fully 11 percentage points above US corporate rates. This is patently absurd policy in a
GIR era, and for two conceptually distinct reasons.

First, for firms operating across borders, incentives exist, via transfer pric-
ing among other instruments, to register profits in, or transfer profits to, lower-
tax jurisdictions, and to register deductions in Canada (where they generate a
larger offset). In effect, taxable income "migrates" and, therefore, significantly
reduces Canadian tax revenues for any given level of economic activity:

> Ireland, with an average corporate income tax rate that is less than one-third
> the rate in Canada [see Table 12], collects more corporate tax revenue as a per-
> centage of gross domestic product (GDP) than Canada. In other words, in
> Ireland corporate profits as a percentage of GDP are at least three times the
> level in Canada. (Mintz 1999: 5)

Phrased differently, competitive corporate tax rates may well *increase* Canada's
corporation tax revenues!

This Irish example also incorporates, to a degree, the second reason:
Canada's high corporate tax rates not only inhibit the inflow of new capital but
also provide incentives for existing Canadian firms to expand elsewhere.
Moreover, high taxes undervalue Canadian firms and, in effect, provide an

Table 12 220

Statutory Corporate Income Tax Rates, Selected OECD Countries, 1996 and 1999

	Corporate Income Tax Rate			
	July 31, 1996	January 1, 1999	Direction of Change	Intention (Year)
	(percent)			
Australia	36.0	36.0	no change	30.0 (2001)
Canada[a]	34.9/43.2	35.0/43.3	no change	
Denmark	34.0	32.0	lower	
France	41.7	36.7/40.0[b]	lower	36.7 (2000)
Germany	56.1	51.9[c]	lower	35.0 - 38.0 (2000)[d]
Ireland	10.0/38.0	10.0/28.0	lower	12.5 (2003)
Italy	53.2	31.3/41.3[e]	lower	
Japan	52.2	48.0	lower	
Netherlands	37.0/35.0	35.0	lower	
Norway	28.0	28.0	no change	
Poland	40.0	34.0	lower	22.0 (2004)
Sweden	28.0	28.0	no change	
Switzerland	35.5	25.1	lower	
Turkey	44.0	33.0	lower	
United Kingdom	33.0	30.0[f]	lower	
United States[g]	39.2	39.2	no change	

a   The rate is a combination of the federal corporate income tax rate (22.1 percent and 29.1 percent, respectively, for manufacturing and others) and the average of provincial corporate income tax rates weighted by provincial GDP by industry. The minor difference between the two years reflects some changes in provincial corporate income tax rates.

b   The rate is a combination of the corporate income tax rate of 33 1/3 percent and surtaxes of 10 percent and 20 percent, respectively. The lower surtax is applied to smaller-scale firms owned mainly by individuals. For 2000 and future years, the lower rate will apply to all firms. See Ernst & Young (1999b) for details.

c   Estimate based on Ernst & Young (1999b). It includes a corporate income tax rate of 40 percent, an average trade rate of 16.75 percent (ranging from 13 percent to 20.5 percent) that is deductible for corporate income tax purposes, and a surcharge of 5.5 percent on corporate income tax payable.

d   The higher rate includes the current solidarity surcharge of 5.5 percent on the assessed corporate tax, which was not included in the latest government proposal for tax reduction. See Ernst & Young (1999a).

e   The higher rate of 41.3 percent includes a general corporate income tax rate of 37 percent and a regional tax of 4.25 percent that is levied on Italian-source income from productive activities, which includes interest payments and labour costs. The general corporate income tax rate may be reduced to 19 percent for qualifying taxable income corresponding to the ordinary remuneration (currently 7 percent) of the net equity increase. However, the average corporate income tax rate for a company may not fall below 27 percent, which, combined with the regional tax rate of 4.25 percent, results in the lower aggregated income tax rate of 31.3 percent.

f   Effective as of April 1, 1999.

g   Estimate based on an average state corporate income tax rate of 6.5 percent (ranging from 1.0 percent to 12 percent).

Reproduced from Mintz (1999, Table 1).

Effective Tax Rates for Domestic Firms in G-7 Countries, 1996, 1999, and 2000

	Manufacturing			Services		
	1996	**1999**	**Proposed 2000**	**1996**	**1999**	**Proposed 2000**
Canada	25.2	25.2	n.a.	33.4	33.4	n.a.
United States	22.6	22.4	n.a.	22.8	22.6	n.a.
United Kingdom	19.8	17.7	n.a.	19.4	17.3	n.a.
Germany	36.9	32.8	20.0	35.8	31.8	19.6
France	25.2	24.4	22.7	27.9	27.0	25.4
Italy[a]	31.2	24.2/17.9	n.a.	35.3	28.0/21.3	n.a.
Japan	31.2	27.6	n.a.	32.8	29.2	n.a.

a The lower effective tax rates are a result of the lower combined corporate income tax rate of 31.3 percent as explained in Mintz, Table 1.
Reproduced from Mintz (1999, Table 2).

invitation for foreign takeovers and foreign relocation which, as already noted, are running at worrying levels. This is woefully inappropriate policy in a GIR era:

> At present, Canada provides few advantages to businesses to create jobs in this country for its well-trained labour force. The "brain drain" will simply follow the "jobs drain" to the United States. (3)

Phrased in a more positive manner, Canada needs GIR-compatible corporate tax rates in order to create in Canada a uniquely attractive domestic environment for growing and maintaining home-based competitive global enterprises. With these home-based multinationals will come the high-value-added jobs (advertising, legal, accounting, finance, computing, R&D etc.) that will reward our investment in the human capital of Canadians.

By way of recommendations for corporate income taxation, Mintz draws from the 1998 *Report of the Technical Committee on Business Taxation* (of which he was Chair) and offers the following set of proposals:

> Canada should undertake a business tax strategy to create a significant advantage for itself in the North American market. Canada may have a relatively small market, but it also has a relatively good pool of educated workers and a stable political environment. Moreover, Canada could offer a significantly better business tax system than that of the United States and at little cost, since business tax cuts, unlike personal tax cuts, are not expensive for the federal or provincial governments.
>   Specifically, we should consider the following strategy:
> ◆ Reduce the general corporate income tax rate from 43 percent to 30 percent by 2004. This would put Canada's level below the average OECD rate and substantially below that in the United States.
> ◆ Broaden the tax base to make the business tax system simpler and more efficient. At the same time, revenues from base broadening would reduce the revenue loss faced by governments so that no more than 2 billion (a conservative estimate) would be needed to cut corporate income taxes. This loss in revenue would be small compared with the loss resulting from personal income tax cuts.
> ◆ Reduce the reliance on inefficient profit-insensitive taxes such as property and capital taxes. Governments should instead impose taxes that are more closely in line with the services provided to businesses. This includes making payroll taxes more closely related to the benefits workers receive from programs these taxes fund. (Mintz 1999: 9-10)

I strongly support these recommendations; I also support Mintz's call for urgency in getting more competitive corporate tax rates. The fact of the matter is that, to borrow a pet phrase from Finance Minister Paul Martin, "come hell or high water" we will eventually have to get our corporate tax rates down to competitive levels. But if we are foolish enough to delay this day of reckoning, we will ultimately have these lower rates but without the "early-mover" advantage. While the politics of implementing a first-mover strategy on the corporate tax front may be difficult (although less so in this era of budget surpluses), the economics would clearly be positive, particularly in terms of generating home-based multinationals and, therefore, fostering the "employ in Canada" tenet of the human capital mission statement.

In his 2000 federal budget, which as already noted presents a blueprint for federal tax reform in the era of budget surpluses, Finance Minister Paul Martin did commit to reducing the federal corporate tax rate from 28 percent to 21 percent over the five-year tax horizon. However, the two-year legislative framework pursuant to the budget was limited to reducing corporate taxes from 28 percent to 27 percent, leaving the remainder of the corporate tax cut until later in the five-year period (and for illustrative purposes, the budget assumes that this will be implemented in year five). Tables 14 and 15 present overviews of the five-year framework and the two-year legislative program, respectively.

This action agenda (Table 15) on the corporate tax front clearly falls into the proverbial "too little, too late" category. In the words of one perceptive critic, backloading the corporate tax cuts in year five means the corporate tax-reduction plan is operating on "government time," whereas business today runs on "Internet time." Ottawa's approach to corporate tax reduction is especially surprising since the "tax costs" of corporate rate reductions are small, as noted in the earlier quote from Mintz. Indeed if Ireland is an appropriate example, there may well be an *increase* in corporate revenues. Along the lines of Mintz's earlier comments, the appropriate policy in a GIR era would have been to reduce Canadian corporate rates *well below* US corporate rates in order to give Canada a first-mover advantage in terms of maintaining, attracting and growing domestic multinationals, let alone in attracting foreign investment. With substantial US corporate tax reductions just around the corner, we are sure to find ourselves in an increasingly non-competitive position on the corporate side. We will then run the serious risk of becoming an "incubator" economy for US and other foreign multinationals and, in the process, we will erode our ability to grow big business within Canada and, in terms of the mission statement,

Table 14 224

Five-Year Tax Reduction Plan

Areas for action	Actions proposed to be implemented over the next five years	Amount of annual tax relief in 2004-05 (millions of dollars)
Eliminate automatic increases in the tax burden due to inflation	• Immediately restore full indexation of the tax system effective January 1, 2000	See below
	• Increase the amount of income Canadians can earn tax-free to at least $8,000 for the basic personal amount and at least $6,800 for the spousal/equivalent-to-spouse amount	2,760[1]
Reduce the high tax burden at the middle income level	• Reduce to 23-percent the 26-percent middle tax rate	3,600
	• Increase the level of income at which the middle tax rate begins to apply from $29,590 to at least $35,000	2,940[1]
	• Increase the level of income at which the top tax rate begins to apply from $59,180 to at least $70,000	730[1]
	• Eliminate the 5-percent surtax	865
Increase support for children	• Increase support for children under the Canada Child Tax Benefit over the course of the next five years, with maximum benefits rising to $2,400 for the first child	2,525[1]
Make the Canadian economy more internationally competitive	• Reduce the corporate income tax rate by 7 percentage points to 21 percent from 28 percent on business income not currently eligible for special tax treatment	2,995
	• Reduce the capital gains inclusion rate from three-quarters to two-thirds	295
	• Postpone taxation of gains on shares acquired under qualifying stock options to when shares are sold rather than when options are exercised	75
	• Allow tax-free rollover of capital gains on qualified investments from one small business to another	75
Other	• Technical measures including other indexation	780[1]
Total		17,640
Of which indexation contributes		6,215

1 Amounts include indexation, based on assumed annual inflation rate of 1.8 percent.
Source: Martin (2000, Table 4.1).

will also erode our ability to "employ in Canada" our human capital. In a word, the approach to corporate taxation in the 2000 federal budget falls well short of being GIR compatible.

On the encouraging side, Finance Minister Martin appears, post-budget, to recognize that there is an urgency here, and he is attempting to assuage concerns by promising a much faster implementation schedule, presumably driven in part by a larger-than-expected budget surplus. While the Department of Finance under Paul Martin has deservedly earned enormous credibility in terms of fiscal issues, the major concern is that Martin's days as finance Minister may be numbered and that the Liberal cabinet is nowhere near as committed as Martin is to following up on these corporate tax reductions. Stay tuned.

Personal Income Taxation
From an international perspective, both upper-middle- and high-level human capital are subject to marginal tax rates that are too high. It is not only that Canada's top marginal tax rates are in the 50 percent range, well above comparable top marginal tax rates in the US, but, as important, that these top marginal rates take effect in Canada at a taxable income below $70,000, even after reflecting the provisions in the 2000 federal budget, whereas the (much lower) top marginal rate in the US takes effect at an income level not far off $400,000 (C$). Moreover, the steep increase in marginal tax rates from the lowest to the middle tax bracket — from 17 percent to 26 percent for the federal rate and from 25.5 percent to 39 percent for the average combined federal-provincial rate (which begins to bite at taxable income levels in the $30,000 range) — has long been recognized as inappropriate. Indeed, part of the original rationale for the introduction of the GST in 1989 was to reduce the middle tax bracket to 24 percent from 26 percent. For various reasons, this reduction did not materialize. The result is that marginal tax rates near 40 percent (federal plus provincial) for taxable incomes in the $30,000 range and 50 percent for incomes as low as $70,000 represent an open invitation for Canada's best and brightest to ply their skills in more favourable tax climes. The traditional Canadian response to this, namely that our system of medicare and lifestyle generally are an important offset to the appeal of lower tax rates elsewhere, particularly south of the border, rings rather hollow since these high-human-capital Canadians will presumably have access

Table 15

Summary of Budget 2000 Tax Measures

Areas for action	Actions proposed to be legislated through the 2000 budget	Amount annually in 2004 (millions)
Eliminate automatic increases in the tax burden due to inflation	• Restore full indexation to the tax system effective January 1, 2000	See below
	• Indexation is expected to result in increases to the amount of income Canadians can earn tax-free to about $8,000 for the basic personal amount and $6,800 for the spousal/equivalent-to-spouse amount	2,015 [1]
Reduce the high tax burden at the middle-income level	• Reduce to 24 percent the 26-percent tax rate effective July 1, 2000	2,410
	• Increase the level of income at which the middle tax rate begins to apply from $29,500 to $32,000	1,885 [1]
	• Increase the level of income at which the top tax rate begins to apply from $59,180 to $64,000	300 [1]
	• Eliminate the 5-percent deficit reduction surtax for incomes up to about $85,000 effective July 1, 2000, and reduce the 5-percent surtax rate to 4 percent on the tax payable on incomes above that level effective January 1, 2001	365

Increase support for children	• Increase the maximum Canada Child Tax Benefit:
	  - to $2,056 by July 1, 2000, from $1,805
	  - to $2,265 by July 1, 2001
	• Increase benefits to middle-income taxpayers through:
	  - increases to the base benefit; and
	  - increases to the level of income at which benefits begin to be reduced
		2,175 [1]

Make the Canadian economy more internationally competitive	• Reduce the corporate income tax rate to 27 percent from 28 percent on business income not currently eligible for special tax treatment, effective January 1, 2001	455
	• Reduce the corporate income tax rate to 21 percent effective January 1, 2001, on active business income between $200,000 and $300,000 earned by a small business	100
	• Reduce the capital gains inclusion rate from three-quarters to two-thirds	295
	• Postpone taxation of gains on shares acquired under qualifying stock options to when shares are sold rather than when options are exercised	75
	• Allow tax-free rollover of capital gains on qualified investments from one small business to another	75
Other	• Technical measures including other indexation	780 [1]
Total		10,930
Of which indexation contributes		6,215

1 Amounts include indexation, based on an assumed annual inflation rate of 1.8 percent.
Source: Martin (2000, Table 4.2).

part IV

through their jobs to excellent health care and associated benefits. Admittedly, while easing the tax load on human capital is only part of the solution to generating an environment where talented Canadians are encouraged to remain in Canada, it is nonetheless an integral part.

In this context, it is instructive to reintroduce the "brain-drain" issue. As I interpret the data, the evidence of a wholesale exodus is simply not there. What is true is that many of the brightest young Canadians are migrating, as are many of those classified as "talent." Suppose this latter category applies only to the top one percent of Canadian income earners. Nortel's CEO John Roth has pointed out (McCarthy 2000), however, this top one percent of income filers (those earning more than $150,000) paid 16 percent of all federal income taxes. Moreover, if these individuals exit, or even a significant number of them do, the likelihood is that they will also take their jobs with them. This tax base is already threatened since, as Roth notes, only 27 out of 160 of Nortel's executives who could choose to live in Canada actually do so. A recent article in the National Post notes, along similar lines,

> Pushed by high taxes and concern over the fate of the Canadian dollar, some of British Columbia's top biotechnology companies are relocating big chunks of their operations south of the border.... So far, the list includes ID Biomedical Corp., Stressben Biotechnologies Corp., and NeuroVir Thereapeutics Inc. (Greenwood 2000)

By way of illustrating the tax differences between BC and Washington State, the article goes on to note,

> The top marginal tax rate in Washington State is just 27 percent and that kicks in at US$250,000. You have to earn a lot of income before you pay 27 percent...
> Compounding the compensation issue is the problem of health care. Senior US executives...have access to the best medical care in the world.

Given that this exodus of jobs and enterprise is unlikely to be reversible, there is an urgency in terms of implementing more compatible tax treatment with the US in order to advance the "employ in Canada" aspect of the mission statement. Delaying the advent of more GIR-consistent tax policy will mean that our resulting diminished economic base will affect our ability to implement the social objectives of the mission statement.

How did the 2000 budget fare in terms of personal income tax reform? The first observation in this direction is that, thanks to the personal income tax provisions, the budget proved so popular with the majority of Canadians that it elicited only one comment in Question Period, after which the opposition refocused their attention on the then-ongoing Human Resources Department fiasco. A large part of the reason for the groundswell of approval for the budget was that, somewhat unexpectedly, Paul Martin indexed the personal income tax system for inflation. Moreover, he did this in a manner that effectively restored the personal and spousal exemptions as well as the thresholds for the tax brackets to those levels that would have prevailed had Canada not abandoned full indexing in the late 1980s. Moreover, as indicated in Table 14, Martin proposed to reduce the middle-income tax rate to 23 percent from 26 percent, with a legislated commitment (Table 15) of an immediate reduction to 24 percent on July 1, 2000. These provisions are not only welcome but also long overdue.

As welcome as full indexation is, it addresses domestic income distribution much more than international competitiveness. My published (2000a) reaction to the 2000 federal budget was that it was a classic "Paul Martin, Sr." budget, one fully attuned to low- and middle-income-distribution concerns within the context of a largely closed economy. Admittedly, this is a bit unfair since the budget did take some initiatives at the high end of the income spectrum. Specifically, the five-year blueprint (Table 14) proposes to eliminate the five percent federal surtax (although the Table 15 "action plan" removed it only for middle-income Canadians); it reduced the capital gains inclusion rate to 66 percent from 75 percent; and, very significantly, it placed the taxation of stock options on a basis comparable to that in the US. These provisions became applicable as of July 1, 2000. By way of elaboration on the stock-option provision, our pre-existing approach was to levy the tax once these options were exercised (i.e., converted into shares). Henceforth however, the tax will apply only after the shares themselves have been sold, as in the US. The reason for labelling this as "very significant" is that a substantial portion of the remuneration of high-level human capital now takes the form of stock options — in some high-tech firms, estimates run as high as 40 percent in terms of the share of equity that relates to stock options. Thus, this is a major factor in the migration of talent to the US. Hopefully, the 2000 federal budget will have levelled this aspect of the playing field.

The bottom line, however, is that the top marginal tax rate has been left intact. At the best of times, it is politically difficult to reduce top marginal rates, and even more so at a time when aspects of our social infrastructure are perceived to be threatened. In this sense, Mr. Martin lost a valuable window of opportunity in terms of decreasing top marginal rates in the context of a budget that was loaded with goodies for low- and middle-tax-rate Canadians (including an increase in the CCTB to $2,400 per child as indicated in Table 14).

There is, however, another far-reaching implication of the 2000 federal budget. By delaying meaningful corporate tax rate reduction and by maintaining the existing top marginal tax rate and only slightly increasing the threshold at which this top rate applies, the federal budget effectively sent the following message to selected provinces: Our focus in the 2000 budget has largely been a social policy focus; if you are concerned with the competitiveness or wealth-creation aspects of the income tax system, feel free to alter your own tax structures accordingly. And they have!

The Provinces and Income Taxation

Under the new tax-on-income regime for the personal income tax (see Chapter 5 or, for more detail, Courchene, 1999b), the provinces are free to design their own rate and bracket structures for their portion of the PIT. As noted, Alberta was quick off the mark in introducing a flat tax or a single-rate tax of 11 percent, more recently reduced to 10.5 percent.[29] As part of this proposal, Alberta increased the personal exemptions from the existing value of roughly $7,000 to nearly $12,000; it also set the spousal exemption at this level. This served to remove a goodly number of Albertans from the tax rolls and lent a significant degree of progressivity to the flat tax, especially at the lower end. However, the principal beneficiaries, dollar-wise, are high-income Albertans.

The important point to note here is that the maximum combined (federal-provincial) top marginal rate in Alberta will now be 39.5 percent (29 percent federal plus 10.5 percent Alberta), absent federal surcharges. (Alberta also removed all of its previous surcharges.) Faced with competitive concerns from its neighbouring province, Saskatchewan reduced its three tax rates to 11 percent, 13 percent and 15 percent. While high-income tax filers face a higher marginal rate in Saskatchewan, the province offset this somewhat by increasing to $100,000 the income threshold where its highest rate takes affect.

Surprisingly, to me at least, Ontario did not react to the "Alberta Advantage" in its 2000 budget. This was in part, presumably, because the Harris government since coming to power in 1995 had already reduced Ontario's personal income tax rate by

nearly 40 percent. In its 2000 provincial budget (Eves 2000), Ontario adopted the following five tax brackets (where the top two reflect the impact of the province's significant surcharge (i.e., the Fair Share Health Care Levy): 6.20 percent, 9.24 percent,
11.09 percent, 13.35 percent and 17.41 percent. In terms of *marginal* tax rates, these
data suggest that the two lowest income classes in Ontario will be better off than similarly situated individuals or families in Alberta. However, this is not likely to carry
over to *average* tax rates, since the Alberta system has much larger exemptions than
Ontario (roughly $12,000 in Alberta and just over $7,000 in Ontario).

This is unlikely to be the last word on PIT reform from Ontario. Apart from
some provocative initiatives dealt with below, Ontario has promised to review its
major healthcare surcharge in its 2001 budget. My hunch is that it will have to reduce
its top marginal rates in response to not only Alberta but also neighbouring US states.

However, Ontario did move aggressively on the corporate income tax front.
The province's current rate for general corporate income taxation is 15.5 percent
and the rate on manufacturing and processing is 13.5 percent. Effective January 1,
2001, both rates will be reduced by 1.5 percentage points — to 14 percent and 12
percent, respectively. Over a six-year period, both rates will fall to eight percent. On
the small business side, the preferential eight percent rate will eventually fall to four
percent, and in the process the income threshold for qualification will be doubled.
There is no doubt that this is primarily a competitive or wealth-creating initiative.
In his budget speech, Ontario Finance Minister Ernie Eves comments on the corporate tax rate reductions as follows:

> [Ontario's corporate tax] will be the lowest general corporate rate in Canada.
> When our tax cut is fully in place, the Ontario and federal corporate income
> tax will also be more than 10 percentage points lower than the average of that
> of the US Great Lakes' states, our biggest competitors for businesses and
> jobs.... I challenge the federal government to match our reductions and make
> us the most competitive jurisdiction in North America. (Eves 2000: 26)

It is important to note that all provinces except Nova Scotia have also
reduced their PIT rates, but none came close to Alberta on the PIT side or to
Ontario on the CIT side.

Implications

The implications of these provincial tax cuts are incredibly far reaching and not
all of them are salutary. Let me begin by noting that these provincial initiatives

can be fully rationalized in the context of emerging economic region-states. If Ottawa has the apparent luxury of focusing primarily on social rather than wealth-creation priorities, selected provinces have no such luxury if they are to prevent their jobs and companies from migrating south. Alberta, of course, has the added fiscal flexibility arising from skyrocketing oil prices, at times exceeding $50 per barrel, so that no other province could hope to match it on the taxation front. Were Alberta to put in place a provincial sales tax, it could then contemplate significant further cuts in income taxation, both corporate and personal. Indeed, it appears that Alberta is about to follow Ontario down the path to corporate income tax reductions.

The second obvious implication is that Alberta and Ontario will become preferred locations for enterprise and employment within Canada. And if the polls are correct, British Columbia's government-in-waiting will ensure that BC joins the other two "have" provinces in terms of generating competitive income tax rates. However, not all provinces are able fiscally or oriented philosophically to follow suit. Therefore, the prospect looms of substantial disparities across provinces in terms of tax rates and, by extension, of growth rates. Of particular importance here is that the generalized tax-cutting across provinces will lower the overall equalization standard.[30] Even if the "have" provinces experience higher growth rates, this will not likely prevent the equalization standard from falling. It is not difficult to foresee that Ottawa, already in a social policy/redistributive role, will feel compelled to enrich the equalization program. This will generate a fascinating internal dynamic — Ottawa abandons wealth creation which is then taken up by the "have" provinces which, in turn, forces Ottawa yet further in terms of a redistributional role, this time across provinces via equalization.

Beyond this, Ottawa is now in the catbird's seat, as it were. Assuming the income tax cuts in Alberta and Ontario do generate an increase in enterprise, jobs and income, Ottawa will reap an even larger share of the overall resulting tax revenues, since its tax rates have remained relatively intact. However, the provinces should really become more important players, not less important players, in the overall tax game, since it is their expenditures on health, education and the like that will surely be under pressure to expand. In other words, the fiscal balance between Ottawa and the provinces is moving in the wrong direction in terms of the principle of fiscal coincidence (i.e., the jurisdiction responsible for spending should also have responsibility for raising the revenues in the first place). It is virtually axiomatic that the "have" provinces will now move into high gear in terms of pressing for major income tax cuts at the federal level.

Another implication is now that the PIT system is on a tax-on-income basis, the Quebec/rest-of-the-provinces anomaly on the tax front will become the focus of attention: Quebec receives an additional 16.5 personal-income-tax points (where a personal income tax point equals one percent of federal income tax revenues collected in that province) than do the other nine provinces.[31] To be sure, all provinces could have opted for these tax points in the 1960s, but only Quebec did. Ottawa can claim this offer has long expired, but the issue will surely be resurrected, especially by the "have" provinces. If Ottawa holds the line on these additional tax-point transfers, and if further tax cuts at the provincial level become problematic in terms of their revenue needs, this will serve to focus the provinces' attentions on some of the underlying parameters of the tax structure, such as the definition of income for tax purposes. This is exactly what Ontario has done.

The 2000 Ontario budget ratchets the federal-provincial tax implications upward a further notch or two. Specifically, Ontario Finance Minister Eves' proposals included: a) an Ontario inclusion rate for capital gains that would fall from the current 75 percent to 50 percent (whereas Ottawa's reduction is only to 66.67 percent); b) an Ontario Research Employee Stock Option Deduction which would exempt from tax the first $100,000 of any resulting income in each year; and c) an Ontario Focused Flow-Through Share Program (OFFTS) which would privilege investment in flow-through shares beyond the existing federal preferences. *All of these proposed measures alter the definition of income for personal income taxation.* Ontario expects the newly created tax collection agency (the Canada Customs and Revenue Agency, CCRA) will collect these taxes for Ontario as part of the revised approach to the tax collection agreements. The implicit, if not explicit, threat is that if the CCRA does not agree to accommodate Ontario, the province will then launch its own, separate, PIT system along Quebec lines, under which it would be free to define income for Ontario tax purposes as it wished. If this happens, the Canadian model of a decentralized yet harmonized PIT system will begin to unravel as other provinces follow Ontario's lead.

While this may be viewed as a collective, federal-provincial negative-sum game, it is nonetheless the case that this is also the ongoing reality. As provinces reach their limit in terms of how much they can decrease tax rates, they will, of necessity, begin to focus on selective tax-base changes that encourage investment, jobs and income in their respective provinces. The underlying problem here is that Ottawa has largely ignored the competitive implications of PIT and CIT reform in favour of internal income-distributional priorities and, in effect, forced the provinces to enact their own competitive measures to protect their economic interests within an integrated North America. In this important sense, the 2000 federal budget was woefully inadequate as a taxation blueprint for a GIR era. Federal Finance has a brief window of opportunity to unwind this error of not reducing top marginal rates and to fast-track the corporate tax cuts. If they let this window pass, the provinces (the "have" provinces in particular) will unwind our prototype of a decentralized and harmonized income tax system. In any event, since income taxation is a prerogative of *both* levels of government under the Constitution, the time has probably come for joint federal-provincial decision making on the income tax front.

The underlying message in terms of taxation is that Canada needs to lower the top marginal tax rates for mobile factors. In this sense, one has to be thankful that the provinces are responding to the challenge. However, the likely resulting distributional and growth implications of transferring the responsibility for tax competitiveness to the provinces will surely come back to haunt us, especially if in the process we drift into a morass of interprovincial tax competition that will undermine the internal economic union and eventually the social union as well. The much preferable approach would have been for the federal government to take the lead here. There is still time for this.

GIR and the Tax Structure

Assume that Canada's tax structure was "optimal" in terms of the dictates of the old paradigm. Now assume that we are in the new GIR paradigm where selected factors have become much more mobile. For any given amount of revenue to be raised, the optimal tax structure has shifted in the direction of lowering tax rates on these mobile factors and raising them on other tax bases, presumably with compensatory changes elsewhere in the policy envelope to address the overall equity issue. If there exists a fiscal surplus, or if one wants to cut taxes in any event, then the obvious approach is to lower the tax rate on mobile factors and to leave other tax rates unchanged. However, this implies, for example, that if the fiscal surplus is only $1 billion, then one is limited to a similar-sized tax cut. But this is the wrong way to approach the tax-structure issue, i.e., limiting changes in the direction of generating a GIR compatible tax structure to the amount of the discretionary budget surplus is a red herring. Tax rates can be altered across tax bases consistent with any desired overall revenue goal.

By way of addressing the proposition that the tax structure should shift away from taxing mobile sources and toward taxing consumption, it is instructive to introduce the notion of the marginal excess burden (MEB) of taxes. The MEB is defined as the "loss of real output which results from the distorting effects of another dollar of taxation on the economy" (Harris 1999b: 7). Table 16 presents MEB estimates for Canada for four tax bases. As the data indicate, raising an extra dollar from corporate income taxation decreases real output by $1.55, and the MEB is 56 cents for personal income taxes. Thus, since a dollar of personal income taxation decreases private spending by a dollar and decreases output by 56 cents, this would justify public spending raised through the PIT system only if the value of such public spending were worth the $1.56 of foregone private spending (8).

In general, the Table 16 data show that the output costs of taxes do indeed vary markedly across various tax bases, from a MEB of 155 cents for corporate taxes to a low of 17 cents for sales taxes. Presumably, much of the "efficiency" of the sales tax, (especially the GST, or value-added variant of sales taxes) is that they are export-import neutral and, hence, an ideal tax in integrated trading environments. It is important to note that these MEB estimates depend in part on how high the tax rate already is on the tax base in question, as well as on how high these tax rates are elsewhere. Utilizing a similar, but not identical, approach to measuring MEB's, Dalhby (1994) notes that the excess burden is much higher for the federal surcharges than it is for the overall marginal-rate structure.

Thus, this evidence lends support to the proposition that the output costs of maintaining high tax rates on personal and especially corporate income taxes are substantial. It also lends support to the proposition that, in terms of the implications for actual output, the emergence of a GIR environment implies that the resulting optimal tax structure would reduce taxes on income relative to consumption. While it is clear that these MEB estimates would suggest that any tax reductions arising from pending budget surpluses should be allocated to more mobile tax bases, it is also the case that even if

Table 16 236

Real Output Loss from an Extra Dollar of Tax (cents)

Corporate income tax	155
Personal income tax	56
Payroll tax	27
Sales tax	17

Source: OECD *Economic Survey, Canada 1997* table 23, which in turn cites the Department of Finance Canada.

Reproduced from Harris (1999, Table 1).

there were no surpluses to allocate, the shift toward a GIR era requires a cor-responding shift in the tax mix. Hence, the underlying message here is that to approach tax cuts on mobile factors only in the context of allocating budget surpluses is far too narrow a perspective. Phrased differently, the time is upon us for a wholesale rethinking of Canada's (federal and provincial) tax structure or tax mix in a GIR era.

Equity, Cohesion and Tax Cuts

I am not foolhardy enough to attempt to make the case that tax cuts on mobile factors can be construed as equitable, in the traditional sense of this term. Nonetheless, I am willing to go as far as to assert that a successful human capital future for all Canadians requires that we create an environment where talent and enterprise can remain in Canada. While this may not imply that policies toward this end (e.g., tax cuts for mobile factors) are equitable *per se*, creating an environment conducive to retaining our human capital and talent is an integral part of generating the social cohesion implicit in the mission statement.

In attempting to buttress this claim, I return to the societal challenge posed by what Reich (1991) refers to as the "symbolic analysts." To recall, these are high-human-capital individuals or knowledge workers who are networking inter-nationally, and who are, increasingly, "seceding from America." They inhabit the same "state" as their fellow citizens, but progressively neither the same economy nor the same social infrastructure. Reich's approach to this "revolt of the elites" is a call for "positive nationalism," as distinct from his concern, even fear, that the global centrifugal forces might push America into zero-sum or even negative-sum nationalism.

I want to argue that the mission statement is a version of this "positive nationalism" and a successful implementation of the mission statement will forge a re-linking of Canada's symbolic analysts to their fellow citizens and to Canada. One aspect of the re-linking is obvious: Canada needs to retain its symbolic ana-lysts and the successful enterprises and corporate headquarters to which they are typically attached, because retaining them shows that rewards exist for develop-ing and enhancing Canadian human capital. But what would link these symbolic analysts to Canada and their fellow Canadians?

I believe important insight in this direction comes from Lester Thurow's recent book, *Building Wealth*:

Without widespread educational skills, no one can build a successful wealth pyramid. At some point, my fellow worker's education becomes as important to my earnings as my own. With them uneducated, a lid is placed on my own potential. I become the equivalent of the Indian software engineer working in Bangalore. I make a nice income relative to those of my illiterate neighbours, but less than those in the developed world with literate neighbours. More important, I am not in charge of the system. I don't make decisions. I am just a hired gunslinger working for an owner I have never met. I can be a marginal part of someone else's wealth pyramid, but I cannot build my own wealth pyramid.

[Thus] skills and education in the bottom two-thirds of the workforce are as important as skills and education in the top third. Neither can reach their potential without help from the other. (Thurow 1999: 144-146)

Thurow goes on to note,

Japan is superbly educated at the bottom but needs creativity at the top. America is superbly creative at the top but needs better skills at the bottom. Only Europe can claim to be well educated at the bottom and creative at the top. (147)

But Canada has a leg up here, even on Europe. We share with continental Europeans the importance of having a generous and inclusive social contract but, unlike Europe, we have married this with the dynamism of the Americans on the economic front. Indeed the thrust of the previous chapter was to design a social infrastructure that will ensure a human capital culture and future for Canadians, one that cuts the link between parental income/status and access to human capital investment since this investment will be a societal commitment to all Canadians and not limited to the private means of individuals. And the ongoing thrust of the present chapter is to generate a domestic economic climate conducive to providing productive opportunities for enterprise and talent alike. Within this societal commitment and framework, those that achieve symbolic-analyst status will recognize that they are building on the human capital base of their fellow Canadians. Thus, it is in their *own* interest to embrace a human capital future for *all* Canadians. This will not mean we will not lose talent to the US. We always have and we always will, given the tremendous range of opportunities that obviously exist in an economy that is more than ten times larger than ours. But it will mean we will have created a domestic economic and social environment that will generate (and foster employment in Canada of) our own symbolic analysts. With the appropriate social infrastructure in place, Canada can become, paraphrasing the "vision" of the Ontario mission statement, the best jurisdiction in the world in which to live, work, invest and raise a family. We will achieve this status if we become a *state of minds*.

G I R   a n d   t h e
D e b t   B u r d e n

N OW THAT PAUL MARTIN HAS TAMED THE FEDERAL DEFICIT AND HIS COUNTERPARTS are doing the same at the provincial level, admittedly with a holdout or two, it is not surprising that attention is turning to Canada's debt burden. There is no question that the debt overhang is compromising the effective operation of Canadian macro policy and, indeed, public policy across the board. This is not at issue. What is at issue is the optimal way to work the debt down to a more acceptable level. In turn, the policy choice is the following: Do we allocate a part of the surplus to pay down the nominal amount of debt outstanding, or do we direct attention toward reducing the debt-to-GDP ratio? Under this latter strategy, the approach would involve ensuring that we would not run deficits (i.e., the absolute level of the debt would not increase), so the debt/GDP ratio would fall in proportion to the rise in GDP. That means a five percent increase in GDP would trigger a corresponding five percent decline in the debt/GDP ratio, assuming an unchanged level of nominal debt outstanding. Not without some risk, my approach would be to opt for the latter strategy, largely because I perceive that the priority for immediate tax reduction and for social spending in line with the mission statement dominates the debt issue. The purpose of this section is to buttress this perspective.

In developing the argumentation for this position and, in particular, in elaborating on the potential risk alluded to above, the appropriate starting point is to recognize the various problems associated with a debt-to-GDP ratio that, across all governments, still hovers near the 100 percent level. The litany of problems would embrace, among others, the following concerns.

First, the presence of a large debt overhang served to complicate the pursuit of the Bank of Canada's conversion to price stability in the late 1980s. Basically, the existence of the debt/deficit overhang meant it was difficult for the Bank to establish policy credibility in domestic and international financial markets since the possibility of eventually "monetizing" the debt remained. The operational implications of this were that Canadian nominal and real rates of interest had to rise significantly, and for an extended period, before they fell back and mirrored our progress on the inflation front. As noted, the fear was that if the initiative ever got off the rails, the debt overhang would provide an incentive for the system to inflate its way out of the dilemma. Thanks to the Bank's policy steadfastness, we have overcome the credibility problem, but not without major intervening costs in the form of higher real interest rates than the Americans (Courchene 1997; Fortin 1999). Had our debt levels been lower, the transition to price stability would have been easier, quicker and less costly. By extension, decreasing the amount of debt outstanding would facilitate our future macro policy.

Second, the presence of high debt meant that when the 1990s recession hit, we were forced into *pro-cyclical* policy response, i.e., we exacerbated the recession by increasing selective taxes. This is the "debt wall" issue. International capital markets took a dim view of Canadian indebtedness, even to the point of putting Canada under a "credit watch," thereby constraining our fiscal room to manoeuvre in response to a domestic economic downturn. Generating a lower debt ratio would restore our fiscal manoeuvrability in any future downturn. In other words, by working down the debt burden, we would provide ourselves with the fiscal freedom to engage in active counter-cyclical stabilization policy in any future downturn.

Third, with debt-servicing running about one-third of program spending, this drives a wedge between the costs of paying taxes on the one hand and the corresponding benefits that taxpayers perceive they are receiving from government expenditures on the other. With debt levels or ratios much lower, this wedge would decline and, with it, Canadians may take a much more positive view of the role of their governments in the economy. This is but another way of saying that as debt-servicing costs decline, more of each tax dollar will find its way into expenditure programs.

For these and other reasons, debt reduction is an important goal. However, as a policy priority, allocating a portion of the emerging "discretionary" fiscal surplus to reducing the outstanding dollar value of the public debt does not, in my view, rank with the tax reduction imperative nor with the priorities on the social front. Thus, the preferable avenue to working down the debt/GDP ratio is to focus on increasing the denominator, namely GDP. Moreover, were we able, via tax cuts

and other measures elaborated below, to generate a rate of growth one-half percent larger than what it would otherwise have been, this would be equivalent to
paying down $5 billion of debt every year (in terms of the combined federal-
provincial debt/GDP ratio).

But this is not the end of the story. At unchanged absolute debt levels, a
five percent annual increase in GDP would decrease the debt/GDP ratio by about
28 percent over five years, and by one-half before 2010. But the ratio would
likely fall by more than this because of the so-called "prudent" approach to budgets adopted by the federal Department of Finance and by some provincial
finance departments as well. Consider the federal approach to what it terms "economic prudence." The process begins by averaging the various private-sector
forecasts with respect to revenues, expenditures and economic variables (i.e.,
inflation, growth, exchange rates) and then applying a degree of "prudence" to
these forecasts. By way only of illustration, if the private-sector consensus (or
average) forecast is that GDP will grow by five percent and interest rates will average five percent, then Finance will base its revenue forecasts on, say, 4.5 percent
and 5.5 percent for growth and interest rates, respectively. Obviously, this provides an operating "cushion," as it were. Beyond this, Finance provides a further
"contingency reserve," typically in the $3 billion range. This contingency reserve
is deficit related, not expenditure related, i.e., if the Finance forecasts come in "on
target," the contingency reserve must be used to reduce the debt: It cannot be
used to finance expenditure. Because economic growth has been unexpectedly
strong in recent years, this prudent approach has led to annual decreases in the
nominal value of debt outstanding, often of an amount larger than the contingency reserve.

Thus, my preferred approach to reducing the debt/GDP ratio is to rely on
GDP growth and budgetary "prudence." The risk to this strategy is that an unex-
pected recession can throw all of this into severe fiscal turmoil. This is always a possibility, although all indications suggest (see GIR and the Economy above) that the
next few years will be growth years. Hence, while not in anyway underplaying the
goal of reducing the debt, the strategy of targeting the economic component of any
projected surplus on tax reduction rather than paying down the debt is appropriate since, failing this, the tax base itself may well migrate south. Obviously, if the
prospective surpluses become massive, as appears to be the case in Fall 2000, then
budgeting, up front, for debt repayment becomes not only possible but desirable.

The October 18, 2000,
Economic Statement[32]

W HILE IT IS NORMAL FOR THE MINISTER OF FINANCE TO PRESENT AN ECONOMIC
Statement in October, this year's *Economic Statement and Budget Update 2000*
was anything but normal. One reason for this is that there has been seismic shift in
the underlying budget parameters over the period from the February 2000 federal
budget to the October 18, 2000, Economic Statement. For example, the February
budget estimated the surplus for fiscal year 1999-2000 to be $5.5 billion. One would
have expected this to be a reasonably accurate estimate of the surplus since the fiscal year-end (March 31, 2000) was just over a month after the budget. When the
final data for the fiscal year became available (Fall 2000), however, the surplus
turned out to be $12.3 billion. Even more dramatic, the Economic Statement fore-
casts cumulative budget surpluses in excess of $120 billion over 2000-01 to 2005-
06, and this forecast incorporates the Table 15 tax rate reductions. These surpluses
pose problems for the above analysis of tax and debt priorities because the analysis
was based on the fiscal parameters underlying the 2000 federal budget.

Another reason why this Economic Statement is out of the ordinary is that
it also serves as the tax and debt planks of the Chrétien Liberals platform for the
November 27, 2000, election. Specifically, the statement incorporates a further
substantial round of tax cuts that become effective January 1, 2001. In other
words, this is really a mini-budget. Admittedly, the possibility exists that the
Liberals could be defeated at the polls and, therefore, the provisions of this mini-
budget would never see the light of legislated day. Nonetheless, they merit highlight since the Economic Statement is appropriately viewed as the latest
installment of the tax reform process that began with the February budget.

For both of these reasons it is important to focus on the highlights of this
Economic Statement, albeit almost as a postscript rather than an integrated analysis, as endnote 32 indicates.

Continuing with Tax Reform

The Economic Statement's approach to tax reform is a combination of accelerating the implementation of the Table 14 five-year plan and of providing further tax
cuts for Canadians. All of the proposed tax cuts listed below are to be in effect as
of January 1, 2001. The provisions include:

- reducing the lowest tax rate to 16 percent from 17 percent;
- reducing to 22 percent the 24 percent tax rate (which the 2000 budget reduced from 26 percent);
- adding a new tax bracket, for incomes between $60,000 and $100,000, that will have a rate of 26 percent. Alternatively, this can be viewed as reducing the top marginal tax rate to 26 percent from 29 percent for incomes between $60,000 and $100,000;
- maintaining the top marginal rate of 29 percent for incomes above $100,000;
- abolishing the federal surtax;
- reducing the capital gains inclusion rate to 50 percent from the 66.67 percent in the 2000 budget;
- introducing more generous rules for stock options and flow-through shares; and
- establishing the timetable for corporate tax cuts proposed in the 2000 budget (see Table 14). The legislated cut to 27 percent from 28 percent on January 1, 2001, will remain. The rate will then fall progressively to 25 percent (on January 1, 2002), to 23 percent (on January 1, 2003) and finally to 21 percent (on January 1, 2004).

These are very significant tax cuts in their own right and they merit further highlight.

The first point to note about these tax reductions is that many of them relate to unfinished business pertaining to the February 2000 federal budget. For example, this mini-budget addresses those provisions of the five-year tax reform plan (Table 14) that were not already addressed in Table 15, e.g., the schedule for corporate tax reductions and the abolition of the federal surtax. Essentially, this is the *acceleration* component of the February budget's tax reform plan.

Second, beyond completing this unfinished business, there is a further round of substantial tax reductions. This is not surprising of and by itself, given the magnitude of the projected surpluses. What are surprising are the income-distributional implications of these tax reductions. Specifically, in light of the above analysis I would have assumed that the Finance Minister would have taken advantage of the massive surpluses to reduce the tax rates on mobile factors. Admittedly, Martin did remove the five percent surtax immediately. However, the corporate tax reductions are implemented very gradually in spite of the rather minimal costs of pursuing an aggressive first-mover advantage over the

Americans. Nonetheless, when fully implemented, Canadian corporate rates will be lower than US corporate rates.

All of the new (i.e., not in Table 14) tax reductions are geared to low- and middle-income Canadians: The top marginal tax rate remains unchanged while all the other rates are reduced. Some of this may relate to electoral politics. Just before the election call, the Canadian Alliance converted their 17 percent single-rate tax into a two-rate version — 17 percent up to $100,000 and 25 percent thereafter. In this light, the mini-budget's reduction of the lowest tax rate to 16 percent from 17 percent is presumably an attempt to "one-better" the Alliance, as it were. Moreover, the reduction of tax rates for those under $100,000 allows the Liberals to claim they are generous to low- and middle-income Canadians but not to high-income Canadians, i.e., the 16 percent to 29 percent tax range compared to the 17 percent to 25 percent range of the Canadian Alliance allows the Liberals to claim the progressivity high road. While this is where they wish to position themselves politically, I also think this is where they want to position themselves ideologically. Hence, it is tempting, and I think appropriate, to argue that they have not bought into the reality that GIR requires lower rates on highly mobile Canadians.

But there is another way, a quite sophisticated way, that one might rationalize their new four-tiered rate structure — 16%-22%-26%-29%. It would go as follows. The personal income tax must be a progressive tax, and the progressivity should come primarily from the federal rate and bracket structure. This view would certainly have been nurtured by Alberta's move to a flat tax or single-rate tax for its PIT. If Ottawa were to flatten its rate structure, and if other provinces were to attempt to follow Alberta's example, the resulting rate and bracket structure for the overall PIT system might embody very little in the way of progressivity. But this is not appropriate for a personal income tax system, or so the argument would go. Therefore, the only way the federal government can ensure that the PIT will be a progressive tax is to embody progressivity in its own portion of the tax. And why not *increase* the degree of progressivity while generally *reducing* tax rates.

This is a very different approach to PIT reform than the one I proffered above, namely that Ottawa should take the lead role in ensuring that our tax rates on mobile factors are competitive. Given, however, that Ottawa has re-affirmed its intent to ensure that its component of the PIT is oriented toward income-distributional goals rather than competitive goals, this becomes in effect an invitation for the provinces to follow Alberta's flat tax approach. Even Albertans with their 10.5 percent single-rate

tax will face a rather progressive tax system overall — 0.0 percent until the federal
exemption is reached; 16 percent until the larger Alberta exemptions are used up;
26.5 percent up to $30,000; 32.5 percent between $30,000 and $60,000; 36.5 per-
cent from $60,000 to $100,000; and 39.5 percent thereafter. Under the former tax-
on-tax approach to the shared PIT, the provinces were forced to *magnify* the
progressivity imposed by Ottawa, since they were required to levy a single tax against
federal tax owing. They are now free to decide the degree of progressivity they wish.
By increasing the progressivity of its own component, Ottawa is effectively ensuring
that the overall PIT system will remain progressive. At the same time, however, it is
probably providing an *incentive* for other provinces, especially those with mobile tax
bases, to follow Alberta's lead and opt for relatively flat tax structures.

Could this be part of the rationale for the increase in federal progressivity
in the mini-budget, and in particular the rationale for maintaining the 29 percent
federal marginal rate? My answer is that is could, but not without an important
caveat: It is the federal government with its large surpluses, and not the
provinces, that can afford to reduce top marginal rates.

At base, the issue is a fiscal-balance issue or, from the provinces' viewpoint,
a fiscal-imbalance issue. Unless the federal government either substantially increases cash transfers to the provinces or transfers additional tax room to the provinces
(e.g., one percentage point of the CHST), the reality is that marginal tax rates for
upper-income Canadians will remain high relative to those for Americans because
most provinces are unlikely to be able to afford such cuts, except Alberta, which has
adequate fiscal flexibility to ensure competitive overall PIT rates. But if the above
choices are the fallback position, why not transfer PIT tax room directly? This could
be done, for example, by reducing each of the four federal tax rates by somewhere
in the five-to-ten-percent range. This would retain the progressivity of the PIT while
allowing the provinces to mount somewhat higher and flatter rate structures of their
own, without foregoing too much in revenues.

Intriguingly, this caveat does not affect my overall assessment. Our inability to provide competitive tax rates for Canada's highly mobile knowledge workers is a national failure and, increasingly, I think, a federal failure.

The Tax Collection Agreements
Earlier in the analysis, I noted that Ontario was proposing to alter the definition
of income for Ontario tax purposes in three areas: capital gains, stock options and

flow-through shares. And if the CCRA then refused to collect Ontario's taxes, the province threatened to establish its own PIT collection system. As I have argued elsewhere (Courchene 1999e), this is in the nature of a credible threat, so that it should perhaps not be surprising that the mini-budget addresses all three of these areas. In terms of the capital gains inclusion rate, it adopts the Ontario 50 per-cent rate. The remaining provisions relating to stock options and flow-through shares may not directly address the Ontario concerns but they are certainly "in the neighbourhood." With these provisions, Ontario's threat to withdraw from the tax collection agreements is no longer credible. A fine finesse!

Debt and GIR

Under the February budget parameters, the above analysis argued that priori-ty should be assigned to tax reduction and to mission-statement-related spending, not to debt repayment. Specifically, the prudent approach to bud-geting along with the contingency reserve would ensure some minimal pay-down on the debt. In tandem with GDP growth, this would reduce the debt/GDP ratio by one-half within nine years, and perhaps much sooner. This treatment of debt as a "residual" is no longer appropriate when the projected surpluses are so large. One has to commit in advance to some debt reduction. The Finance Minister has done exactly this for fiscal year 2000-01 — a com-mitment to pay down the debt by at least $10 billion dollars. Moreover, apart from the monies "sheltered" in the form of prudence and the contingency reserves, the government will announce, each fall, whether more of that year's surplus should be dedicated to debt paydown, depending on the economic circumstances at the time. High marks here!

Spending and GIR

Setting aside the backtracking on EI, which clearly runs counter to a human cap-ital future for Canadians, the spending in the mini-budget is in all the "right" areas — the $21.1 billion over five years for health; $2.2 billion on early child-hood development as well as an increase in the CCTB; and close to $2 billion on education, research and innovation. What is lacking, however, is a credible com-mitment to a human capital future. If the pundits are correct, this will become woefully evident in the election spending promises, by which time this book will be in press.

Monetary Policy

W ERE ONE TO JUDGE FROM THE AMOUNT OF MEDIA COVERAGE DEVOTED TO THE conduct of monetary policy, i.e., the *lack* of media coverage, one would be led to assume that monetary policy must be one of Canada's success stories. There is, of course, more than a kernel of truth in this. Market interest rates and inflation rates have been consistently lower in the mid- to late 1990s than in any other post-war period. But given that this is also the case for the Americans and most of our other trading partners, it remains surprising that more of our deteriorating economic position *vis-à-vis* the Americans does not take the form of placing some of the blame on the steps of the Bank of Canada.

My own retrospective on the macro mix, and the Bank of Canada policy in particular, is that we stepped too hard on the monetary brakes in the late 1980s. Specifically, the immediate result of the Bank of Canada's shift toward a price-stability strategy in 1988 was a sharp rise in Canadian nominal and real interest rates and a dramatic appreciation in the Canadian dollar (from 70 US cents per Canadian dollar in 1986 to 89 cents in 1991). This led in turn to a mushrooming of deficits and debt, in part from the debt-servicing implications of high interest rates and in part because the sharp interest-rate/exchange-rate increases clobbered economic activity, simultaneously reducing tax revenues and triggering compensatory expenditures like welfare and EI. To make matters worse, the already constrained fiscal positions led, in pro-cyclical fashion, to a series of tax increases at both levels of government which not only further complicated the economic picture but, *inter alia*, fed into the "overtaxed" nature of the Canadian economy (Fortin 1999).

In the more recent period, Canada reversed this policy mix: Fiscal policy became very tight and, as compensation, we allowed the exchange rate to fall dramatically from a high of 89 cents in 1991 to a low of 63.5 cents in the summer of 1998, which returned to the 67-69 cent range at the time of writing. To be sure, we are benefiting from the ongoing and prolonged economic boom, but not to the degree that has been true for the Americans, in large measure because of the wild swings in terms of our macro mix over the last decade.

While these are my own views of the demand-side problem (Courchene 1997; 1999a), they are broadly consistent with those of Fortin (1999), who argues that it is the monetary side that has contributed to the "underemployed" nature of the Canadian economy in comparison with the US economy. One of

Fortin's ongoing concerns is that the Bank of Canada has embraced a target range for inflation that is too low (especially compared to the US implicit range) and been too concerned about the cost of allowing the unemployment rate to fall below the rate which, *in the past*, would have triggered inflationary tendencies. In contrast, the US Federal Reserve "has not hesitated to keep interest rates low enough to actively 'test and probe' levels of unemployment below six percent," the non-inflationary level of unemployment generally accepted in the United States until that time (Fortin 1999: 47).

Phrased differently, for most of the 1990s the Bank of Canada has been overly concerned with a resurgence of inflation and, therefore, has maintained a policy stance that has likewise been overly restrictive in terms of the employment dimension. Intriguingly, this may also relate to the paradigm-shift perspective of this study in the following sense: What has been surprising to analysts and policymakers alike is the degree to which the prolonged boom, especially in the US, has failed to ignite inflation forces. This may be the result of enhanced global integration of production. It may also relate to the emerging role of the Internet and e-commerce as triggering new cost-effective business organizational forms for both production and distribution. (The manner in which the GIR era is influencing the business cycle and the inflation-unemployment trade-off has been highlighted in *GIR and the Economy* above.) In this light, among the various recommendations offered by Fortin (1999: 52) is that the Bank of Canada should not attempt to achieve a "more ambitious inflation target" than the US Federal Reserve. I concur.

Are Flexible Exchange Rates Consistent with GIR?

BEYOND THE IMPORTANT MESSAGE EMANATING FROM THE ABOVE DISCUSSION — THAT more attention and research needs to be addressed to the implications of the post-1988 policy thrust of the Bank of Canada — another issue has risen as GIR has increasingly become the bedrock of the new economic order. This relates to the appropriate currency arrangements for small open economies that are highly integrated trade-wise with the global economy and, in Canada's case, with the United States.

The particular concern here is not only the sharp decline in the value of the Canadian dollar (from a peak of 89 cents in 1991 to a trough of 63.5 cents in the fall of 1998) but also the extremely high degree of exchange-rate volatility since 1976 when the Canadian dollar was trading at a premium against the US dollar. Supporters of flexible rates and of the Bank's approach to exchange-rate flexibility correctly emphasize that the recent rapid increase in exports to the US, as reflected in figures 2 and 3 and Table 1, are to a large degree the result of the depreciation of the Canadian dollar. However, there is another side to this depreciation. As Richard Harris and I have argued in several recent articles (e.g., 1999), this dramatic fall in the value of the Canadian dollar has, among other aspects, reduced Canadian's standard of living and purchasing power vis-à-vis the Americans; generated bargain-basement prices for Canadian assets which, in turn, are significantly contributing to the ongoing buyout of corporate Canada; and, arguably, contributed to the shortfall in Canadian productivity relative to US productivity.

Much of the criticism of our analysis, from the Bank of Canada among other quarters, is that Canada remains much more dependent on resources and commodities than does the US, so it is appropriate for the exchange rate to fall in line with the fall in commodity prices. Our response is that the new economic order will be driven by human capital, not resource capital, and that the former requires much more in the way of stable and predictable cost structures. Moreover, by attempting to privilege the commodity sector via exchange-rate policy, we Canadians are providing disincentives for the inevitable transition from our traditional resource-based economy and society to a knowledge and human capital future. This is a fundamental concern. As a result of exchange-rate volatility and misalignment, Canada may latch on to an inferior allocation of resources. We comment on this important issue as follows:

> The dynamics of the response to a particular misalignment vary significantly with the human capital intensity of the sector in question. In the case of overvaluation, firm exit (or relocation) is the ultimate response. With a serious undervaluation, such as Canada is now experiencing, the process works quite differently. The immediate effect of the depreciation is to shift income in Canada from wages to profits. With real wages in the United States rising relative to those in Canada, skilled labour begins to migrate. Many firms will resist raising wages in the short run and would rather use the depreciation to cut prices and build market share. If the low exchange rate persists, most firms will ultimately come to realize that the situation is unsustainable in the longer term:

they will either have to raise real wages for their skilled workers or follow them to the United States.

Do new firms not enter or expand during periods of undervaluation? There is some evidence this does occur in traditional sectors. For firms whose business is based on skilled labour, the difficulty is that, during periods of exchange rate undervaluation, skilled labour markets become very tight. New entry, based on a cost advantage due to an undervalued exchange rate or on wages that might be temporarily low in domestic currency, is very risky. The net impact is that firms may exit in periods of overvaluation, and workers may exit in periods of undervaluation. For a smaller country, building comparative advantage in human-capital-intensive industries becomes quite difficult if both firms and highly skilled labour are mobile between the two countries. The irony is that repeated periods of exchange rate misalignment are likely to result in the shift of Canadian comparative advantage toward industries that are resource and/or capital intensive, and in an employment base that is both less diversified and less human capital intensive than would be the case with exchange rate stability. (Courchene and Harris 1999: 10)

By way of a hypothetical example related to the above, would BC now be more like high-tech Washington (Microsoft, Amazon.com etc.) if the BC-Washington exchange rate (and the Canada-US exchange rate) had been fixed at, say, 80 cents at the inception of the Free Trade Agreement? We believe the answer is *yes*.

Our bottom line is two-fold. The first is that Canada needs far greater exchange-rate stability (*vis-à-vis* the US dollar) in order to maintain our heightened degree of trade, to receive our appropriate share of US investment and to ensure that we can compete in the emerging high-tech and human capital arenas where enterprise is footloose and requires stable and predictable cost structures. A corollary to this point is that our economic prospects may well become seriously compromised if our macro authorities view exchange-rate depreciation as a response to the GIR challenge, i.e., if we use the depreciation as a substitute for lowering taxes on mobile factors, for example.

Our second point is both much more forward-looking and, admittedly, much more subjective. Specifically, we foresee an era of global currency integration or consolidation, so much so that the global system is likely to eventually coalesce around two or three key currencies. Hence, the ultimate choice facing Canada and Canadians may not be whether we choose between a flexible exchange rate or fixed exchange rates, but whether we simply use the US dollar as our currency (i.e., opt for "dollarization") or we attempt, along Euro lines, to work with the US and perhaps other nations in the Americas to create a common North American currency or a North American Monetary Union (NAMU). Much of our analysis is directed to the prospects for, and characteristics of, such a NAMU.

Now that I have broached the concept of a NAMU, and more generally the issue of the evolution of exchange rate relationships in the Americas, it is instructive to place this issue in a much larger perspective. I believe the advent of the Euro represents a watershed in the annals of economic and financial history. Admittedly, some of the factors triggering the Euro had to do with concerns and issues specific to Europe — a move toward an integrated economic space replete with some overarching political institutions, an attempt to provide a bulwark against the possibility of ever reliving the hostilities of the twentieth century etc. However, now that the Euro is largely in place, it also, and powerfully, signals the fact that currencies have become a "supranational" public good, replacing national currency regimes. Euroland will quickly extend well beyond the original eleven countries and the Euro will become a global currency that will challenge the role of the US dollar in global portfolios.

Even more speculatively, I do not believe that having one's own currency will feature prominently in what "nationalism" in the 21st century will be all about. An aside is warranted here, since many Canadians assume that fixing the exchange rate or participating in a NAMU would threaten our identity and sovereignty across a wide swath of policy areas. There is no evidence that this is the case. To see this, it is useful to recall that it was during the Pearson years when we Canadians broke sharply with the Americans and creatively implemented our east-west social contract. Among the initiatives we put in place were our comprehensive equalization program, the Canada Assistance Plan, the arrangements for medicare, the Canada and Quebec Pension Plans etc. Yet, *throughout the Pearson years we had a fixed exchange rate with the US dollar*, i.e., *we followed American monetary policy*. Thus, abandoning domestic exchange rate flexibility during this period clearly did not curtail either our *desire* or our *ability* to foster policies that have made Canadians socio-economically unique in the upper half of North America.

Whatever view one takes with respect to the desirability or achievability of a North American monetary union, the above discussion of the possible evolution of Canada's currency arrangements serves a larger purpose in the context of this monograph. Earlier, I asserted that GIR need not affect the *goals* we Canadians set for ourselves, but it will affect the *instruments* we employ to achieve these goals. The key point is that flexible exchange rates and monetary independence are in the nature of *instruments, not goals*. The ultimate goal of monetary policy is to generate an environment within which we can best achieve our overall societal goals, whether cast in terms of economic competitiveness and social cohesion or in terms of the paramount goal of becoming a human capital society. I believe achieving this goal in a GIR-era requires currency integration. Others may disagree. Indeed, the majority of Canadians appear to disagree. If so, this must be because they harbour the view that flexible exchange rates will contribute to achieving our societal goals. It must *not* be because Canadians view flexible rates, in and of themselves, as a societal goal. They are not.

To this point in the discussion of the interaction between GIR and competitiveness within an overarching human capital context, the emphasis has been on generating the appropriate constellation of macro-economic parameters — taxes, debt-reduction, monetary and exchange-rate policy. While this is a necessary condition for success in the new global order, it is not sufficient: We cannot neglect the broad range of other policies relating to competitiveness — industrial policy, trade policy, competition policy, regulatory policy and the like. A detailed assessment of these areas is well beyond the scope of this monograph and, indeed, beyond my analytical ability. What serves as the concluding section to this chapter are a few reflections on how these policy areas may be made more conducive to both the emerging GIR era and the human capital mission statement.

GIR, Human Capital and Competitiveness

D RAWING FROM THE ANALYSIS IN EARLIER CHAPTERS, THERE ARE AT LEAST THREE perspectives that ought to inform our approach to policies related to industrial policy and competitiveness. The first addresses the inherent dynamics and creative-destruction characteristics of the new order. Specifically, if we are really committed to an innovative culture on the competitive front, then the burden of proof relating to the acceptability of new processes, products and organizational arrangements must rest with the advocates of the status quo, not with the innovators. The associated principle was enunciated earlier, but it merits reiteration in this context: *Government should adopt, as a principle, the presumption that any private-sector initiative is permissible, unless it can be demonstrated to run counter to the public interest.* This is the *sine qua non* of an entrepreneurial and innovative culture.

The second theme is that we should lever off our demonstrated strengths. In the economic turmoil associated with the new global order, countries are lucky if they have a few domestic industrial "winners" they can parlay into successful global competitors and, in the process, can incubate and grow associated global players. In the previous chapter, I noted that one of Canada's obvious domestic winners — our healthcare sector — must be repositioned as one of our major economic sectors and export platforms in the GIR era. Later in this section, I will focus on the possibilities of levering off the Canadian banks as an essential motor of the Canadian economy.

The third theme is that the time has come for our industrial and competitive policies to embrace the concept of 21st-century Canada as a "state of minds" and, therefore, to tilt *all* such policies, where feasible, in directions that are consistent with a human capital society. This is not intended to interfere with the GIR requisites that our policies in these areas become state-of-the-art (e.g., by adopting best practices from elsewhere in the world). Rather, the intention is that where there are degrees of freedom in terms of policy design, this freedom be utilized to ensure that the policy or policies in question contribute to the "develop, enhance and employ in Canada" tenet of the human capital mission statement.

By way of an example here, our approach to competition and mergers policy should embrace all of these principles. Assessment of a prospective merger's impact on competition should recognize that most (but admittedly not all) markets are now international if not global. Moreover, the assessment should be forward-looking in terms of assessing where the "puck" is going to be, not where its been, to fall back on the Gretzky dictum. In addition, the burden of proof should be on the regulators, or the government, to demonstrate that the merger runs counter to the public interest and not on the merging parties to demonstrate that the proposal advances the public interest. Finally, some version of the human capital mission statement should become an integral part of the philosophy underpinning competition policy and mergers/takeovers.

In terms of the potential for levering off our strengths, the banking sector provides an interesting case study. Consider the following, admittedly controversial approach to banking. Drawing from recommendations in the 1990 Senate of Canada report, *Canada 1992, Toward a National Market in Financial Securities* (for which I served as scribe and consultant), suppose we allowed (*not* required) the chartered banks to restructure themselves as a publicly held holding company and in the process we also opened up the ownership limits somewhat. One arm of the holding company would relate to their existing banking and securities activities. With the other arm, the banks could engage in any commercial activity they wished. Note that because of the holding company structure, there would be a separation of banking and commerce, i.e., non-bank-related commercial activities would not be financed by the banks' insured deposits base. With this structure in place, the banks would then be

- ◆ Allocated powers to operate in a wide range of commercial activities — activities that many of their international competitors now engage in. For example, I have never understood why the banks are denied full leasing powers. Why would we deny this power to banks when we allow huge foreign-based commercial/financial conglomerates such as Ford and General Electric to hold sway here?

- ◆ Encouraged to help grow domestic start-ups in the commercial sector, i.e., to play an incubator role. What I have in mind here is that the banks would be able to take an ownership position sufficient to warrant a presence on the emerging company's board of directors. This would bring some of the vast expertise of the banks to bear on the operations of these small- and medium-sized firms. If the prospects look impressive, presumably the banks would take a role in developing the company further. If not, they would simply exit. While the banks are allowed, under current legislation, to undertake these activities within certain limits, the thrust of this recommendation would be to remove any such constraints.

- ◆ Encouraged, relatedly, to have their senior personnel become more active on the boards of directors of small Canadian enterprises. Few Canadians have the wealth and breadth of experience that exists in the upper echelons of our nationwide banks. We would indeed be levering off our strengths if this human capital could play a role in growing our innovative companies into larger ones.

I hasten to add that all of this would be "permissive" legislation. The banks and their boards of directors may well prefer to "stick to their knitting," as it were, and not take advantage of these new powers. This must be their prerogative.

It may well be that this brief case study more appropriately should have focused on our high-tech successes such as Nortel and JDS Uniphase or on the impressive global range of Bombardier. But banking is, intriguingly, the quintessential GIR industry since, at base, it is an increasingly sophisticated telecomputational and information network where the distinction between what is domestic and what is international in their operations is becoming progressively blurred. To revert to the earlier analogy, banks progressively operate in the space of flows rather than the space of places and, increasingly, the bank "branch" will eventually be "decentralized" to the home PC. By way of a final comment on the banking sector, the prevailing "big cannot buy big" philosophy toward mergers is puzzling since our banks are small players on the international scene when the comparison is made with the above three companies.

In any event, the important message is that we should review our entire constellation of policies relating to industry, trade and competitiveness with an eye toward infusing them with the spirit, not the letter, of the above three themes.

Conclusion

B Y WAY OF A CONCLUDING COMMENT, IT IS INSTRUCTIVE TO RECALL THE TRILOGY of Canadian policy challenges articulated by Pierre Fortin in his 1999 C.D. Howe Benefactors Lecture. His concern that Canadians are "overtaxed" and "underemployed" were addressed in the first few sections of this chapter. Much of the remainder of the above analysis attempts to address the third of his concerns, namely that Canadians are "underproductive." Enhancing productivity is clearly the key to ensuring that Canadians' living standards will grow. Part of the productivity challenge was addressed in the previous chapter where the emphasis was placed on ensuring that our information/Internet infrastructure became in effect the "pan-Canadian railway" of the 21st-century information era. In terms of this information and productivity challenge, the recent paper by Porter and Martin (2000), which updates their 1991 study of Canada's competitive prospects, serves as an appropriate summary of much of the thrust of this chapter. Their "concluding thoughts" run as follows:

◆ Relentless innovation and upgrading of productivity are the keys to international competitiveness in the modern economy.

◆ While Canada has some firms that belong in the ranks of the world's best, the overall economy is not where it needs to be, or even on the right course.

◆ In 1991, Canada chose the familiar and comfortable path of replication, benchmarking and operational improvement. In 2000, the nation must choose the alternative path of innovation and bold strategy.

◆ Canadian firms must understand that competing in Canada alone will eventually destroy them. They must decide to compete globally, based on unique products and processes.

◆ This road will be profoundly worrisome, even frightening at times, but it is necessary for Canada to prosper and not continue to slowly decline relative to other leading nations.

◆ Canada's governments — federal, provincial, municipal — cannot simply follow other countries and states and exhort Canada's firms to engage in challenging new modes of operation. Instead, Canada's governments also must get out of their comfort zones in order to pursue innovative and bold strategies to provide a leading macroeconomic context and a uniquely favourable microeconomic environment for business.

◆ Only if both businesses and governments together choose to challenge themselves to new ways of thinking and competing will Canada truly prosper in the new millennium. (Porter and Martin 2000)

To this, I would like to re-emphasize that to be successful in the new economic order requires us to abandon our old paradigm ways, namely "the familiar and comfortable path of replication, benchmarking and operational improvement," as Porter and Martin stress. This is not the stuff of the new economic order. Yet I believe it is also the case that success in a GIR environment will not come with a tax cut here or there, or with a policy designed to foster innovation or with a creative approach to institution design. In order to reap the benefits of these and similar initiatives, our policies have to be embedded within a framework that captures the essence of the new global order. This essence is the human capital mission statement.

I turn, finally, to the enduring Canadian issue — federal-provincial relations — and more generally to how Canadian federalism might accommodate GIR, in particular, the human capital imperative.

GIR, Canadian
Federalism and
Human Capital

Introduction

T HIS FINAL SUBSTANTIVE CHAPTER FOCUSES ON THE POLITICAL ASPECTS, ESPECIALLY
the federal-provincial and institutional aspects, of the range of challenges
and opportunities generated by the new global order. The underlying thrust is
that the inherent flexibility of both the structure and the processes of Canadian
federalism constitute an enormous asset in addressing the dictates of the new
order. Phrased differently, I buy fully into the recent observation by Kenichi
Ohmae (2000) that federalism is the most "cyber-compatible" approach to
governance in the GIR era.

To be sure, the decade or so following the *Constitution Act, 1982*, where we
sought constitutional solutions to what were inherently political and institutional
challenges, was not our finest federalism hour. Nonetheless, for most of the post-
war period we Canadians proved to be absolute masters of the art of federalism and
recently we appear to be rekindling these innate abilities, as reflected in the AIT and
SUFA arrangements, among others. Thus, the first section of this chapter is intended
to celebrate our achievements in terms of making the structures and processes of
federalism work toward our common weal. In effect, this is a levering-off-our-
strengths introduction to the emerging institutional and process challenges associated with implementing the human capital mission statement.

The analysis then focuses on the "who should do what" issue in terms of
implementing GIR-compatible policies. Part of this analysis will rejoin the observations in the concluding section of Chapter 8, namely that in order to maintain
political saliency across citizens, Ottawa will look longingly at key policy aspects
relating to the implementation of the mission statement — aspects that have

traditionally fallen in the provincial domain. But these policy areas are for the provinces to lose. If the provinces, individually or collectively via the APC process or SUFA, cannot deliver a human capital future for all Canadians, then Ottawa will, and *should*, play a dominant role. As an ardent decentralist, this is a tough line for me to take. Nonetheless, at stake is our socio-economic future in an information era; this must trump the politics of federalism. My guess, however, is the provinces can and will pull their appropriate weight in the fascinating tug-of-war to determine who-does-what in the new global era. As the above few sentences suggest, the analysis will be more indicative than definitive. This is appropriate since there is no single best way to achieve a human capital society and future in a federation as culturally and economically diverse as Canada.

The final section of the chapter will return to the Chapter 2 discussion of the emerging role of cities in the Canadian federation and in the division of powers. Focus will be directed to the recent charter for the city of Toronto and, more generally, to the jurisdictional implications arising from the new and exciting role of cities, especially global city-regions, as powerful motors of economic growth and export platforms in the 21st century.

Celebrating Canadian Federalism

C ANADA PROBABLY RANKS AS THE MOST CENTRALIZED OF ALL FEDERATIONS IN TERMS of how our central governing institutions operate. There is essentially no meaningful role for provincial input at the centre. In particular, we lack the equivalent of a triple-E second chamber that characterizes most federations, e.g., the United States and Australia. And Germany, for example, has the Bundesrat, which is composed of direct representatives of the governments of the respective Länder and which must approve all legislation pertaining to the Länder. In our federation, the Ottawa-appointed Senate does not serve as a House of the Provinces. Beyond this, Ottawa alone decides on appointments to national institutions like the Supreme Court, the Bank of Canada, the various other national agencies and, as noted, the Senate itself.

Lacking said input at the centre, and following the more or less universal principle that nature abhors a vacuum, regional interests in the Canadian federation have, by default and of necessity, come to be articulated through the provinces and their respective premiers. On many issues therefore, the provinces become the *de facto* opposition to much of federal legislation, such as the health-care funding associated with the 2000 federal budget. Thus, Canadian govern-ance has perforce been structured along the lines of "interstate federalism," as distinct from the "intrastate federalism" that characterizes those federations with adequate and integrative subnational input at the centre. As noted, this has led to our extensive reliance on federal-provincial diplomacy or "executive federalism" — the hundreds of annual meetings between officials from both orders of gov-ernment, recently extended in certain areas to embrace officials from the First Nations. While executive federalism is frequently, and somewhat appropriately, criticized for its behind-closed-doors approach to the management of federal-provincial interdependencies, the very structure of our system implies that this will be an enduring feature of Canadian federalism.

As prelude to the governance challenge arising from the dictates of GIR, it is important to emphasize that Canadians have managed most aspects of our fed-eration in an incredibly creative way. Phrased somewhat differently, the overarch-ing constitutional framework has proven in most areas to be amazingly flexible.

A few examples will suffice. Without much if any resort to formal consti-tutional change, we dramatically centralized revenues during the Second World War. In the post-war period, we again proceeded to decentralize revenues via cre-ative instrumentalities that serve as instructive models for decentralized federa-tions everywhere. Our approach to tax-sharing in the personal and corporate income tax systems is worthy of special emphasis. While close to 40 percent of Canada's personal income taxes accrue to the provinces, the nature of this decen-tralized tax system is that it is fully harmonized in terms of the definition of the tax base. Moreover, it is compliance-friendly in that there is only one tax form for citizens to fill out. With the new tax on income approach that begins on January 1, 2001, the provinces will have full rate and bracket flexibility, but the underly-ing harmony of the tax system will remain since the tax base will remain harmo-nized (unless some provinces opt for the Quebec approach of mounting their own tax collection systems).

This reference to Quebec and its separate personal income tax system raises another fascinating feature of the Canadian federation: its inherent asym-metry across provinces, one aspect of which is "opting out." In the 1950s, Quebec mounted its own, separate, provincial income tax system, i.e., it opted out of the tax collection agreements as was its right under the Constitution. But it was this opting out by Quebec that allowed Ottawa and the nine other provinces to forge the shared and harmonized approach to the personal income tax system alluded to in the previous paragraph. If Quebec were somehow forced to remain within the overall system, the "compromise" tax reality would almost surely *not* be the existing decentralized yet harmonized model. In other words, opting out has allowed both Quebec and the rest of Canada to pursue their preferred options. Unlike much of the ongoing rhetoric in our federation, my view is that opting out is more akin to a creative solution than a problem.

On the corporate tax side, Quebec, Ontario and Alberta have their own tax systems in place. Yet all provinces have agreed to a set of mutually created rules that allocate the profits of multi-province corporations across the respective provinces. Hence, we escape the zero taxation and double taxation problems that frequently arise in the US corporate tax system. And this cooperation with respect to the corporate tax system is a result of a *voluntary* collective agreement adhered to by all parties.

Beyond this, Canadians have been innovative in a wide range of other areas relating to the workings of federalism. The initial equalization program was a product of ordinary federal legislation, but equalization became such a hallmark of Canadian federalism that the principle was enshrined in the *Constitution Act, 1982*. Arguably, however, the most significant provisions in the *Constitution Act, 1982*, were those embodied in the *Canadian Charter of Rights and Freedoms*. This represents a path-breaking innovation for a parliamentary federation, since the Charter overrides parliamentary supremacy in selected areas. In other words, it marries aspects of the American "checks and balances" approach with the "parliament-is-supreme" concept of the Westminster model. Our uniquely Canadian accommodation process here is the "notwithstanding clause" — the ability of legislatures to temporarily override the courts, i.e., to place limits on the courts' interpretation of the Charter, so long as these limits "can be demonstrably justified in a free and democratic society."

At the more mundane, but no less important level, we have formally passed powers upward (the constitutional amendments relating to Unemployment Insurance and Old Age Pensions), Ottawa has unilaterally transferred powers downward (training), the provinces and Ottawa acting together have implemented the Canada Pension Plan (replete with Quebec's "opting out," but compatible, QPP) and so on. Moreover, the manner in which we have altered the magnitude of, and incentives within, the federal-provincial transfer system is tantamount to an effective reworking of the division of powers. For example, tilting federal-provincial transfers toward *conditionality* effectively centralizes the federation, since Ottawa can, via the transfers, impose its own (or pan-Canadian) views on provincial spending. Likewise, tilting the transfer system toward *unconditionality* enhances provincial priorities and flexibility, i.e., it is decentralizing.

The evolution of our approach to implementing these intergovernmental transfers is highly revealing. In the 1950s and 1960s, we instituted a series of shared-cost and conditional programs that served to convert the various provincial programs in the health and welfare areas into "national" systems. In other words, conditional transfers to the provinces delivered our version of the welfare state. As these programs became established and attracted a receptive citizen constituency in each province, Ottawa was able to convert many or most of these programs into unconditional grants, as befits a decentralized federation.

Another highly illustrative example of Canada's innate creativity in terms of working within the constitutional framework relates to the investment industry, i.e., the various stock markets and the investment dealers. Given that this area relates to financial capital, the most mobile of factors, no newly formed federation would ever dream of assigning this function to the subnational level. Yet regulation of the securities industry in Canada rests (for various historical reasons) entirely with the provinces. Albeit not without some problems along the way, Canada has far and away the most efficient capital markets of any small- or even medium-sized economy. All of this is a result of the provinces acting in a pan-Canadian manner, even including the recent rationalization of the roles of Canada's various stock exchanges. It may well be the time is approaching when the optimal approach will be to transfer powers in this area upward to Ottawa. In the interim, this represents a key area in which the provinces have delivered pan-Canadian public goods and services to consumers, investors and corporations alike.

More recently, triggered by the *Report To Premiers,* executive federalism led to the creative CCTB, which in turn paved the way for SUFA which formally

Figure 12 264

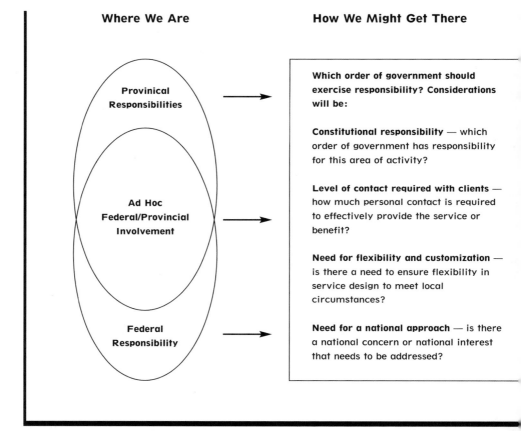

Where We Are

Provincial
Responsibilities

Ad Hoc
Federal/Provincial
Involvement

Federal
Responsibility

How We Might Get There

Which order of government should exercise responsibility? Considerations will be:

Constitutional responsibility — which order of government has responsibility for this area of activity?

Level of contact required with clients — how much personal contact is required to effectively provide the service or benefit?

Need for flexibility and customization — is there a need to ensure flexibility in service design to meet local circumstances?

Need for a national approach — is there a national concern or national interest that needs to be addressed?

* There will always be areas in which both governments should operate, and the aim should be for a process of effective and respectful cooperation in these areas. Cooperation means that major decisions on program design, financing and delivery should be made through agreement by both orders of government, with delivery of programs by one or the other.
Note: Federal/territorial cooperation should also address the need to clarify responsibilities as proposed in this chart while reflecting the financial arrangements for the delivery of social programs to Aboriginal residents of the territories.

Source: Report To Premiers (1996, 9).

Clarifying Federal/Provincial
Responsibilities for Social Programs

Where We Would Like to Be

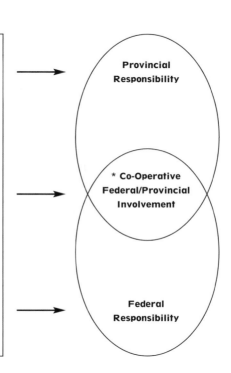

Existence of delivery vehicles — does one order of government already have an efficient delivery system in place?

Extent to which an order of government already delivers services to a client group — is one order of government already significantly involved in delivering services to this target group?

Relationship with other programs — are related programs required to effectively manage the service?

Effectiveness in achieving desired outcomes — can delivery by one government produce more effective outcomes?

Provincial
Responsibility

* Co-Operative
Federal/Provincial
Involvement

Federal
Responsibility

recognizes the federal spending power but subjects it to the "federal principle," i.e., it spells the end of unilateral federalism in areas of exclusive provincial jurisdiction. Relatedly, one of the most exciting features of evolving Canadian federalism has been the revitalization of the Annual Premiers Conferences (APCs), which is serving to nudge the provinces into a pan-Canadian vision regarding several policy areas that fall under exclusive provincial jurisdiction. Ottawa is playing this "managing interdependence" game as well, via its most welcome "Team Canada" initiative that involves the provinces in an area of exclusive federal jurisdiction — trade and commerce, and external economic relations generally.

Finally, but hardly exhaustively, the federal-provincial AIT and SUFA represent new governance instrumentalities in terms of managing interdependencies on the economic and social union fronts, respectively.

The underlying messages here should be clear. First, we Canadians, acting with and through our governments, have excelled in terms of ensuring that our governance structures have been able to accommodate both domestic and international social and economic challenges. Second, we must again draw on our innate creativity to ensure that Canadian governance is up to the task of redesigning our policies and processes to accommodate, and excel, in the knowledge/information era.

Approaches to Policy Interdependencies

I N THE REPORT TO PREMIERS (1996), A MAJOR PART OF THE FOCUS WAS TO RETHINK Canadian governance, as it related to social policy, along the lines of both the subsidiarity principle and the division of powers. Figure 12, reproduced from the Report, reflects this focus. It is a "disentanglement" model — it carves out larger areas for sole federal or provincial responsibility and converts the large "ad hoc federal/provincial involvement" area into the much smaller "cooperative federal/provincial involvement." (Compare the left column, "where we are," with the right column, "where we would like to be.") My quarrel with the vision explicit in Figure 12 is this sort of conceptual reworking of the federal-provincial policy interface will not lead to more scope for Ottawa and the provinces to legislate in a "watertight compartments" approach to the division of powers. Admittedly, policy duplication can and should be minimized, but policy overlap or entanglement is, in my view, synonymous with decentralization, especially so in the context of the human capital mission statement. Indeed, even resorting to the principle of subsidiarity would *not* lead to a classification of policy areas that would make them either exclusively provincial or exclusively federal. Rather, subsidiarity is an inherently crosscutting concept. In virtually every policy area, both levels of government have a role to play. Perhaps monetary policy is an exception, but external affairs, for example, is not since provincial governments have trade "embassies" in various capitals and have formal arrangements with other subnational governments relating to trade, cultural and student exchanges, and other areas (e.g., Ontario and Baden-Würtemberg, and Quebec and Bavaria). At the provincial level, Quebec's oversight of its civil law system comes close to a watertight compartment, but Ottawa controls the related Supreme Court appointments. And so on.

Arguably, Figure 13[33] is a preferred stylized vision of these policy interdependencies. Interprovincial agreements like SUFA can be viewed as corresponding to the inner circle of Figure 13 ("jointly decided common objectives and minimum common standards"). However, Figure 13 makes clear that even arrangements like SUFA and AIT are embedded within other policy areas and, more importantly, the need for coordination and harmonization extends well beyond these formal intergovernmental agreements or arrangements. This inevitable interdependency serves to put emphasis on federalism as a "process" as well as a structure, as noted earlier.

Richard Zuker (1997) approaches this unavoidable entanglement by calling for what he refers to as "reciprocal federalism." Zuker's key point is that provincial policies and legislation can become more effective if Ottawa also legislates in an appropriate manner. Likewise, federal policies can become more effective if the provinces embrace consistent legislation. It is here that subsidiarity should prove to be a constructive principle to inform the implementation of policy responsibilities. Phrased differently, there are incentives for both levels of government to legislate in a complementary and even cooperative manner.

The above detour may border on esoteric, but its relevance in the context of embracing a common mission statement for federal Canada should nonetheless be apparent. To this I now turn.

Figure 13   268

Division-of-Powers
Interdependencies

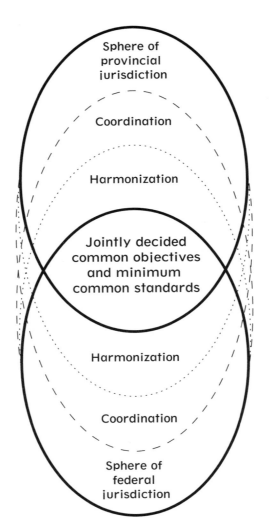

Source: See endnote 33

Federalism and the
Mission Statement

S UCCESSFUL IMPLEMENTATION OF THE HUMAN-CAPITAL-BASED MISSION STATEMENT
obviously requires a philosophical and policy commitment on the part of
both levels of government. It transcends creative intergovernmental instrumentalities (like AIT on the competitiveness front and SUFA on the social cohesion
front) to extend to a far wider range of programs and policy areas. Most of all it
commits the federal and provincial "minds of state" to work together to ensure
that Canada becomes a "state of minds."

At one extreme, this probably calls for a restructuring of government
bureaucracies to ensure that relevant policy decisions are informed by the commitment to develop, enhance and employ in Canada the human capital of
Canadians. Earlier I suggested that the positioning of the human capital and
informatics aspects of our competitiveness prospects under the overarching
Industry Canada banner should be reversed, along with similar changes in
provincial bureaucracies that would give pride of place to human capital.

At the other extreme, the commitment to the mission statement must go
beyond governments and involve citizens. Despite being negotiated in a behind-
closed-doors fashion, SUFA calls for an impressive degree of citizen involvement
in the future evolution of the agreement (Mendelsohn and McLean 2000). My
earlier suggestion that the mutual recognition of provincial credentials be converted to a version of citizens' occupational mobility rights (by placing the burden of proof on governments and not on citizens) would clearly advance this
objective. Even more obviously, so would a joint governmental agreement to
embrace some version of a human capital bill of rights for our children.

Were the provinces to buy into the vision of a human capital mission statement, it would nonetheless remain critical that they be allowed considerable flexibility in terms of policy implementation. This is the essence of federalism, since it
allows provinces to design their policies in line with the preferences of their citizens.
It becomes much more important in the context of the mission statement since we
are in effect charting unknown territory. There is no comprehensive model in place
anywhere in the world that we can simply import. Perforce, we will be engaged in a
"learning by doing" process. With the advent of a tax on income approach to the personal income tax system, the provinces will be well-placed to engage in a creative set

of initiatives on the economic and social fronts, with the their income tax systems as a core instrument for delivery and reconciliation. Moreover, in both AIT and SUFA we have in place a set of overarching principles that will serve to ensure that these provincial initiatives will fall within overall societal objectives.

For this process of provincial "doing" to carry over into provincial "learning," we need much more in the way of information-gathering and assessment in terms of these provincial initiatives. For some policy areas, the obvious place for this to occur is at the pan-provincial level. This in turn opens the way for the reinvigorated APC process to play the leading role as a clearing house on both the information-collection and assessing-outcomes fronts. A working example of this pan-provincialism is the Council of Ministers of Education and their *Shared Priorities in Education at the Dawn of the 21st Century*, the "action plan" of which focuses on five themes: accountability, quality of education, accessibility, mobility, and responsiveness to learner needs. In other areas, Ottawa may be best positioned to take the lead role. For example, as federal Health Minister Allan Rock notes,

> Health Canada is going to launch the Canada Health Network, which is really a network of 380 reputable organizations who have Web sites with reliable data about health, health treatments, health care, and health outcomes. Under the seal of approval of Health Canada, through the Canadian Health Networks, you will be able to gain access to information you can trust about a wide range of subjects of practical importance to Canadians. Our partners are growing week by week. The number of sites is burgeoning and soon it will be a remarkable collection of practical and useful information you can trust. (Rock 1999: 10)

To succeed fully, however, this must eventually become a joint federal-provincial venture.

Hence, what is required in terms of the mission statement is, first, a societal commitment to a human capital future and, second, some similar overarching infrastructure that collects and disseminates, monitors and assesses policies and programs related to the human capital development of Canadians.

Who Does What?

WE NOW COME TO THE *MOST* DIFFICULT "WHO DOES WHAT" ISSUE: ON THE ONE hand, internalizing or managing the policy interdependencies and, on the

other, legislating or otherwise coordinating the pan-Canadian or infrastructure
dimensions of the mission statement. By way of motivating this issue, let me reiterate
my underlying fear as it relates to the implications of GIR. I am confident that our *economic* infrastructure will eventually fall into line with the forces of GIR. We will get
our corporate tax rates down. We will lower our top marginal rates. We will become
a more dynamic and innovative society. Globalization and the information revolution
will make this so. But if at the same time we fail to embed this process of economic
liberalization within a GIR-consistent domestic *social* infrastructure, we will also
import much of what we dislike about the US social contract — income polarization,
an increasingly *Me Inc.* society, and an erosion of key aspects of our east-west social
contract. Above all, this is the motivation underpinning the mission statement.
Returning to the issue at hand, the provinces are clearly at the forefront in terms of
ensuring that Canadians have access to a GIR-consistent social infrastructure since
they oversee most of the key policy areas — health, welfare, education, training and,
arguably, early childhood development. As valuable and critical as these provincial
policy areas are, they need to be embedded within a pan-Canadian strategy.

There are two polar approaches to this division-of-powers and interdependency issue. The first would be for an APC-like process to take the lead role
in managing policy interdependencies and in addressing pan-Canadian or infrastructure issues. The second would be for Ottawa to move into this breach. But
neither of these polar approaches would deliver fully on what is required: the former because the APC does not have the *legislative ability* to provide the pan-
Canadian framework required, the latter because Ottawa lacks the *implementation
ability* to generate GIR-consistent social infrastructures.

Hence, we need some version of the earlier vision of "reciprocal federalism." A key process innovation toward this end should probably involve the revitalization of the First Ministers' Conference to meet on an annual basis to assess
the overall progress in ensuring that Canada becomes a *state of minds*. The appropriate model for such an FMC would ideally embody aspects of the ongoing APC
process: a fixed meeting date each year, open processes for establishing the
human-capital-related agenda, ample time for the preparation (and pre-FMC
release) of federal and provincial position papers, and a chair that rotates in some
acceptable manner across first ministers.

At the more general level, it is undoubtedly the case that a societal commitment
to the mission statement would be tantamount to a *de facto* reworking of aspects of the

governance of the federation and of the division of powers. This is hardly a persuasive argument against embracing the mission statement, since a *de facto* reworking of powers would characterize virtually *any* approach we took to addressing the GIR challenge. Indeed, the federation is already in a division-of-powers flux with the recent devolution of aspects of tourism and mining to the provinces, let alone the significant downward transfer of powers relating to training. And at the more philosophical level, we are witnessing dramatic changes in the manner in which Ottawa is viewing its role in the federation. As reflected in the shift away from the Canada Assistance Plan's approach to welfare and toward an increased emphasis on the tax-transfer system, via the CCTB, Ottawa is assuming a larger responsibility for the well-being of Canada's children. This initiative, along with the Millennium Scholarship program among others, signals a conscious Ottawa decision to have a *direct relationship with Canadians* rather than transferring funds *through the provinces*, and is replete with an increase in federal visibility and accountability for these programs.

However, the underlying issue transcends visibility and accountability *per se*. As noted in the concluding section of Chapter 8, GIR has ushered in a new political and electoral dynamic. Old-style politics relating to resource-based economic development is losing its lustre in terms of both competitiveness and nation building. GIR politics will progressively relate to knowledge-based initiatives, where citizens and human capital, not physical/resource capital, are at the forefront. This is what competitiveness and nation building will be all about in the new millennium. With the transfer of these old-style policy areas to the provinces (forestry, mining etc.) and with the recent federal emphasis on a *direct* relationship with citizens, Ottawa has recognized fully that there has been a sea change in what constitutes electoral currency. While this is great news in terms of the likelihood that Ottawa may buy into a human capital future for Canadians, it is troubling news on the federal-provincial front. Armed with dramatic surpluses, the federal government appears perched to make significant forays into policy areas that have traditionally, and constitutionally, fallen under provincial jurisdiction.

In some areas, such as internal adjustment and distribution, a larger federal role or presence is probably warranted. To see this, recall the adjustment associated with the mid-1970s energy price increase. Canadians flocked to energy-rich Alberta and this province reaped the production and tax-revenues associated with these migrants. When the energy-price-bubble burst, however, many of these same migrants returned to their home provinces and some fell back on provincial welfare.

Not to put too fine a point on this, should booming provinces be entitled to the productive return of migrants while their home provinces remain saddled with their
eventual income support? It seems to me that labour-force adjustment has *national*
dimensions; there should be a larger role for Ottawa in the process.

Indeed, the manner in which Ottawa is approaching this distribution issue
appears to be appropriate. Specifically, it is playing a larger role in terms of income
support for children (via the personal income tax system, which is constitutionally appropriate). This in turn leaves income support for adults as a provincial
responsibility, which allows the provinces to mount comprehensive school-to-
work and welfare-to-work subsystems. And for poorer provinces, the equalization
program provides "reasonably comparable" resources toward this end.

At another level (i.e., in terms of economic competitiveness) however, federal policy may well be heading in the wrong direction. By transferring to the
provinces much of the responsibility for ensuring that tax rates on mobile factors
remain competitive, Ottawa is triggering a process that may well serve to unwind
key aspects of social Canada. As noted in the previous chapter, the resulting
implications could run the gamut from an increasing divergence in tax rates
across provinces to the likelihood of greater regional disparities alongside a
decline in the equalization standard, a fall in provincial tax revenues in the face
of pressing needs on the social front and/or a tendency for provinces to push for
changes in the tax structure (i.e., in the definition of income), any or all of which
carries potential destructive implications for the preservation of the internal economic and social union. If Ottawa's strategic game expects that the citizens of
these cash-strapped provinces will now look to the burgeoning federal surpluses
and invite the federal government to play a more important social role in their
lives, Ottawa has not reckoned with the reactions of the provinces, and not only
Quebec. Unless additional federal funding (preferably tax-point transfers, but at
least in the form of relatively untied cash transfers) is forthcoming, selected
provinces will begin to focus on rethinking and reworking their social systems.

This is wrong-headed federal policy. Ottawa should not abandon its traditional role as the lead player in ensuring Canada's competitive future. To turn the
responsibility for reducing tax rates on mobile factors over to the provinces, or to
those selected provinces whose tax bases are particularly at risk, is to generate a
substantial transfer of effective power in the federation to selected provinces, with
rather dramatic implications for the east-west solidarity of provinces and citizens

alike. This does not mean that the provinces should not aggressively pursue their competitive positions within an integrated NAFTA environment. They should, and one would expect they will, given their economic-region-state focus. But provincial competitiveness should take place within an overarching framework where Ottawa remains the lead player.

The underlying problem here is straightforward. Despite the federal rhetoric (e.g., Chrétien's "third way" speech in Berlin (2000)), Ottawa has not bought into the essence of GIR, let alone the human capital mission statement. While much of the thrust of this chapter has been that we Canadians have been excellent at tailoring our federal structures and processes to addressing internal and external forces, this "process" dimension of our creativity cannot get off the ground unless and until we collectively buy into a human capital future.

Thus, the larger and overarching message is clear. If there is a *collective will* to embrace a human capital future for Canadians, there clearly is a *collective way*, as our achievements in creative federalism have amply demonstrated.

Assuming that collectively we buy into a human capital future, the reality is that even without additional powers associated with ensuring competitive tax rates, enormous responsibility will rest with the provinces in terms of delivering on this goal. It is they who control the key programs relating to the social dimension of the mission statement. Far and away the most appropriate and efficient way for them to proceed here is to make the human capital mission statement the priority item on the agenda of their ongoing Annual Premiers' Conferences. If they make significant progress toward this goal on both the social and the competitiveness fronts, they will force Ottawa to buy into the process in much the same manner in which Ottawa was forced to buy into the CCTB and SUFA initiatives. On the other hand, if the provinces do not respond to this challenge, then Canadians will and should ask Ottawa to play a larger role. In this important and strategic sense, the ball is currently in the provinces' court.

Quebec and the Mission Statement

EVEN IF THE MAJORITY OF CANADIANS WERE TO BUY INTO THE MISSION STATEMENT, surely the entire project would run aground because Quebec and Quebecers would not be party to this national or pan-Canadian exercise, or so the story would go. After all, Quebec is not a signatory to SUFA (in part because SUFA explicitly recognizes the federal spending power). Moreover, in the implementation of any human capital mission statement, Quebec would clearly insist on special powers, since among other issues, language and culture are intimately intertwined with human capital development and Quebec would not defer to an enhanced role for federal infrastructure in the context of implementing a knowledge/human-capital-based society.

Despite the foregoing observations, Quebec is unlikely to derail our collective march toward a human capital future. It may be the case that we will have to resort to creative instruments to accommodate Quebec's aspirations in this regard, but the larger and more important reality is that Quebec society is under even more pressure than is English Canada in terms of coming to grips with the implications of GIR. Hence, I believe Quebec will become a leading advocate of a human capital future for its citizens. Many of its policies already reflect this thrust — its creative family policy and the fact that until recently it had the lowest corporate tax rate in Canada.

By way of making this case, I shall draw upon a recent series of eight lengthy op-ed articles by Alain Dubuc, editorialist-in-chief for the Montreal's *La Presse*. Dubuc begins his series by noting that Quebec politics is trapped in a cul-de-sac, the prisoner of its long-standing political debate. He then traces the history of this political debate and, in passing, the history and prospects of Quebec's federalists and separatists. All of this makes for fascinating insight into the heart and soul of Quebec and Quebecers. However, what is of relevance here is his final essay, *The Way Ahead*. Dubuc's vision for the future of Quebec is, *inter alia*, along the following lines:

> Considering Quebec's needs, potential and challenges, including the impasse in which it now finds itself, leads us to the conclusion that its future will depend on fighting three battles: in education, culture and the new economy....
>
> The first objective is education, which appears now to be the essential condition for global economic success. For it is through education that a society can develop a skilled labour force, encourage research and train people who will be able to think and adapt. Education, which is intimately tied to language and values, remains one of the building blocks of identity....
>
> The second objective is the economy, specifically the many variations of the economy of the future. This knowledge economy will allow Quebec to achieve genuine prosperity and close the large gaps that, despite its recent successes, remain. The development of the knowledge economy requires that we have a

very clear definition of our priorities in research, human resources and the development and use of the new technologies. It also requires that we re-examine the institutions and practices that hinder our development, particularly the sacred "Quebec model," whose tax system rigidity and complacency act as a brake on innovation and growth....

The final objective is culture...But while all governments have reasserted the importance of culture, they have systematically treated it as a poor relation in budgetary decisions. Quebec's specificity justifies significant intervention in the development and diffusion of creative productions, but also of the library networks, language learning, literacy and efforts to stimulate intellectual development....

If Quebec succeeds in these new strategic areas, the terms of the debate on the national question will also change. A project that gives Quebec a dynamic economy, explosive cultural life and outstanding human resources will provide it with a remarkably protective bulwark. Success in all these fields is the most powerful and convincing expression of national self-affirmation. (Dubuc 2000: 26-28)

This is a remarkable statement. It buys fully into the cohesion and competitiveness imperatives of the new economy and it embeds all of this within a knowledge/human capital future for Quebecers. To be sure, Alain Dubuc is not the government of Quebec. But his words represent the winds of change in Quebec as the province wrestles with its future in the context of the new global order.

Thus, Quebec will in my view be anything but a laggard when it comes to "opting-into" (albeit perhaps selectivity) a pan-Canadian project along the lines of the mission statement.

I now turn to the final substantive issue, namely revisiting the role of cities in the structure of federalism. Indeed, Alain Dubuc's reflections on the key role of Montreal provide a natural lead-in for the discussion of cities and the division of powers:

Montreal must be the crucible for this knowledge-based society. At present, the metropolis is the victim of a regionalism that is compromising its development. The future of Quebec will be jeopardized if Montreal's essential role is not recognized by all Quebecers. (27)

Cities, Federalism and GIR

IN CHAPTER 2 WE SAW THE FORCES OF GIR CONSPIRING TO ALTER THE FUNDAMENTAL economic geography of cities and, in particular, those urban agglomerations that comprise what has come to be referred to as global city-regions. These global city-regions are emerging as the primary economic motors of the information economy. There is no possibility that Ontario could succeed as a North American region-state without the emergence of Toronto[34] as a dynamic global city-region. And the above quotation from Alain Dubuc makes a similar claim for the Quebec-Montreal relationship. Indeed, one can go further here: Canadian competitiveness in the GIR era depends on the economic vitality and dynamism of its key city-regions — Montreal, Toronto, Calgary and Vancouver among several others. Thus, city-regions are emerging as key competitive nodes in the networking of international economic activity in the GIR era. Moreover, these cities find themselves on the front lines when accommodating many federal policies. This is abundantly evident in terms of immigration, which sees most newcomers to Canada settle in Montreal, Toronto and Vancouver. Relatedly, it is also clear that these cities are in the forefront of implementing Canada's federal multicultural policies. In other words, cities are emerging as key players in both the competitiveness and cohesion dimensions of the new global economy. Thus, the issue is not so much *whether* they will be able to extricate themselves from their current "constitutionless" status as wards of their respective provinces, but rather *how* they will increase their autonomy and forge more formal linkages with both levels of government.

Toward this end, Appendix C reprints a background report from the city of Toronto entitled *Comparison of Powers and Revenue Sources of Selected Cities*, which is part of a larger report designed to forge a new relationship with both Ontario and Canada. This report presents comparative data on cities in Canada (and elsewhere) in terms of their constitutional status, access to revenues and intergovernmental funding arrangements. That Toronto should be in the forefront of this movement is hardly surprising since the newly amalgamated megacity generates nearly a quarter of Canada's GDP — and almost one third of Canada's GDP within a one-hour's driving radius of Pearson International Airport. Despite Toronto's economic role, arguably it remains the most politically constrained of all of Canada's large cities. That all of this relates to the new global order is clear:

> If Toronto is to continue to be a wealth creator that benefits Ontario and Canada in the face of severe competition from neighbouring North American cities in the context of NAFTA, the city requires:

- recognition as an independent, responsible and accountable order of government with the power to act on local matters; and
- long-term financial stability. (Toronto 2000)

While what follows will have a Toronto focus, the analysis is intended to be much more general. For example, the Canada West Foundation has launched *The Western Cities Project*. The Foundation's June 2000 report on *Financing Western Cities: Issues and Trends* deals with most of the issues highlighted below in the context of seven western Canadian cities. In any event, the ensuing analyses of selected issues relating to Canada's cities are designed as complementary thrusts to the overarching goal of this monograph — Canada's large cities and global city-regions can become *national* focal points in terms of ensuring that Canadians can develop, enhance and employ in Canada their human capital. I begin with infrastructure issues.

Building Infrastructures

Canadian cities are in need of a substantial infusion of GIR-consistent infrastructure:

> Toronto can help Canada become economically dynamic only through greater integration with the US economy. To do so, however, it must go head to head with some very substantial cities south of the border that are in the midst of a renaissance spurred on by massive investment...To maintain our ranking...in the face of well-capitalized US urban competition will require both a strategy and a scale of public and private financial investment not now evident. (Berridge 2000)

These US cities have benefited from very substantial *federal* government infrastructure spending. As noted in Appendix C, the US federal government has introduced a Transportation Equity Act for the 21st century (TEA-21) with a total budget of $217 billion. Major US cities are accessing this fund to undertake large-scale transportation infrastructure programs. The Appendix C report notes that an American urban region the size of the GTA would receive roughly $42 million annually under TEA-21 in base funding. This is essentially a non-starter, politically, in Canada since our federal government must go *through the provinces* with respect to municipal initiatives. Ottawa is mounting a modest infrastructure program, but it requires provincial matching and will presumably be subject to provincial priorities. Thus, as part of wrestling with its infrastructure deficit, a "fundamental strategic goal for the Toronto area must be to become financially self-sufficient, not only from an operating perspective, but in generating a significant portion of capital requirements for new investment" (Berridge 2000). As noted in the next section, Toronto has limited fiscal capacity to meet its operating budget, let alone embark on infrastructure spending.

But the solution to the infrastructure challenge goes well beyond the financial issue. Again, Berridge merits quotation:

> Toronto also desperately needs the management capacity for urban regeneration that is characteristic of every other world city. We have no development corporations for public-private projects comparable to the agencies typically responsible for transforming waterfront and industrial lands in US and British cities.

Relatedly,

> Toronto cannot remain a competitive global city without the active involvement of the business, financial and voluntary sectors. All successful cities have broadened the constituency commitment to productive management of their urban future beyond the narrow framework of homeowner-based local politics. Without such business intelligence and community resources, no effective business plan can be realized. How we achieve this may be Toronto's biggest challenge. (Berridge 2000)

Ironically, this infrastructure challenge can be viewed as more of a problem for Queen's Park than for Toronto, in the following sense. Queen's Park knows only too well that without state-of-the-art physical and social infrastructure for its cities, Ontario will never succeed as a powerful North American region-state. Hence, it has two polar options. The first is to ensure that Toronto can generate its needed infrastructure, via provincial-municipal transfers or via bestowing the city with enhanced taxation/financing capacity. If Queen's Park fails to do so, then the second option will come into play: In league with other Canadian cities, Toronto will aggressively lobby the federal government to begin to deal *directly* with the infrastructure challenges facing Canada's cities. The fact that the US federal government is very actively engaged in this area will strengthen the cities' position with Ottawa, whatever the constitution might say. Hence the dilemma for Queen's Park and, by extension, for other provinces too.

Fiscal Flexibility

Now that I have broached the finances of cities, there are three general approaches to placing the fiscal positions of Canada's cities on a more secure footing. The first is to upload selected expenditure categories to the provincial level. An obvious candidate here is "social housing" (at least for Toronto) which should appropriately be a provincial, if not national, responsibility in any event. Indeed, if the earlier analysis is correct — that region-states will focus more on wealth creation than on income-distribution concerns — then there probably is a rationale for a greater federal presence on the distributional front. However, to the extent that any such uploading leads to a compensating decrease in provincial grants to cities and local governments, this will do little to ameliorate the financial straightjacket, although it will help cushion the fiscal implications of an economic downturn.

A second approach relates to the general area of cost containment and, in particular, to a more extensive approach to user fees. In terms of the latter, Toronto could follow the increasing trend to extend user fees to other services, such as garbage collection. Along similar lines, Berridge notes,

> [Toronto and the GTA] have to decide what activities the city-region should *not* finance off the tax base, scrutinizing all the operating municipal services businesses — electricity, water and waste water, garbage, transit — and creating new organizations largely able to meet their own needs. Toronto is one of the few world cities that still operates these services as mainline businesses. The ability to use the very substantial asset values and cash flows of these municipal businesses is perhaps the only financial option to provide the city-region with what is unlikely to be obtainable from other sources: its own pool of re-investment capital. Such an urban infrastructure fund would have remarkable leverage potential, both from public-sector pension funds and from other private-sector institutions. (Berridge 2000)

But this has never been the Canadian way. We pride ourselves in our universal, no-user-fee, medicare system and are extremely loath to rely on user fees elsewhere in the policy arena, lest they become the thin edge of the wedge in terms of spreading to the health system. This is yet another reflection of the fact that we Canadians are having a difficult time making the transition from the former resource-dominated and behind-tariff-walls paradigm to the new realities of the emerging global order. Arguably, Berridge's comments are the way of the future.

The third and most obvious avenue for achieving fiscal flexibility is to gain access to new revenue sources. The area under some discussion is for the GTA to share in the provincial motor fuels tax, along the lines of current practice in the greater Vancouver area. "The ability...to receive a share of the fuel tax (and possibly license fees and other transportation-related charges) to fund road and

transit improvements would increase Toronto's financial self-sufficiency and its
ability to pay for transit and transportation needs in the region" (Slack 2000).
Beyond this option, Slack notes that city-regions like Stockholm and Frankfurt
have access to a share of income taxation. Allocating a portion of the provincial
sales tax is yet another potential option. Appendix C presents a survey of
Canadian and foreign cities' access to various sorts of taxes.

It may not be surprising that none of these options is even on Queen's
Park's radar screen. What is surprising is that they have not featured prominently, except for the fuel tax, in terms of the priorities of Toronto and the GTA.

In my view, the underlying issue here is political, not economic. Until
recently, Toronto and the GTA were locked into the constitutional mindset that
they are creatures of the province. However, with the creation of the megacity and
with the potential for the Greater Toronto Services Board to evolve into a GTA-
wide instrument for integrating physical and human capital infrastructure, the
political dynamics of Toronto and, by extension, of Ontario are about to change.
Enter *The Toronto Charter*.

The Toronto Charter and Political Evolution

With over 4.5 million residents, the GTA has a larger population than all but two
Canadian provinces — Ontario (or the rest of Ontario) and Quebec. If and when
the GTA embraces a "unity of purpose" and conceives of itself as an integrated
global city, it may well become a political arrangement that will be able to rival
Queen's Park in selected policy areas. And if the GTA were ever to become a single
political entity, it would not take long before it would probably harbour aspirations
of becoming a city-province along the lines of the German city-länder —
Hamburg, Bremen and Berlin. Presumably, the province would veto any such
aspirations, but the fallback position would certainly be a degree of GTA self-
determination that Queen's Park could no longer ignore. But even without political amalgamation, the Toronto megacity will possess a cadre of civil servants that
will have sufficient informational, analytical and implementation capacity to generate approaches to policy and program development that would rival those emanating from Queen's Park. Of and by itself, this will change the political dynamics
between the GTA and the province.

With the promulgation of *The Toronto Charter*, this political evolution has
already begun. The Charter was developed by a working group that included

academics, journalists, urban planners, business people and professionals, community workers, bureaucrats and politicians under the leadership of Alan Broadbent. A city charter is not novel in the Canadian context — Vancouver, Winnipeg, Montreal and Saint John all have charters, and Newfoundland's new Cities Act is the equivalent of a charter for its two major cities. Table 17 spells out the provisions of *The Toronto Charter*.

As is very obvious, this is a rethinking and repositioning of Toronto within the Canadian federation. The starting point is to view Toronto (or the Toronto region) as a separate "order of government" in the federation. From this perspective, much of the rest of the charter follows rather axiomatically. In particular, Toronto should then be entitled to

- ◆ be a player in the federal-provincial relations arena;
- ◆ powers over a large range of policy areas, driven by the principle of subsidiarity (some of these powers would be concurrent and some exclusive);
- ◆ fiscal autonomy; and
- ◆ develop more formal relations with other levels of government.

While the formal Charter, as reproduced in Table 17, has not been adopted by Toronto, the city is well along the way in terms of embracing the substance and spirit (if not the letter) of the Charter and is now beginning the sure-to-be-prolonged set of discussions with Ontario, Canada, the Association of Municipalities of Ontario and the Federation of Canadian Municipalities. Although this is currently a Toronto-focused initiative, it will not be long before other cities will latch on to key aspects of the substance and spirit. In an important sense, therefore, we are now launched into a fascinating process that will likely end up with a rethinking and reworking of the role of cities in the federation.

Implications

The reality of the new global order is that cities, especially those that fall into the category of global city-regions, have become major international players on the economic front. It is only natural that with this enhanced economic status, these city-regions will begin to strive toward some comparable recognition on the political front. Indeed, the more Toronto and the GTA embrace the concept of themselves as dynamic economic motors having to go head-to-head with competing North American global city-regions, the more likely that Queen's Park will

The Greater Toronto Charter

Article One	The Greater Toronto Region form an order of government that is a full partner of the Federal and Provincial Governments of Canada.
Article Two	The Greater Toronto Region, and its municipalities, be empowered to govern and exercise responsibility over a broad range of issues, including: *child and family services; cultural institutions; economic development and marketing; education; environmental protection; health care; housing; immigrant and refugee settlement; land-use planning; law enforcement and emergency services; recreation; revenue generation, taxation and assessment; transportation; sewage treatment; social assistance; waste and natural resource management; and water supply and quality management.* with the exception of those matters as are mutually agreed upon with other levels of government that are best assigned to another level.
Article Three	The Greater Toronto Region have the fiscal authority to raise revenues and allocate expenditures with respect to those responsibilities outlined in Article Two.
Article Four	The Greater Toronto Region be governed by accessible, democratic governments, created by their citizens and accountable to them for the exercise of the governments' full duties and responsibilities.
Article Five	The Greater Toronto Region continue to fulfill its obligation to share its wealth, innovation and other assets with the rest of Canada, through appropriate mechanisms developed in concert with other levels of government.

be pressured to accommodate this via a greater degree of self-determination. The interesting issue is whether this should trigger formal constitutional change. I think not. Even the bold provisions of *The Toronto Charter* could be implemented *institutionally* via a deft approach to the delegation of powers on Ontario's part, should the process ever get this far. More importantly, this is inherently an evolutionary process, one that requires learning-by-doing and political and institutional flexibility, not constitutional rigidification.

Nonetheless, the underlying message, indeed the underlying dynamic, is that Canada's cities *will* carve out a larger economic, social and political role within the Canadian federation. Rather than resorting to formal constitutional change, the appropriate way to proceed is by way of creative governance structures and instrumentalities that will accommodate the rising economic and political star of Canada's city-regions. This is of critical importance to the successful pursuit of the mission statement, since these cities are now perched atop Canada's human capital pyramid.

Going Forward

G LOBALIZATION AND THE KNOWLEDGE/INFORMATION REVOLUTION ARE SIGNALLING the advent of a new societal order, one with profound and pervasive implications for citizens, for markets, for governments and, therefore, for public policy. This new global order is a truly remarkable watershed in the annals of human history and, as is the case with all great transformations, it carries with it both enormous opportunities and daunting challenges. The role of chapters 2 through 8 is to analyze and isolate these opportunities and challenges in general terms as well as in relation to Canada and Canadians. The remainder of the analysis assesses the resulting implications for public policy — indeed, for the evolution of Canadian society — and evolves toward highlighting two defining features of the new global order. First, central to this new era is a truly exciting development: the democratization of information and the emergence of information-empowered individuals as dominant players in the economic and political arenas. Second, the inexorable march of GIR has presented us with a historically unprecedented window of opportunity: With knowledge now at the cutting edge of competitiveness and with enhancing the education and skills of all Canadians as the keys to addressing inequality, a societal commitment to a human capital future is emerging as the principal avenue by which to promote both economic competitiveness and social cohesion. These two fundamental realities of GIR lead directly to the conclusion of this analysis: To succeed in the 21st century, Canada must become *a state of minds*.

Readers interested in a review of the main findings, implications and conclusions of the analysis are referred to the *Overview and Executive Summary* in Chapter 1. For present purposes, two aspects of the competitiveness-cohesion nexus merit highlight.

The first is a personal reflection on the preceding analysis. At many points during the drafting of the policy sections — essentially Part IV but aspects of Part III as well — I felt that forging and/or forcing a linkage that required policy to address both cohesion and competitiveness resulted in a compromise to both cohesion and competitiveness. What I mean here is I was certain an unconstrained approach to competitiveness would have dominated the version of competitiveness that arose from the mission statement. And with even more certainty I felt this was true for social policy and social cohesion. Perhaps it is natural for an author to become overly influenced by what he/she has just written, but I now have come to the view that embracing the mission statement and its implications is actually the first-best approach to competitiveness and to social cohesion. In other words, if one were free to design a competitive economy, the optimal approach to so doing would be along the mission-statement or Part IV lines. And surprisingly, perhaps, I now think this is even more true for the social side, in part because of the obvious: equal access to a human capital future is essential for social cohesion, and in part because of the not-so-obvious: our social infrastructures must be viewed as major economic and export platforms or we will never achieve state-of-the-art social programs for Canadians. No doubt, someone will point out exactly where and how I may have gone astray here, but in the interim we have an exciting and indeed quite remarkable result — *the optimal way to pursue both economic competitiveness and social cohesion in their own right is to pursue them in tandem!*

The second observation is related. In spite of the complementarity of the social and economic goals, their policy challenges differ markedly. Dealing first with competitiveness, the very nature of the NAFTA/information-revolution combination means you and I will have access to state-of-the-art private-sector goods and services across an increasingly wide range of areas. This being the case, and unless we take leave of our senses, it follows that Canadian policy will obviously want to ensure that Canadian-based operations and human capital are competing in an arena at least as favourable as that of our trading partners, particularly the Americans. This leads to the equally obvious conclusion that our tax rates on mobile factors must become competitive. What is not so obvious is whether our rates will become competitive *before* too much of our financial, investment and human capital migrates to sunnier climes, which will depend on how we progress on the social side.

The challenges and politics on the social side are much more complex and difficult. The outputs of social programs are inherently non-tradeable internationally, so best practices elsewhere need not influence the evolution of our own policies toward the social envelope. We have no choice but to be the architects of our own social infrastructure. Moreover, we are charting unknown territory in the sense that there is no single best approach to a human capital future, let alone to the design of individual social programs. However, we have federalism as an ally here. It allows for creative provincial experimentation and its consequent learning-by-doing, obvious assets to the evolution of social infrastructure consistent with a human capital society and economy. Nonetheless, unlike the case for competitiveness, the problem here is that no overriding force on the social front is driving us in the direction of a human-capital future. If while focusing our attention on becoming more competitive with the Americans we satisfy ourselves with mere tinkering or "muddling through" on the social policy front, we are likely to fall into the trap of (unintentionally) embracing the US vision of social policy. (Pressures in this direction already exist.) Therefore, we need some clear and upfront signal of our collective commitment to a human capital future. My choice here would be a credible commitment to a human capital "bill of rights" for our children. This would galvanize Canadians in terms of embracing the implications of the mission statement. It would also serve to generate a collective confidence with respect to the future that would allow us to pursue a first-mover advantage on the competition front.

As I pen these final comments, I am acutely aware of the shortcomings of the foregoing analysis. For one thing, I made (implicit) promises I did not deliver on — my claim in Chapter 3 that the GIR era will ultimately be citizenship-enhancing was not taken up in the policy section. While I believe this to be true, I pass the baton to the political scientists. Moreover, and again along citizenship lines, there is virtually no reference to our First Nations, and precious little to the importance of duality as an abiding principle in Canada-Quebec relations. More generally, the economic policy section (Chapter 14) is far narrower than are the Part II implications for the economy. Finally, I readily admit there is too much about Ontario and Toronto in the foregoing analysis and not enough about the other regions, provinces and cities of Canada. Mea culpa.

Books, thankfully, have an end, but by its very nature, there is no conclusion to this work. One obvious reason is that globalization and the knowledge/information revolution are far from running their full course, so "going forward" is the appropriate way to convey the message that Canada's response to the GIR challenge is also in its infancy. There is a second reason why *Going Forward* is an appropriate title for this final chapter: Canada and Canadians have not yet made the collective commitment to become the most human-capital-oriented economy and society on earth.

My final comments should hardly come as a surprise. Canada in the millennium must become a state of minds. We can achieve this goal only if we commit ourselves to making the dramatic transformation from a resource- and physical-capital-based economy and society to a human-capital-based economy and society. In the words of the mission statement, our collective challenge is to

> Design a sustainable, socially inclusive and internationally competitive infrastructure that ensures equal opportunity for all Canadians to develop, to enhance and to employ in Canada their skills and human capital, thereby enabling them to become full citizens in the information-era Canadian and global societies.

Canadians recall with pride Sir Wilfrid Laurier's prophetic claim that the 20th century would belong to Canada. If we embrace the mission statement and make Canada a state of minds, *the 21st century will belong to Canadians.*

1   Given the interrelated nature of the GIR
     challenge for governments, markets and cit-
     izens (let alone the three interfaces), it is
     inevitable that a degree of arbitrariness will
     enter the analysis. For example, the reality
     that GIR is leading to a polarization of mar-
     ket incomes could be dealt with in terms of
     the implications for citizens, for markets or
     even for governments. Indeed, given the
     many implications that have to be allocated
     in terms of the Figure 1 categories, it is
     probable that each reader would choose a
     unique assignment.

2   The mushrooming of debt/GDP ratios was
     also fairly widespread among OECD
     nations and even beyond. McKinnon
     (1997), among others, links this debt
     explosion to the demise of the Bretton
     Woods fixed-exchange-rate system and the
     consequent removal of an external disci-
     pline on expenditure-intent governments.
     Relatedly, one of the reasons why Italians
     have been such strong supporters of the
     Euro is that the common currency will *inter
     alia* force Italy to come to grips with its
     huge deficit, its inflation and its spending
     (McKinnon 1997; Friedman 1999: 150).
     Indeed, it already has.

3   The "innovative milieu" is comprised of a
     set of relations that unite a local production
     system, a set of actors and representations
     and an industrial culture. Together, these
     generate a localized dynamic process of col-
     lective learning. Specialized labour mobility
     inside the local labour market, innovation
     imitations and interfirm cooperation link-
     ages, common codes and conventions, and
     a sense of belonging are the basic con-
     stituent elements of the local *milieu*
     (Camagni 2000: 9).

4   For a much broader range of perspectives
     relating to citizenship and democracy in the
     new global order, see Simeon (1997) and
     Kymlicka (1997) and references therein.

5   Note, however, that the actual drafting of
     these directives is in the hands of the
     European Commission. In EU jargon, the

     Commission proposes and the Council
     disposes.

6   Arguably, Greenpeace was involved in
     many areas much earlier, but I view this as
     a powerful organization-led lobby, whereas
     Maude Barlow's initiative (along with oth-
     ers, such as banning land mines) was more
     citizen-based. Perhaps this is drawing too
     fine a line.

7   For purposes of this book, I am defining
     MNCs as being subject to host-country con-
     straints and controls whereas TNEs are not so
     constrained. For example, under the "national
     treatment" provisions of the FTA, an
     American corporation can do in Canada any-
     thing and everything that a Canadian corpo-
     ration can do. In effect, an American or
     Mexican corporation has the rights of a
     "domestic" Canadian corporation. Note also
     that MNE is used interchangeably with MNC.

8   This section draws heavily from Courchene
     and Telmer (1998: Chapter 9).

9   Note that I am defining "integration" in
     terms of the *volume* of trade. As Helliwell
     (1998) has emphasized, corrected for
     income levels and distance, the internal
     Canadian market is much more integrated
     (in an efficiency sense) than is the cross-
     border market. Indeed, east-west trade
     (interprovincial trade) is ten times larger
     than north-south trade (international trade)
     for comparable income densities and dis-
     tances. But because the US is so large, the
     gross flows tell a very different story.

10   It is important to note that these trade data
     are gross flows of goods and services, not
     value-added. This is probably most impor-
     tant for the auto sector. For example, each
     car exported from Ontario is recorded as
     the full value of the car, even if many of the
     component parts were initially imported.
     This means the ratio of exports to GDP
     could, in principle, exceed 100 percent, as
     this ratio does in many "flow-through"
     economies (such as Singapore).

11   Not all analysts would agree with this. For
     example, Savoie (forthcoming, 2001)

argues that Confederation, and national policy initiatives in particular, did not serve the Maritime provinces well.

12   A recent study (commissioned by New Brunswick) by Boyd Company Location Consultants (1995) compares New Brunswick to 25 US cities in terms of a range of factors relating to call centre operations. New Brunswick comes out on top or near the top in terms of most categories (telecommunications costs, fringes, office space costs, weekly wages, energy costs etc.).

13   Much of what follows will constitute a summary, often with direct quotations, of an insightful, recent book by Dani Rodrik (1997). However, this is a poor substitute for reading this valuable treatise.

14   Note that "liberalism" is employed here in its British meaning, i.e., freer markets.

15   In more centralized federations such as the US and Australia, there is less need for an agreement on internal trade since the courts have interpreted their respective federal trade and commerce powers (or interstate commerce clauses) in a very expansive way. One of the differences is that Canada, unlike the US or Australia, has a list of exclusive provincial powers which, in turn, constrains the scope of Ottawa's trade and commerce power.

16   This section is based on Courchene (1995-96).

17   Except in the context of competitive federalism, dealt with later in the chapter.

18   The wording is adapted from the Ontario Securities Commission *Report on Implications for Canadian Capital Markets of the Provision by Financial Institutions of Access to Discount Brokerage Services* (1983: 16) which, in turn, drew from my research report to the Commission (Courchene 1984).

19   Richards (1998) presents an insightful analysis of this impediment to public-sector adjustment.

20   I must declare a potential conflict of interest here. This section on the BCNI initiative was written in the summer of 1999, based on the April 1999 BCNI documentation. Subsequently (August 1999), I was asked (and accepted) to serve on the BCNI advisory committee related to this initiative. I attended the September 1999 advisory committee meeting and the January 2000 meeting. All of the references to the BCNI initiative are restricted to the April, 1999 documentation, well in advance of my involvement. Relatedly, while readers might assume that because of my book, *From Heartland to North American Region State*, I was closely associated with the Ontario mission statement, the truth is I was totally unaware of this initiative until three months after it was published. Nonetheless, it is the case that, after the fact, I applaud both initiatives.

21   This is only one of many possible approaches one could take toward implementing policies designed to increase equality of access to human capital formation.

22   Under the 50-50 EPF cost sharing, one half of the federal share was in the form of cash transfers. Hence, the 25 cent sharing figure in this section.

23   Note that the 25 percent ceiling referred to in the next-to-last bulleted entry corresponds to the original EPF federal cash-transfer funding share (see endnote 22).

24   Since Kent's article is in the form of an "internal memo" to the Prime Minister, the "we" and "our" in the quotation relates to the federal government.

25   As this manuscript was going to press, the Chrétien Liberals reversed themselves and "loosened" EI, as it were. The accepted rationale for this move is that it would serve the Liberals' election interests in Atlantic Canada.

26   Readers wishing more detail with respect to the range of training available to the Canadian forces can consult *Marching To a Different Drummer* (Courchene and Campbell 1995).

27   This could be extended to include a minimum personal income tax on high-income citizens.

28   While this section draws largely from Mintz
      (1999), an alternative, and generally simi-
      lar, framework and approach can be found
      in Olewiler (1999).

29   The operational principle underpinning
      Alberta's tax reform was that *all* Alberta
      taxpayers would be better off under the
      new tax system. However, Alberta brought
      down its budget *before* the federal budget.
      The reduction of the middle income tax
      rate in the federal budget meant the exist-
      ing system (defined to include the 2000
      federal budget) would leave some middle-
      income taxpayers better off than they
      would be under Alberta tax reform. Hence,
      Alberta lowered its flat rate from 11 per-
      cent to 10.5 percent to ensure that all tax-
      payers would benefit.

30   The equalization standard is the product of
      the all-province average tax rate and the
      average per capita tax base in the five des-
      ignated provinces (Ontario, Quebec, British
      Columbia, Manitoba and Saskatchewan).
      (For more details, see Courchene 1994:
      Chapter 4.)

31   This Quebec tax abatement works as fol-
      lows. Ottawa reduces or "abates" federal tax
      owing by Quebecers by 16.5 percent.
      Quebec then increases its PIT rates to take
      advantage of the vacated federal tax room.
      Thus, compared with their fellow
      Canadians, Quebecers pay less federal per-
      sonal income tax and more in provincial
      income tax. It is important to note that,
      overall, this is revenue neutral for both
      Quebec and Ottawa: Ottawa reduces
      Quebec's cash transfers (e.g., from equaliza-
      tion) by the value of the abatement.

32   The pre-election mini-budget, or Economic
      Statement, came much too late in this
      book's production process to have its provi-
      sions integrated fully into the analysis. Yet
      the implications of the Economic Statement
      are of utmost importance to the issues
      being addressed in Part IV of this book.
      The "hold-the-press" compromise was to
      add a single section that would summarize

the main provisions as they relate to chapters 13 and 14 and to use endnotes to
update Chapter 15, if needed.

33   Figure 13 comes from an unidentified
      handout that fell somehow into my pos-
      session. I have tried unsuccessfully to find
      the author.

34   The new megacity of Toronto has a popula-
      tion of roughly 2.5 million. The Greater
      Toronto Area (GTA) includes Toronto as
      well as the regions of Durham, Peel, Halton
      and York. The population of the GTA is 4.5
      million. The reference to Toronto as a "glob-
      al city-region" relates primarily to the GTA.

Arthurs, Harry (1999) "Constitutionalizing Neo-Conservatism and Regional
    Economic Integration: TINAx2," in Thomas J. Courchene (ed.), *Room To
    Manoeuvre? Globalization and Policy Convergence* (Queen's University: The
    John Deutsch Institute for the Study of Economic Policy), pp. 17-74.

Banting, Keith G. (1997) "The Internationalization of the Social Contract," in
    Thomas J. Courchene (ed.), *The Nation State in a Global/Information Era:
    Policy Challenges* (Queen's University: The John Deutsch Institute for the
    Study of Economic Policy), pp. 255-86.

Bastien, Richard (1981) *Federalism and Decentralization: Where Do We Stand?*
    (Ottawa: Supply and Services Canada).

Beach, Charles M. and George A. Slotsve (1996) *Are We Becoming Two Societies?
    Income Polarization and the Myth of the Declining Middle Class in Canada*
    (Toronto: C.D. Howe Institute).

Beauchesne, Eric (1999) "US Firms on Buying Spree in Canada", *The Ottawa
    Citizen* (July 9), p. D3.

Bell, Daniel (1987) "The World and the United States in 2013", *Daedalus*, vol.
    116, no. 3 (Summer), pp. 1-31.

Berridge, Joe (2000) "There's No Need to Sit and Wait for a Handout," in Mary
    Rowe (ed.), *Toronto: Considering Self-Government* (Owen Sound: The
    Ginger Press).

Biggs, Margaret (1996) *Building Blocks for Canada's New Social Union*, Working
    Paper F02 (Ottawa: Canadian Policy Research Networks).

Bliss, Michael (2000) "Sick and Tired of It", *National Post* (January 12), p. A18.

Boyd Company Location Consultants (1995) *A Comparative New Brunswick and
    U.S. Cost Analysis for Call Centre Operations* (Princeton, N.J.: Boyd
    Location Consultants).

Breton, Albert (1990) "Centralization, Decentralization and Intergovernmental
    Competition," 1989 MacGregor Lecture (Queen's University: Institute of
    Intergovernmental Relations).

Brock, Kathy (2000) "Sustaining a Relationship: Insights from Canada on
    Linking the Government and the Third Sector," School of Policy Studies
    Working Paper Series, Number 2000/1 (Queen's University: School of
    Policy Studies).

Business Council on National Issues (1999) "The Canada Global Leadership
    Initiative" (Ottawa: BCNI).

Cable, Vincent (1995) "The Diminished Nation State: A Study in the Loss of Economic Power," *Daedalus*, vol. 124, no. 2 (Spring), pp. 23-53.

Camagni, Roberta (2000) "Economic Role and Spatial Contradictions of Global Cities: The Functional, the Cognitive and the Evolutionary Context", prepared for the Global City-Regions Conference (UCLA, October 21-23, 1999), forthcoming in Allen Scott (ed.) *Global City-Regions* (Oxford University Press).

Canada West Foundation (2000) "Great Expectations: The Ideal Characteristics of Non-Profits", Alternative Service Delivery Project Research Bulletin, no. 3, (Calgary, Alberta: Canada West Foundation).

Carnoy, Martin and Manuel Castells (1996) "Sustainable Flexibility: Prospective Study on Work, Family, and Society in the Information Age," Working Paper no. 11 (University of California, Berkeley: Centre for Western European Studies).

Castells, Manuel (1989) *The Information City: Information Technology, Economic Restructuring and the Urban-Regional Process* (Oxford: Blackwell Publishers).

Castells, Manuel (1996) *The Rise of the Network Society* (Oxford: Blackwell Publishers).

Castells, Manuel (1997) *The Power of Identity* (Oxford: Blackwell Publishers).

Castells, Manuel (1998) *End of Millennium* (Oxford: Blackwell Publishers).

Chrétien, The Honourable Jean, Prime Minister of Canada (2000) "The Canadian Way in the 21st Century" paper presented to the Berlin Conference hosted by Chancellor Gerhard Schröder on "Progressive Governance in the 21st Century," June 2-3.

Cooper, Sherry (1999) *The Cooper Files* (Toronto, Ontario: Key Porter Books Limited).

Courchene, Thomas J. (1984) "A Real Secure Industry or a Real Securities Industry," (Submission to the Ontario Securities Industry in respect of its Review of Discount Brokerage), mimeo, Department of Economics, University of Western Ontario, London, Ontario.

Courchene, Thomas J. (1989) *What Does Ontario Want? The Coming of Age of Robarts' Confederation of Tomorrow Conference* (York University: Robarts Centre For Canadian Studies).

Courchene, Thomas J. (1992) "Mon pays, c'est l'hiver: Reflections of a Market Populist," *Canadian Journal of Economics*, Vol. 25 (November), pp. 759-91.

Courchene, Thomas J. (1994) *Social Canada in the Millennium: Reform Imperatives and Restructuring Principles* (Toronto: C.D. Howe Institute).

Courchene, Thomas J. (1995) "Glocalization: The Regional/International Interface," *Canadian Journal of Regional Science*, Vol. XVIII:1 (Spring), pp. 1-20.

Courchene, Thomas J. (1995-96) "Corporate Governance As Ideology," *Canadian Business Law Journal*, Vol. 26, pp. 202-10.

Courchene, Thomas J. (1996) *ACCESS: A Convention on the Canadian Economic and Social Systems* (Toronto: Ministry of Intergovernmental Affairs), reprinted in *Canadian Business Economics*, Vol. 4, no. 4 (Summer 1998), pp. 3-26.

Courchene, Thomas J. (1997) "The International Dimension of Macroeconomic Policies in Canada," in M.U. Fratianni, D. Salvatore and J. von Hagen (eds.), *Macroeconomic Policies in Open Economies*, Handbook of Comparative Economic Policies, Vol. 5 (Westport, CT: Greenwood Press), pp. 495-537.

Courchene, Thomas J. (1998) *Renegotiating Equalization: National Polity, Federal State, International Economy*, Commentary, no. 113 (Toronto: C.D. Howe Institue).

Courchene, Thomas J. (1999a) "Towards a North American Common Currency: An Optimal Currency Area Analysis," in Thomas J. Courchene (ed.), *Room To Manoeuvre? Globalization and Policy Convergence* (Queen's University: The John Deutsch Institute for the Study of Economic Policy), pp. 271-334.

Courchene, Thomas J. (1999b) "National versus Regional Concerns: A Provincial Perspective on the Role and Operation of the Tax Collection Agreements," *Canadian Tax Journal,* Vol. 47, no. 4, pp. 861-89.

Courchene, Thomas J. (1999c) "From Heartland to North American Region State." Acceptance remarks for the 1999 Donner Prize, *Policy Options Politique*, Vol. 20, no. 4 (July-August).

Courchene, Thomas J. (1999d) "Fair Shares Federalism and the 1999 Federal Budget," *Policy Options Politique*, Vol. 20, no. 3 (April), pp. 39-46.

Courchene, Thomas J. (1999e) "The PIT and the Pendulum: Reflections on Ontario's Proposal to Mount its Own Personal Income Tax System," in Robert Young (ed.), *Stretching the Federation: The Art of the State in Canada* (Queen's University: Institute of Intergovernmental Relations), pp. 129-86.

Courchene, Thomas J. (2000a) "A Paul Martin, Sr., Budget," *Policy Options Politiques*, vol. 21, no. 3 (April), pp. 17-20.

Courchene, Thomas J. (2000b) "A Mission Statement for Canada," *Policy Options Politiques*, vol. 21, no. 6 (July-August), pp. 6-14.

Courchene, Thomas J. and Richard G. Harris (1999) *From Fixing To Monetary Union: Options for North American Currency Integration*, Commentary 127 (Toronto: C.D. Howe Institute).

Courchene, Thomas J. and Robert Campbell (1995) "Marching To a Different Drummer: Exploratory Research on the Potential for a Military Role in the Training of Civilian Canada," in Roy Hogg and Jack Mintz (eds.), *Who Pays the Piper? Canada's Social Policy* (Queen's University: The John Deutsch Institute for the Study of Economic Policy), pp. 87-146.

Courchene, Thomas J. and Colin R. Telmer (1998) *From Heartland To North American Region State: The Social, Fiscal and Federal Evolution of Ontario* (Toronto: Faculty of Management, University of Toronto).

Crane, David (1997) "Trade Patterns Eroding Our Nation," *The Toronto Star* (January 5), p. F2.

Dalhby, Bev (1994) "The Distortionary Effect of Rising Taxes," in William B.P. Robson and William M. Scarth (eds.), *Deficit Reduction: What Pain, What Gain?* (Toronto: C.D. Howe Institute), pp. 43-72.

Davenport, Paul (2000) "Universities, Innovation and the Knowledge-Based Economy," Industry Canada Distinguished Lecture, CERF/IRPP Conference on "Creating Canada's Advantage in an Information Age," available on the IRPP website — www.irpp.org.

Davidson, James Dale and Lord William Rees-Mogg (1997) *The Sovereign Individual* (New York: Simon and Schuster).

Delottinville, P. (1994) *Shifting in the New Economy: Call Centres and Beyond* (Toronto: Copp Clark Longman).

Decter, Michael B. (2000) *Four Strong Winds: Understanding the Growing Challenge to Health Care* (Toronto, Ontario: Stoddart).

Dobell, Rod (2000) "Social Capital and Social Learning in a Full World" paper prepared for an HRDC/OECD symposium on *The Contribution of Human and Social Capital to Sustained Economic Growth and Well Being* (Quebec City), March 19-21.

Drucker, Peter (1986) "The Changed World Economy," *Foreign Affairs* 64
    (Spring), pp. 1-17.

Drucker, Peter (1989) *The New Realities* (New York: Harper Row).

Drucker, Peter (1993) *Post-Capitalist Society* (New York: Harper Business).

Dubuc, Alain (2000) "We Must Break this Vicious Circle," *Policy Options
    Politiques* (June), 8-28. This is a translation of eight full-page editorials in
    La Presse in February of 2000.

Elkins, David (1995) *Beyond Sovereignty: Territory and Political Economy in the
    Twenty-First Century* (Toronto: University of Toronto Press).

Eves, Ernie, Ontario Minister of Finance (1998) *Ontario Economic Outlook and
    Fiscal Review* (Toronto: Queen's Printer for Ontario).

Eves, Ernie, Ontario Minister of Finance (2000) *2000 Ontario Budget: Balanced
    Budgets — Bright Futures,* budget speech (Queen's Park: Queen's Printer
    for Ontario).

Fortin, Pierre (1999) *The Canadian Standard of Living: Is There a Way Up?* C.D.
    Howe Institute Benefactors' Lecture (Toronto: C.D. Howe Institute).

Freeman, C. and C. Perez (1988) "Structural Crisis of Adjustment," in G. Dosi
    et al., (eds.) *Technical Change and Economic Theory* (London: Pinters
    Publishers).

Friedman, Thomas (1999) *The Lexus and the Olive Tree: Understanding
    Globalization* (New York: Farrar, Strauss and Giroux).

Friedrichs, Carl (1968) *Trends of Federalism in Theory and Practice* (New York:
    Praeger).

Fry, Earl (1998) *The Expanding Role of State and Local Governments in US Foreign
    Affairs* (New York: Council on Foreign Relations Press).

Fukuyama, Francis (1995) *Trust: The Social Virtues and the Creation of Prosperity*
    (London: Penguin Books).

Garrett, Michael (2000) "Towards a New Relationship with Ontario and
    Canada," memo from CAO of City of Toronto (June 6).

Gertler, Meric (2000) "Self-Determination for Toronto: What are the Economic
    Conditions, and Do they Exist?", in Mary Rowe (ed.), *Toronto: Considering
    Self-Government* (Owen Sound: The Ginger Press).

Gibbins, Roger (1997) "Democratic Reservations About the ACCESS Models,"
    in Harvey Lazar (ed.), *Assessing ACCESS: Towards a New Social Union*
    (Queen's University: Institute of Intergovernmental Relations), pp. 41-44.

Goldman Sachs (2000) "Technology and the New Global Economy," *CEO Confidential* (March).

Grady, Patrick and Katie Macmillan (1998) "Why Is Interprovincial Trade Down and International Trade Up?", *Canadian Business Economics*, Vol. 6, no. 4, pp. 26-35.

Graham, Katherine A., and Susan D. Phillips (1998) "Who Does What in Ontario: The Process of Provincial-Municipal Disentanglement," *Canadian Public Administration*, Vol. 42, no. 2 (Summer), pp. 175-209.

Graham, Stephen (1994) "Networking Cities: Telematics in Urban Policy in a Critical Review," in *International Journal of Urban and Regional Research*, Vol. 18, no. 3, pp. 416-32.

Gratzer, David (1999) *Code Blue: Reviving Canada's Health Care System* (Toronto: ECW Press).

Greenwood, John (2000) "B.C. Biotechs Fleeing South," *National Post* (July 26), pp. C1, C6.

Hall, Michael H. and Keith G. Banting (2000) "The Nonprofit Sector in Canada: An Introduction," in Keith Banting (ed.), *The Nonprofit Sector in Canada: Roles and Relationships* (Queen's University: School of Policy Studies), pp. 1-28.

Hall, Michael H. and L. G. Macpherson (1997) "A Provincial Portrait of Canada's Charitable Sector," *Research Bulletin*, Vol. 5, no. 2 (Toronto: Canadian Centre for Philanthropy).

Hardin, Hershell (1974) *Nation Unaware: The Canadian Economic Culture* (Vancouver: J.J. Douglas Ltd.).

Harris, Richard G. (1993) "Trade, Money, and Wealth in the Canadian Economy", Benefactors Lecture, Toronto, C. D. Howe Institute.

Harris, Richard G. (1999a) *Determinants of Canadian Productivity Growth: Issues and Prospects*, Discussion Paper Number 8 (Ottawa: Industry Canada).

Harris, Richard G. (1999b) "Making a Case for Tax Cuts" (Ottawa: Business Council for national Issues), mimeo.

Harris, Richard G. (2000) *The Knowledge-Based Economy: Facts and Theories*, Framework Paper 00-02, Queen's Management Research Centre for Knowledge-Based Enterprises (Queen's University: School of Business), mimeo.

Helliwell, John (1998) *How Much Do National Borders Matter?* (Washington: The Brookings Institution).

Helpman, Elhanan (ed.) (1998) *General Purpose Technologies* (Boston: MIT Press).

Horsman, Mathew and Andrew Marshall (1994) *After the Nation State: Citizens, Tribalism and the New World Disorder* (London: Harper Collins).

Huntingdon, S. (1991) "A New Era In Democracy's 'Third Wave'," *Current* (September), pp. 27-39.

Industry Canada (2000) "A Regional Perspective on Canada-US Standard of Living Comparisons," *MICRO*, Vol. 7, no. 1, pp. 5-6.

IRPP Task Force on Health Policy (2000), *Recommendations To First Ministers*, (Montreal: IRPP).

Kent, Tom (2000) *What Should Be Done About Medicare* (Ottawa: Caledon Institute).

Kneebone, Ron and Ken Mackenzie (1998) "Stabilizing Features of Fiscal Policy in Canada," in T.J. Courchene and T.A.Wilson (eds.), *Fiscal Targets and Economic Growth* (Queen's University: The John Deutsch Institute for the Study of Economic Policy), pp. 191-235.

Kymlicka, Will (1997) "The Prospects for Citizenship: Domestic and Global," in Thomas J. Courchene (ed.), *The National State in a Global/Information Era: Policy Challenges* (Queen's University: The John Deutsch Institute for the Study of Economic Policy), pp. 315-25.

Lasch, Christopher (1994) "The Revolt of the Elites: Have They Cancelled Their Allegiance to America?" *Harper's* (November), pp. 39-50.

Lecoq, Bruno (1991) "Organisation industrielle, organisation territoriale: une approche intégrée fondée sur le concept de réseau," *Revue d'Économie Régionale et Urbaine*, 34:321-342.

Letourneau, Raynauld and Martine Lajoie (2000) *A Regional Perspective on the Canada-US Standard of Living Comparison*, Occasional Paper No. 22 (Ottawa: Industry Canada).

Lipsey, Richard and Cliff Bekar (1995) "A Structuralist View of Technical Change and Economic Growth," in Thomas J. Courchene (ed.), *Technology, Information and Public Policy* (Queen's University: The John Deutsch Institute for the Study of Economic Policy), pp. 9-76.

Martin, Honourable Paul, Minister of Finance (2000), *Better Finances, Better Lives: The Budget Plan 2000* (Ottawa: Finance Canada).

McCarthy, Shawn (2000) "Tax Break for Options a First Step, Roth Says," *Globe and Mail, Report on Business* (January 17), pp. B1, B2.

McKenna, Honourable Frank and Donald Savoie (1995) "Challenging the Status Quo in Canadian Federalism," mimeo.

McKinnon, Ronald I. (1997) "Monetary Regimes, Government Borrowing Constraints and Market-Preserving Federalism: Implications for EMU," in Thomas J. Courchene (ed.), *The Nation State in a Global/Information Era* (Queen's University: The John Deutsch Institute for the Study of Economic Policy), pp. 101-42.

Mendelsohn, Matthew and John McLean (2000) "SUFA's Double Vision: Citizen Engagement and Intergovernmental Collaboration," *Policy Options Politique*, vol. 21, no. 3 (April) pp. 43-46.

Mendelson, Michael (2000) "The Emancipation of Cities," in Mary Rowe (ed.), *Toronto: Considering Self-Government* (Owen Sound: The Ginger Press).

Ministerial Council on Social Policy Renewal and Reform (1996) *A Report To Premiers* (This Report can be obtained from the intergovernmental secretariat of any province).

Mintz, Jack M. (1999) "Why Canada Must Undertake Business Tax Reform Soon," C.D. Howe *Backgrounder* (Toronto: C.D. Howe Institute) (November 4).

Monahan, Patrick J. (1995) "To the Extent Possible: A Comment on Dispute Settlement in the Agreement on Internal Trade," in Michael Trebilcock and Daniel Schwanen (eds.), *Getting There: An Assessment of the Agreement on Internal Trade* (Toronto: C.D. Howe Institute), pp. 211-18.

Newfoundland Royal Commission on Employment and Unemployment (1986) *Building on Our Strengths* (St. John's: Queen's Printer for Newfoundland).

Newhouse, John (1997) "Europe's Rising Regionalism," *Foreign Affairs*, vol. 76 (January/February), pp. 67-84.

Ohmae, Kenichi (1990) *The Borderless World* (New York: Harper Business).

Ohmae, Kenichi (1993) "The Rise of the Region State," *Foreign Affairs,* Vol. 72, pp. 78-87.

Ohmae, Kenichi (2000) "How Regions Can Prosper from Globalization," Keynote Address to Global City Regions Conference (UCLA, October 1999)

Olewiler, Nancy (1999) "National Tax Policy for an International Economy: Divergence in a Converging World?," in Thomas J. Courchene (ed.), *Room to Manoeuvre? Globalization and Policy Convergence* (Queen's

University: The John Deutsch Institute for the Study of Economic
    Policy), pp. 345-82.

Ontario Economic Council (1976) *Issues and Alternatives* (Toronto: Ontario
    Economic Council).

Ontario Hospital Association (1999) "Investing in the Future of Canada's Health
    Care System" (Submission to the House of Commons Standing
    Committee on Finance for the Federal 2000 Budget) (September 17).

Ontario Jobs and Investment Board (1999) *A Road Map to Prosperity: An
    Economic Plan for Jobs in the 21st Century* (Toronto: Ontario Jobs and
    Investment Board).

Ontario Securities Commission (1983) *Report on the Implications for Canadian
    Capital Markets of the Provision by Financial Institutions of Access to Discount
    Brokerage Services* (Toronto: Data Line).

Ostry, Sylvia (1997) "Globalization and the Nation State," in Thomas J.
    Courchene (ed.), *The Nation State in a Global/Information Era: Policy
    Challenges* (Queen's University: The John Deutsch Institute for the Study
    of Economic Policy), pp. 57-66.

Ostry, Sylvia (2001) "Perspectives on the Evolution of the Global Trading
    System," in Thomas J. Courchene (ed.), *Money, Markets and Mobility:
    Celebrating the Ideas and Influence of the 1999 Nobel Laureate, Robert A.
    Mundell* (Queen's University: The John Deutsch Institute for the Study of
    Economic Policy).

Paquet, Gilles (1995) "Industrial Evolution in an Information Age," in
    Thomas J. Courchene (ed.), *Technology, Information and Public Policy*,
    Vol. 3 of the Bell Canada Papers on Economic and Public Policy
    (Queen's University: The John Deutsch Institute for the Study of
    Economic Policy), pp. 197-230.

Pauly, Louis (1999) "The 'Culture' of Multinational Corporations and
    Implications for Canada," in Thomas J. Courchene (ed.), *Room To
    Manoeuvre? Globalization and Policy Convergences* (Queen's University: The
    John Deutsch Institute for the Study of Economic Policy), pp. 89-116.

Porter, Michael and Roger Martin (2000) "High Taxes, Timid Exporters Crush
    Canadian Wealth," *The Ottawa Citizen* (January 25), p. D10.

Quarter, J. (1992) *Canada's Social Economy* (Toronto: James Lorimer).

Reich, Robert (1991) *The Work of Nations* (New York: Alfred A. Knopf).

Report of the GTA Task Force (1996) *Greater Toronto* (Toronto: Queen's Printer for Ontario). This report is referred to as the *Golden Report*, after its Chair, Anne Golden.

Report To Premiers: see Ministerial Council on Social Policy Renewal and Reform (1996).

Richards, John (1998) *Retooling the Welfare State: What's Right, What's Wrong, What's to be Done?* Policy Study 31 (Toronto: C.D. Howe Institute).

Rock, Alan (1999) "Speaking Notes for Alan Rock, Minister of Health, at the Empire Club" (Toronto, September 30).

Rodrik, Dani (1997) *Has Globalization Gone Too Far?* (Washington: Institute of International Economics).

Ruggie, J.G. (1995) "At Home Abroad, Abroad at Home: International Liberalization and Domestic Stability in the New World Economy," *Millennium: Journal of International Studies*, 24, no. 3, pp.507-26.

Safarian, Edward (1980) *Ten Markets or One? Regional Barriers to Economic Activity* (Toronto: Ontario Economic Council).

Salamon, Lester M. (1987) "Of Market Failure, Toward a Theory of Government-Nonprofit Relations in the Modern Welfare State," *Journal of Voluntary Action Research* (16).

Saskatchewan Personal Income Tax Review Committee (1999) *Final Report and Recommendations* (Regina, Saskatchewan: Ministry of Finance).

Savoie, Donald (2001) Wrestling Economic Development: Taking Stock of the McKenna Approach in New Brunswick (forthcoming).

Scherer, Christoph (1996) "The Economic and Political Arguments For and Against Social Clauses," *Intereconomics* (January-February), pp. 9-20.

Schuller, Tom (1999) "The Complementary Roles of Human and Social Capital," paper presented to the HRDC/OECD conference *The Contribution of Human and Social Capital to Sustainable Economic Growth and Well-Being in Canada*, March 19-21, Quebec City, mimeo.

Scott, Allen J., John Agnew, Edward W. Soja and Michael Storper (2000) "Global City-Regions," background paper for Global City Regions Conference (UCLA, October 1999), forthcoming in conference volume from Oxford University Press.

Segal, Hugh (1999) "Towards a New Definition of Citizenship: Beneath and Beyond the Nation State" paper prepared for the Canada/United

Kingdom Colloquium (Newcastle, County Down, Northern Ireland), (November 18-20).

Shapiro, Bernard J. and Harold T. Shapiro (1996) "Universities in Higher Education: Some Problems and Challenges in a Changing World," in Thomas J. Courchene (ed.), *Policy Frameworks for a Knowledge Economy* (Queen's University: The John Deutsch Institute for the Study of Economic Policy), pp. 81-108.

Simeon, Richard (1972) *Federal-Provincial Diplomacy* (Toronto: The University of Toronto Press).

Simeon, Richard (1997) "Citizens and Democracy in the Emerging Global Order," in Thomas J. Courchene (ed.), *The Nation State in a Global Information Era: Policy Challenges* (Queen's University: The John Deutsch Institute for the Study of Economic Policy), pp. 299-314.

Slack, Enid (2000) "The Road To Financial Self-Sufficiency for Toronto: What Are the Impediments and How Can They Be Overcome," in Mary Rowe (ed.), *Toronto: Considering Self-Government* (Owen Sound: The Ginger Press).

Smiley, Donald V. and Ronald L. Watts (1985) *Intrastate Federalism in Canada* (Toronto: University of Toronto Press).

Stanbury, William and Ilan Vertinsky (1995) "Assessing the Impact of New Information Technologies on Interest Group Behaviour and Policymaking," in Thomas J. Courchene (ed.), *Technology, Information and Public Policy* (Queen's University: The John Deutsch Institute for the Study of Economic Policy), pp. 293-380.

Standing Senate Committee on Banking, Trade and Commerce (1990) *Canada, 1992: Toward a National Market in Financial Services* (Ottawa: Senate of Canada).

Standing Senate Committee on Social Affairs, Science and Technology (1999) *Final Report on Social Cohesion* (Ottawa: Senate of Canada).

Storper, Michael (1995) "The Resurgence of Regional Economics Ten Years Later", *European Urban and Regional Studies*, Vol. 2, no. 3, pp. 191-221.

Strange, Susan (1988) *States and Markets* (London: Pinter).

Strange, Susan (1995) "The Defective State," *Daedalus*, vol. 124, no. 2 (Spring), pp. 55-74.

Sulzenko, Andrei (2000) "Challenges and Opportunities of Canada's Growing North American Linkages," luncheon address to the Roundtable on

North America Integration (Ottawa, September 6) (Ottawa: Industry Canada), mimeo.

Technical Committee on Business Taxation (1998) *Report of the Technical Committee on Business Taxation* (Ottawa: Department of Finance).

The Economist (1993) "Towers of Babble" (December 25), pp. 72-74.

The Economist (1999) "A Survey of E-Business" (June 26).

The Economist (2000a) "The Next Revolution: A Survey of Government and the Internet" (June 24).

The Economist (2000b) "A Survey of E-Commerce" (February 26).

Thurow, Lester (1992) *Head to Head: The Coming Economic Battle Among Japan, Europe, and America* (New York: William Morrow and Company Inc.).

Thurow, Lester (1993) "Six Revolutions, Six Economic Challenges," *The Toronto Star* (January 28), p. A21.

Thurow, Lester (1995) *The Future of Capitalism* (New York: William Morrow and Company Inc.).

Thurow, Lester (1999) *Building Wealth: The New Rules for Individuals, Companies and Nations* (New York: Harper Business).

Toronto (2000) "Towards a New Relationship with Ontario and Canada", *Issue Note* (Toronto: Chief Administrator's Office), p. 3.

Toulin, Alan (2000), "Poorest U.S. State Ahead of Canada," *National Post* (August 2), pp. A1, A4.

Tourraine, Alain (1996) "La Globalizacion como ideologia," *El Pais* (December 22).

Tuohy, Carolyn (1994) "Health Policy and Fiscal Federalism," in Keith Banting et al. (eds.) *The Future of Fiscal Federalism* (Queen's University: School of Policy Studies) pp. 189-212.

United Nations (1990) *Regional Economic Integration and Transnational Corporations in the 1990s: Europe 1992, North America and Developing Countries*, United Nations Centre on Transnational Corporations, series A, no. 15 (New York: United Nations).

Vardy, Jill (2000) "Canada Lags in E-Commerce Race," *Financial Post* (January18), pp. C1, C8.

Vincent, Carole and Frances Wooley (2000) *Taxing Canadian Families: What's Fair and What's Not* (Montreal: Institute for Research on Public Policy).

Watts, Ronald L. (1999) *The Spending Power in Federal Systems: A Comparative Study* (Queen's University: Institute of Intergovernmental Relations).

Weinstein, Michael (2000) "Mobility and the American Dream," *International Herald Tribune* (February 21), p. 10.

Williamson, Shane (2000) "A Perspective on the International Migration of Skilled Workers," paper presented to IRPP and CERF Conference "Creating Canada's Advantage in an Information Age" (Ottawa, May 4-6).

Wolfe, David (1997) "The Emergence of the Region State," in Thomas J. Courchene (ed.), *The Nation State in a Global/Information Era: Policy Challenges* (Queen's University: The John Deutsch Institute for the Study of Economic Policy), pp. 205-40.

Wolfe, Robert (1999) "Regulatory Diplomacy: Why Rhythm Beats Harmony in the Trade Regime," in Thomas J. Courchene (ed.), *Room To Manoeuvre? Globalization and Policy Convergence* (Queen's University: The John Deutsch Institute for the Study of Economic Policy), pp. 191-238.

Wolfe, Robert (2000) "Confronting the Aftermyth of Seattle: Canada Must Set Key Trade Priorities Now," *Policy Matters,* Working Paper Series (March).

Zuker, Richard (1997) "Reciprocal Federalism: Beyond the Spending Power," (Ottawa: The Caledon Institute), mimeo.

AIT	Agreement on Internal Trade
APC	Annual Premiers' Conference
Battle in Seattle	Refers (in specific terms) to the massive protests in Seattle associated with the WTO meeting. More generally, an attempt by citizens and NGOs to put a human face on globalization.
BCNI	Business Council on National Issues
CAP	Canadian Assistance Plan (the former cost-sharing program for welfare)
CCED	Child Care Education Deduction
CCRA	Canada Customs and Revenue Agency (the successor to Revenue Canada)
CCTB	Canada Child Tax Benefit
CGLI	Canada Global Leadership Initiative (a year-long research project launched by the BCNI that examined Canada's economic performance and economic challenges)
CHST	Canada Health and Social Transfer
CIT	Corporate Income Taxation
CRTC	Canadian Radio-television and Telecommunications Commission
EU	European Union
FDI	Foreign Direct Investment
FTA	Free Trade Agreement (between Canada and the US)
FMC	First Ministers' Conference
GATT	General Agreement on Tariffs and Trade
G-20	International organization made up of the G7 countries, the World Bank, the IMF, the European Community and eleven other countries, designed to coordinate global economic policies.
GIR	Globalization and the Knowledge/Information Revolution
GTA	Greater Toronto Area
MAI	Multilateral Agreement on Investment (an aborted attempt to deregulate key aspects of foreign direct investment, FDI)
MEB	Marginal Excess Burden (the loss of real output which results from the distorting effects of another dollar of taxation on the economy)

MNC	Multinational Corporation (used in the text to designate those corporations that are subject to host-country constraints)
MNE	Multinational Enterprise (same as MNC and in contrast to TNE)
NAFTA	North American Free Trade Agreement (between Canada, Mexico and the US)
NAIRU	Non-Accelerating Inflation Rate of Unemployment (the equilibrium rate of unemployment that is consistent with stable inflation)
NAMU	North American Monetary Union (a plan to develop a North American currency similar to the Euro)
NCBS	National Child Benefit Supplement
NGO	Non-Governmental Organization
NTP	New Techno-Economic Paradigm
OAS/GIS	Old Age Security / Guaranteed Income Supplement (Canada's publicly funded system of retirement benefits)
OECD	Organization for Economic Cooperation and Development
OJIB	Ontario Jobs and Information Board
PAGVS	Panel on Accountability and Governance in the Voluntary Sector
PIT	Personal Income Taxation
PSE	Post-Secondary Education
SUFA	Social Union Framework Agreement (a common name for *A Framework to Improve the Social Union of Canada*)
TEA-21	Transportation Equity Act for the 21st Century (a $217 billion US fund and federal initiative designed to undertake major transportation infrastructure programs)
TINA (1)	There Is No Alternative (see TINA (2))
TINA (2)	Trapped In North America
TNE	Transnational Enterprise (used to describe those foreign corporations that are not subject to host-country constraints)
VSTF	Voluntary Sector Task Force
WTO	World Trade Organization

Appendix A
A Primer on Human Capital,
Social Capital and Social Cohesion

Human Capital

T RADITIONALLY, ECONOMISTS HAVE FOCUSED ON FOUR FACTORS OF PRODUCTION: land, labour, capital and enterprise/entrepreneurship. At base, the recent focus on human capital implies that the factor called "labour" is far from homogeneous: It has become increasingly common to distinguish between unskilled labour on the one hand and skilled labour (or human capital) on the other. For example, Reich (1991) focuses on what he refers to as "routine workers" at one end of the spectrum and "symbolic analysts" or knowledge workers at the other end. Therefore, "human capital" refers to the stock of skills and knowledge embedded in people. And an *increase* in human capital means an *increase* in this stock of skills and knowledge.

So why not simply refer to this component of the labour force as "knowledge workers?" Why refer to it as "human capital?" For several important reasons. First, the reference to "capital" is critical because this component of labour has characteristics that are typically associated with physical capital. There are costs to accumulating both physical and human capital. Thus, like physical capital, one has to "invest" in human capital. This investment also generates an income stream, or a "return" on the human capital investment. Presumably the greater the return, the more individuals will invest in their own human capital, and the greater the incentive for society to invest in the skills and knowledge of its citizens. Also, like physical capital, the stock of human capital will depreciate over time and can be rendered obsolete by technological advances. Finally, but not exhaustively, human capital is progressively becoming more mobile across borders. Admittedly, this degree of mobility falls way short of that of, say, financial capital. Nonetheless, for these and other reasons, one can make the case that individuals embodying high-level human capital are more like physical capital than they are like unskilled labour. As a result, the set of policies needed to ensure Canada can attract and retain human capital are not unlike those required to attract and retain physical capital.

For many of this text's references to human capital, readers would not be far off the mark by assuming these are knowledge workers. Nonetheless, for some purposes, the fact that this knowledge is in fact a *stock* of human capital becomes critical.

While I argue the essence of the emerging GIR reality is that of a human capital society, others would argue we are really entering a knowledge-based economy (Harris 2000). I agree with this: Canada's future must be that of a knowledge-based economy and society. In particular, it is important to distinguish tradeable knowledge as intellectual capital (e.g., information and explicit knowledge) from human skills, tacit knowledge and wisdom, which are inherently embodied in a single person, i.e., human capital. Nonetheless, the focus on Canada becoming a human capital society is intended to capture *both* types of knowledge. In other words, if we are successful in generating a human capital society, we will also have bought fully into a knowledge-based economy and society. Harris elaborates on this linkage as follows:

> [Economists place] a lot of importance on the role of human capital formation in the growth process, and these variables find considerable support in various growth and productivity studies. Human capital appears as an engine of growth in two ways. One, it serves to facilitate knowledge spillovers, which raises the productivity of all factors. Or, in more conventional language, being more skilled makes it more likely that you will transmit what you know to others, who will then do the same and so on. Two, higher skills enter directly into the production of new technology (product and process innovation) and are necessary to facilitate the adoption of new technology. (Harris 1999: 14)

In this and other senses, I make an implicit link between a human capital society and a knowledge-based society.

Finally, while there are important societal returns arising from an increased level of human capital, the bulk of the returns will rest largely with the individual that has the human capital. Now, the distribution of human capital is far from equal across our citizens; left to the interplay of market forces (and private means), this will not result in a societally equitable distribution of earnings. For this reason, the focus on a human capital mission statement for Canada places priority on equality of access or of opportunity for all Canadians to develop and enhance their human capital potential.

From Human Capital To Social Capital

R ECENTLY, AN IMPORTANT INTERDISCIPLINARY LITERATURE FOCUSING ON "SOCIAL capital" has emerged, in part as an extension of human capital. Whereas human capital, as noted above, relates to the knowledge, skills, competencies and other attributes embodied in individuals, social capital is generally defined "in terms of *networks, norms and trust*, and the way these allow agents and institutions to be *more effective in achieving common objectives*" (Schuller 2000: 3, emphasis original). Dobell reflects on the human capital/social capital linkage as follows:

> The issue of human capital is not only a matter of investment in skills and productive capacity: it is also investment in understanding and social capacity — capacity to participate in ongoing social processes and cultural practices, perhaps particularly around risk perceptions. The issue of social capital is distinct from human capital and relates to the features of a society which make it possible to arrive at collective decisions which will stick, which will be implemented and which will command continuing allegiance and hence see continuing compliance. (Dobell 2000: 4)

In this sense, then, social capital is an important societal asset. Moreover, most of the burgeoning literature recognizes that an increase in human capital is generally associated with an increase in social capital. Dobell (3) notes "a key role" [in developing social capital] is played by continuing education or lifelong learning in building human capital (and hence creating capacity to participate in deliberative processes).

Social Cohesion

I N THIS MONOGRAPH, I SELDOM EMPLOY THE TERM SOCIAL CAPITAL. IN ITS PLACE, I USE "social cohesion," where social cohesion is assumed to embody the above concept of social capital *and* embody the concept of equality of opportunity. Specifically, the human capital mission statement (Chapter 11) is designed to encompass both economic competitiveness and social cohesion. A more detailed treatment of the concept of social cohesion in the Canadian context appears in Chapter 13.

Appendix B

Globalization and the Knowledge/Information Revolution: Variations on the New Techno-Economic Paradigm (TEP)

	Variations on the New TEP	Definition
A.	Noting is "overseas" any longer (Ohmae 1990: vii).	The increasing internalization of production, initially in manufacturing, but increasingly in services as well.
B.	Shift from multinational enterprise (MNEs) to transnational enterprises (TNEs).	TNEs no longer subject to host-country controls, unlike MNEs.
C.	Globalization as the inter-nationalization of cities.	Economies of scale and scope associated with the information revolution imply that international cities have become the connectors outward to, for example, London, New York, and Tokyo, and inward to their regional hinterlands.
D1.	Globalization as the knowledge/information revolution: Knowledge.	Knowledge is increasingly at the cutting edge of competitiveness.

Characteristics	Policy Implications/Challenges
Decouples firms from the factor endowments of any single country.	• Wreaks havoc on national welfare states that have geared incentives to National production systems. • What is the nature of a welfare state when production is international?
Two polar models: the "national treatment" model, as under the FTA and NAFTA, and the "single-country (home-country) rule" model as in the European Union (EU). In theory at least, the former is sovereignty enhancing while the latter implies policy homogenization.	• Canadians eventually will realize that the genius of the FTA lies in the sovereignty-enhancing national treatment principle. • It is the international private sector that is globalizing, not the public sector. Pressures mount for governments to transfer powers upward so that political space is more contiguous with economic space.
• Represents one way in which the "institutional structure" is globalizing. • May be a temporary phenomenon as the spread of the information revolution allows for a greater dispersion of economic power and activity.	• An integral part of the process by which power is being transferred downward from nation-states. This is especially so since, in Canada at least, international cities are "constitutionless". • An integral part of the regional/international interface.
• Skilled labor is more like capital than like traditional labor. • Disappearing middle class. • Shift in the "wealth-generating process" (Harris 1993). • For resources to remain important, they must embody knowledge (or high-value added techniques).	• Dramatic implications in all countries with respect to the distribution of income. • Even resource-rich economies must make the transition to human-capital-based economies and societies. • Social policy, as it relates to human capital and skills formation, is indistinguishable from economic policy.

	Variations on the New TEP	**Definition**
D2.	Globalization as the knowledge/ information revolution: Information.	Compresses both time and distance in terms of economic activity and, therefore, enhances global integration.
E.	Globalization as consumer sovereignty (Ohmae 1990).	"Performance standards are now set in the market place by those that buy the products, not those that make or regulate them" (Ohmae 1990: dustjacket).
F.	Globalization as regime theory.	In a sense, this is the oldest form of globalization. Regimes are the formal or institutional devices through which economic and political actors organize and manage their interdependencies.
G.	Globalization as ultra mobility.	Enhanced mobility is generic in that it underpins all conceptions of globalization as well as virtually all conceptions of a new TEP shift.

Source: T.J. Courchene (1995) "Glocalization:
The Regional/International Interface",
Canadian Journal of Regional Science XIII, 7 (Spring).

Characteristics	Policy Implications/Challenges
Privileges individuals in the sense that they now have the ability to access, transmit, and transform information in ways that governments of all stripes are powerless to prevent.	• Arguably, this is inherently decentralizing. • The information revolution will also redraw the boundary between what is feasible in the public and private sectors — for example, it will eventually relegate the Canadian Radio-television and Telecommunications Commission to the sidelines, just as facsimile transmissions are marginalizing the post office.
This is a variant of information revolution in D2 in that it implies that "receptors," rather than "transmitters," are in the driver's seat.	• Obviously, this transfers power from governments to consumers. • Of more interest here, however, is that, while the information revolution privileges citizens as "consumers," it tends to disenfranchise them as "citizens," since an important set of decisions relating to them is beyond the purview of the nation-state.
Regimes have long been with us — in energy, airlines, minerals, and so on. They set standards, perform allocation functions, monitor compliance, reduce conflict, and resolve disputes.	Regimes restrict the autonomy of nation-states. Now, however, regimes are spreading into "soft" areas such as non-tariff barriers, the environment, social charters, and rights for indigenous peoples.
Since taxation or regulation of mobile factors becomes more difficult, and since globalization or ultra mobility implies an increase in the number and range of factors and commodities that are mobile, this constrains the instrument set available to policy authorities. In tandem, with the spread of free-trade arrangements, this constrains policymakers from using allocative instruments to deliver distributional goals.	Arguably, the optimal jurisdictional space for taxation has increased relative to that for spending. Thus, one now speaks of EU-wide corporate taxes, or carbon taxes, for example. Yet, the optimal spending jurisdiction has not yet become EU-wide. This creates the specter of EU financial transfers to member states — that is, an internationalization of Canadian-style fiscal federalism.

Appendix C

Comparison of Powers and Revenue Sources of Selected Cities

A Background Report prepared by:
Chief Administrator's Office, Strategic & Corporate Policy Division
June 2000

Constitutional Status/City Powers

T HE STATUS OF A CITY GOVERNMENT AND ITS LEGISLATIVE POWERS ARE IMPORTANT determinants of a city's ability to meet needs within its boundaries. A city's legislative toolkit helps or hinders the city's flexibility, creativity and nimbleness in solving problems in a rapidly changing environment.

Constitutional Standing

While Canadian municipalities remain "creatures of the province" under the *Constitution Act, 1867*, many cities in other countries are formally recognized within national constitutions.

- The Constitution of the Federative Republic of Brazil, 1988, recognizes municipalities as a specific order of government, gives municipalities special taxing powers and defines how other taxes are to be shared.

- Almost all European local governments are formally recognized constitutionally:
  - Germany's constitution specifically recognizes municipalities and their responsibilities for local affairs. Municipalities are involved in decision-making at the national table.
  - Municipalities in the Netherlands are recognized in the constitution and a ministry of urban affairs exists. In addition, there is a growing awareness that rules and conditions prevent municipalities from operating efficiently.
  - Municipalities in Sweden have constitutional standing.

United States – Home Rule Status

◆ Several U.S. states provide municipalities with the option to adopt Home Rule status or remain under general law. Home Rule status is a legal right that grants greater discretionary authority to local governments by allowing them to draft, adopt and amend constitutional Charters and govern their own affairs without legislative interference by the state government. Home Rule allows municipal governments to take independent action and offers protection from arbitrary action by the State. While the provision is intended to increase local autonomy, it does not prevent the State from controlling the fiscal capacity of local governments.

→ The Home Rule Charter in New York asserts that municipalities can pass laws which supersede general state laws as long as the laws passed by municipalities concern "municipal property, affairs and government" and are limited to local matters. If a dispute arises, the matter is generally settled by the courts. The Charter contains a Bill of Rights and a Statute of Local Governments.

Trends in Canada

In response to increasing responsibilities and expectations placed on local governments along with changing urban conditions, many Canadian provinces have amended their Municipal Acts to give municipalities broader powers and greater flexibility.

◆ In 1995, the Alberta government approved the Alberta Municipal Government Act (Bill 31) in response to growing demands placed on municipal governments as a result of provincial downloading and the reduction of provincial funding. The Act introduces two significant concepts: natural personal powers and spheres of jurisdiction. Provisions for greater fiscal flexibility in municipal investment and borrowing are also embedded in the Act.

◆ In 1996, the Government of British Columbia and the Union of British Columbia Municipalities (UBCM) signed a protocol of recognition for local government in British Columbia that explicitly recognizes local government as an "independent, responsible and accountable order of government." The following year, the parties agreed to a set of principles to guide the reform of the Municipal Act. The aim of reform is to give municipalities broad powers to respond to the evolving needs of their communities. The Government of

British Columbia adopted a multi-year phased approach to overhaul the Municipal Act within three to four years:

→ 1998 – Local Government Statutes Amendment Act, 1998 (Bill 31) – recognizes local government as an independent, responsible and accountable order of government; facilitating public-private partnerships; and providing flexible broad corporate powers.

→ 1999 – Local Government Statutes Amendment Act, 1999 (Bill 88) – includes amendments in open meetings, elections, campaign financing, service powers, taxes, fees and charges (more flexible authority to impose a parcel of taxes, fees and charges), and tax collection.

◆ Newfoundland's House of assembly enacted a new Cities Act, which took effect on April 1, 2000. The more noteworthy features of the Cities Act are as follows:

→ the Preamble recognizes that each city is an order of government and is autonomous;

→ the Preamble stipulates that each city "must have adequate powers and financial and legal resources (a) to ensure good government and services locally, (b) to meet existing and future community needs, (c) to apply creative, innovative and entrepreneurial solutions, (d) which ought not to be altered unilaterally, without consultation with other orders of government";

→ Newfoundland must consult with the mayor of a city before the province "enacts, amends, repeals or makes legislation, regulations, policies, programs or orders that affect the city" (section 2);

→ each city is given natural person powers;

→ the power given to each city "is stated in broad terms to give the city adequate power to provide good government and services, as the council considers appropriate, in response to existing and future local issues and needs and to give the council (a) full discretion in the exercise of its powers to meet local conditions, (b) the right to determine the local public interest" (section 46);

→ the only limits on a city's powers are that it not be inconsistent with a federal or provincial enactment, that it be within the province's competence and it not be expressly excluded from the city's competence by a statute (section 47); and

→ the cities are given fifteen spheres of power in which they can act or exercise power, subject to the province's right to establish standards for services in three spheres: natural environment, safety and protection of people and protection of property including fire and police services, and structures, including buildings, fences and signs (section 48).

◆ Also in Newfoundland, a new Municipalities Act was passed by the House of Assembly in the 1999 spring session, and recently took effect on January 1, 2000. The new legislation removes many restrictive provisions contained in the former Act and provides support in fostering self-reliance and independence among local governments. The Act increases municipal autonomy in administration and financial management, expands taxation and collection capacities, and expands and provides new authorities for service delivery and municipal controls.

Municipal Governments' Access to Financial Resources

What Others Are Doing

◆ Local Income Tax

→ Manitoba allocates revenues from two percentage points of the personal income tax and one percentage point of the corporate income tax for distribution to municipalities in the form of a per capita grant.

→ Section 1301 of the New York State Tax Law allows New York cities with populations in excess of one million to impose a local income tax (New York City and Yonkers). The personal income tax is imposed on residents only.

→ Municipalities in Pennsylvania have access to local earned income taxes. Local income taxes generate 20 percent of municipal revenues and represent about one-sixth of local government tax revenues.

→ Local governments in Germany receive 15 percent of national income and wage tax revenues (shares may differ according to municipalities). The state governments distribute revenues to local governments in originating municipalities (where the taxpayer resides).

- → Municipalities and counties in Sweden are able to levy their own income tax and rely heavily on this tax as a major source of revenue. Local income taxes account for roughly half of total local revenues. In addition, municipalities receive one-quarter of their funding from the central government; the remainder of funding comes from fees and charges.
- ◆ Local Retail Sales Tax
  - → In British Columbia, legislation provides that the province share retail sales tax revenues with the municipalities.
  - → New York City is entitled to a portion of state sales tax.
  - → Municipalities in California have access to the sales tax.
- ◆ Business Tax
  - → In Frankfurt, Germany, the business tax (Gewerbesteuer) is a tax on corporate profits. The base is determined by central government and the individual municipalities set the local rate. The business tax accounts for two-thirds of Frankfurt's tax revenues, and roughly a quarter of total revenue.
- ◆ Hotel and Motel Occupancy Tax
  - → The hotel tax is an additional levy that transfers a tax to non-residents (visitors) who use municipal services. Municipalities have the option to "piggy back" on the existing provincial retail sales tax rate or administer their own independent tax. A number of U.S. cities have implemented a hotel occupancy tax.
- ◆ Gasoline Tax
  - → In most cases, revenues from a gasoline tax are earmarked for local roads and public transit. The tax affects both residents and visitors.
  - → For every one litre of gasoline sold in Ontario, the provincial government collects almost 15 cents.
  - → It is estimated that every cent of taxes levied on a litre of gasoline raises revenues between $19 million and $28 million. In the GTA, each cent per litre would generate annual revenues ranging from $47 million to $53 million.
  - → Montreal's Agence Metropolitaine de Transport (AMT) is partially funded by a 1.5 cent/litre gas tax (total raised: $47 million).
  - → Greater Vancouver's TransLink (Vancouver Regional Transit System) is partially funded by a 4 cent/litre gas tax (total raised: $79 million).

→ Public transit in the U.S. is receiving 2.8 cents per gallon (0.7 cents/litre) from gas taxes to reduce deficits (Transportation Equity Act for the 21st Century). It is estimated that American transit systems will receive more than $29 billion from gas taxes over the next five years.

→ Different U.S. states collect different tax rates:

  • The state of Michigan collects 19 cents per gallon gas tax and diverts 1.5 cents to a Comprehensive Transportation Fund.

  • The state of Florida diverts 8.8 cents per gallon to a Transportation Trust Fund.

  • New York State provides subsidies to transit systems based on the Petroleum Business Tax. The tax is measured by the quantity of various petroleum products refined or sold in the state or imported for sale or use in the state. The state collects approximately 10 cents per gallon.

◆ Automotive License Fees

→ Montreal's Agence Metropolitaine de Transport (AMT) is partially funded by a $30 car registration fee, annual revenues: $43 million.

◆ Land Transfer Tax

→ Approximately one-third of all municipalities in Nova Scotia levy a land transfer tax at a rate of 0.5 to one percent of the value of the transferred property.

→ Municipalities in Quebec can levy a land transfer tax at the rate of 3/10 of one percent on the first $50,000 of sale price and 6/10 of one percent on the excess.

Intergovernmental Funding Arrangements

◆ The Transportation Equity Act for the 21st Century (TEA-21) is the largest infrastructure investment program in the United States with a total budget of $217 billion. Major U.S. cities are undertaking major transportation infrastructure programs under this program. It is estimated that an American urban region the size of the GTA would receive approximately $42 million annually under TEA-21 in base funding. Similarly, an American urban region comparable to the size of City of Toronto would receive about $22 million annually under TEA-21.

♦ The Community Development Block Grant (CDBG) is the eighth largest federal grant program in the U.S. The program funds urban improvement projects that specifically benefit low and moderate income families. It is estimated that an American urban region the size of the GTA would expect to receive $155 million annually under CDBG. Similarly, an American urban region comparable to the size of the City of Toronto would receive approximately $81 million annually under the CDBG.

♦ The Home Investment Partnership Program (HOME) is the largest federal block grant to state and local governments with more than $1 billion allocated to cities and states annually. The aim of the program is to create affordable housing for low-income households. Funds are used to rehabilitate sites, demolish, rehabilitate or build housing for rent or ownership. It is estimated that an American urban region the size of the GTA would receive $46.5 million under HOME annually. An American urban region comparable to the City of Toronto would receive $24 million annually.

♦ The Big Cities Policy in the Netherlands is a bilateral funding agreement between the Dutch government and the four big cities: Amsterdam, Rotterdam, Utrecht and The Hague. The aim of the policy is to increase the financial resources of the big cities through the joint development of programs. Earmarked funds are channelled from central government to the cities for the construction of major infrastructure, house building, public transportation, improving quality of life in urban areas, economic development and job creation. The allocation of funds is based on plans submitted by each city. City councils propose projects that reinforce the city's economic structure and boost employment. Forty percent of funds from the policy are specifically earmarked for Amsterdam. Although the cities are not completely free to spend earmarked funds as they wish, they are free to spend resources as efficiently and integrally as possible on the specific purpose agreed to.

♦ The financial relationship between the central and local governments in the Netherlands is clearly defined in the *Financial Relations Act, 1929*. The Act provides for a special fund known as the Municipal Fund. The Fund, which is fed by central tax revenues, transfers central government funds to municipalities in the form of a General Grant. Through this tax sharing system, payments are made to municipalities on the basis of certain allocation criteria. The Fund is administered by the Council for Municipal Finance, a neutral advisory body to the Vereniging van Nederlandse Gemeenten (Association of Dutch Municipalities).

◆ Trilateral Funding Agreements in Canada

→ The Vancouver Agreement is a trilateral agreement between the City of Vancouver, and the Provincial and Federal governments. All three orders of government work together, within their own jurisdictions and mandates, and with communities in Vancouver, to promote and support sustainable economic, social and community development. The initial goal and focus of the Agreement is to work with residents in neighbourhoods in and around the Downtown Eastside to develop a healthy and sustainable community.

→ The Winnipeg Development Agreement (WDA) is a $75 million tri-partite agreement between the City of Winnipeg and the Provincial and Federal governments. The goal is the work with communities and businesses to support long term sustainable economic development in Winnipeg. Under the agreement, the City can implement projects under programs it administers. The WDA was due to expire on March 31, 2000.

**For further information or additional copies of this report, please contact:
Phillip Abrahams at 416-392-8102 or e-mail at pabraham@city.toronto.on.ca
Please visit our Web site at www.city.toronto.on.ca**

AGMV Marquis

MEMBRE DU GROUPE SCABRINI

Québec, Canada
2001